Beyond a Joke

Also by Michael Pickering

VILLAGE, SONG AND CULTURE

EVERYDAY CULTURE (co-edited with Tony Green)

ACTS OF SUPREMACY: THE BRITISH EMPIRE AND THE STAGE, 1790–1930 (with J. S. Bratton, Richard Cave, Heidi Holder and Brendon Gregory)

HISTORY, EXPERIENCE AND CULTURAL STUDIES

RESEARCHING COMMUNICATIONS: A PRACTICAL GUIDE TO METHODS IN MEDIA AND CULTURAL ANALYSIS (with David Deacon, Peter Golding and Graham Murdock)

STEREOTYPING: THE POLITICS OF REPRESENTATION

CREATIVITY, COMMUNICATION AND CULTURAL VALUE (with Keith Negus)

Beyond a Joke

The Limits Of Humour

Edited by
Sharon Lockyer and Michael Pickering

First published 2005 by
PALGRAVE MACMILLAN
Houndmills, Basingstoke, Hampshire RG21 6XS and
175 Fifth Avenue, New York, N.Y. 10010
Companies and representatives throughout the world

PALGRAVE MACMILLAN is the global academic imprint of the Palgrave
Macmillan division of St. Martin's Press, LLC and of Palgrave Macmillan Ltd.
Macmillan® is a registered trademark in the United States, United Kingdom
and other countries. Palgrave is a registered trademark in the European
Union and other countries.

ISBN 13: 978–1–4039–3942–5   hardback
ISBN 10: 1–4039–3942–X   hardback

This book is printed on paper suitable for recycling and made from fully
managed and sustained forest sources.

A catalogue record for this book is available from the British Library.

Library of Congress Cataloging-in-Publication Data
Beyond a joke : the limits of humour / edited by Sharon Lockyer and
Michael Pickering.
      p. cm.
   Includes bibliographical references and index.
   ISBN 1–4039–3942–X
     1. Wit and humor–Social aspects. 2. Wit and humor–Philosophy.
I. Lockyer, Sharon, 1974– II. Pickering, Michael

   PN6149.S62B49 2005
   809.7–dc   2005051278

10   9   8   7   6   5   4   3   2   1
14 13 12 11 10 09 08 07 06 05

Printed and bound in Great Britain by
Antony Rowe Ltd, Chippenham and Eastbourne

Contents

Notes on Contributors

Michael Billig is Professor of Social Sciences at Loughborough University. His background is in social psychology and among his interests have been the study of extreme right-wing ideology, nationalism and psychoanalytic theory, and currently also in the connections between theories of humour and social theory in general. He is the author of *Social Psychology and Intergroup Relations*, 1976; *Fascists: A Social Psychological View of the National Front*, 1978; *L'Internationale Raciste: de la Psychologie à la 'Science' des Races*, 1981; *Ideology and Social Psychology*, 1982; *Arguing and Thinking*, 1987, new edn 1996; *Ideological Dilemmas: A Social Psychology of Everyday Thinking*, 1988 (with Susan Condor, Derek Edwards, Mike Gane, David Middleton and Alan Radley); *Ideology and Opinions: Studies in Rhetorical Psychology*, 1991; *Talking of the Royal Family*, 1992 (new edn 1999); *Banal Nationalism*, 1995; *Freudian Repression*, 1999; *Rock'n'Roll Jews*, 2000 (2001); and *Laughter and Ridicule: Towards a Social Critique of Humour*, 2005.

Deborah Chambers is Chair of Communication Studies at the University of Newcastle. She has taught and researched in Australia as well as the UK. She is the author of *Representing the Family*, 2001; *Women and Journalism*, 2004 (with Linda Steiner and Carole Fleming); *The Practice of Cultural Studies*, 2004 (with Richard Johnson, Parvati Raghuram and Estella Tincknell); and *New Social Ties: Contemporary Connections in a Fragmented Society*, (2005).

Frances Gray is Senior Lecturer in Drama at Sheffield University. She has been Visiting Professor at Allegheny College, Pennsylvania, and the Universities of Lodz and Krakow, as well as a Studio Manager for BBC Radio. She is the author of *John Arden*, 1982; *Noel Coward, Second Wave: Women's Plays at the Albany Empire*, 1990; *Women and Laughter*, 1994; and *Women, Crime and Language*, 2003. In 1994, Frances was awarded First Prize in the *Radio Times* Awards For Radio Comedy, for *Sally, Jo and Harris of the Yard*.

Dennis Howitt is Reader in Applied Psychology at Loughborough University. He is the author of 16 books and numerous articles in the fields of race, forensic psychology, mass communications and statistics.

He is co-author (with Kwame Owusu-Bempah) of *The Racism of Psychology: Time for Change*, 1994; and *Psychology Beyond Western Perspectives*, 2000.

Sharon Lockyer is Lecturer in Media Studies at De Montfort University. Previously she taught at Loughborough University, where she was awarded her PhD for a thesis entitled *An Eye to Offensiveness: The Discourse of Offence and Censure in Private Eye*. She has written articles on the ethics of humour and was the recipient of the *International Society for Humor Studies* Emerging Scholar Award 2004.

John Morreall is Professor of Religious Studies at the College of William and Mary and President of Humorworks Seminars (www.humorworks. com). He was President of the *International Society for Humor Studies* in 2004–5. He has also taught at Northwestern University, Illinois, and at Pennsylvania State University. His books include *Taking Laughter Seriously*, 1983 (still in print, translated into Japanese and Turkish); *The Philosophy of Laughter and Humor*, 1987; *Humor Works*, 1997; and *Comedy, Tragedy, and Religion*, 1999. From 1988 to 1999 he was Review Editor of *Humor: International Journal of Humor Research*. As a consultant, he has done presentations on the benefits of humour for over 400 organisations in North America, Europe and Japan. His clients include ING, IBM and the World Bank.

Kwame Owusu-Bempah is Reader in Psychology at Leicester University in the School of Social Work. His research in the area of race extends over twenty years, has yielded numerous publications in academic and professional journals, as well as in edited volumes. He is co-author (with Dennis Howitt) of *The Racism of Psychology: Time for Change*, 1994; and *Psychology Beyond Western Perspectives*, 2000.

Jerry Palmer is Professor of Communications, London Metropolitan University and Visiting Professor in the Sociology Department, City University. He has been Senior Research Fellow at Wesleyan University, Connecticut, USA, and Visiting Professor at Copenhagen University and Arhus University. He is the author of *Thrillers*, 1978; *The Logic of the Absurd: On Film and Television Comedy*, 1987; *Potboilers*, 1991; *Taking Humour Seriously*, 1994; *Design and Aesthetics*, 1996 (co-edited with Mo Dodson); *Spinning into Control: News Values and Source Strategies*, 2000; and *Media War: The Iraq Crisis*, 2004 (with Howard Tumber).

Michael Pickering is Reader in Culture and Communications at Loughborough University. His most recent publications include *History, Experience and Cultural Studies*, 1997; *Researching Communications: A Practical Guide to Methods in Media and Cultural Analysis*, 1999 (with David Deacon, Peter Golding and Graham Murdock); *Stereotyping: The Politics of Representation*, 2001; and *Creativity, Communication and Cultural Value*, 2004 (with Keith Negus).

Ken Willis is an English teacher currently working in Liverpool. He has recently been awarded his PhD for a thesis on the pragmatics and politics of humour.

Introduction:
The Ethics and Aesthetics of Humour and Comedy

Michael Pickering and Sharon Lockyer

Introduction

Two years ago, as we were planning this book, a story made the headlines. It was featured in all the major newspapers in Western Europe. Silvio Berlusconi, the Italian prime minister and billionaire media magnate, had begun his term as president of the European parliament in Strasbourg with an ill-judged and highly offensive remark. He had rounded accusingly on the German MEP, Martin Schulz, with the suggestion that he should take a part as a guard in a film about Nazi concentration camps. Most of those present were appalled, though Berlusconi beamed broadly after delivering his insult. Berlusconi is renowned for possessing the gift of the gaffe, but this was a comic blunder of enormous proportions. He was widely condemned for his crude national stereotyping and crass moral insensitivity, but he then managed to slip further into the mire by claiming that in his own country, Holocaust jokes have been 'doing the rounds' for years because Italians knew how to laugh about 'that kind of tragedy'. His attempt at damage limitation only succeeded in causing offence further afield, among Italy's Jewish community and Jewish people around the world. Even in his own country, the newspaper *La Stampa* pronounced Berlusconi's remark poisonous, and said: 'A joke can ruin everything.' The implication was that there are times when humour, or attempted humour, is not only inappropriate but also disastrous for the various social identities and relations that are drawn into it.

The incident was reproduced on that evening's television news. Following his response to Martin Schulz, Berlusconi's grin seemed intended to signify that his remark was just a joke and nothing more. This of course was disingenuous, but it relied upon the commonplace notion that a joke is *sui generis* and shouldn't be registered within the same schema of understanding as serious discourse. Jokes do have their own generic and discursive characteristics, and are dependent on the time and place in which they are made or reproduced, but does this mean that they have no reference at all to anything beyond the comic frame in which they are uttered? Clearly not. The Berlusconi story is just one example of an attempt (or apparent attempt) at humour that proved seriously offensive. It was an extreme example, for we don't normally make unwarranted comparisons between our adversaries and prison camp warders. It was also a very poor joke. But everyone has encountered cases of jokes that seriously backfire. They go badly wrong, and maybe even achieve the opposite of humour, so raising concerns about the value or context of comic transgression.

For many people, there are certain jokes that are beyond a joke. Berlusconi's bungled attempt at ironic wit within a key political arena dedicated to European integration was an obvious example of a 'joke' that can, at least potentially, 'ruin everything'. The cause of cross-national reconciliation, and the task of coming to terms historically with the greatest race crime of the twentieth century, certainly suffered a severe jolt. Others disagreed, and were prepared to defend Berlusconi. They even included Jewish people. Vox pop interviews by Sophie Arie in Rome were reported in *The Guardian* on 4 July, 2003: 'I was stunned,' said Federica, 33, climbing on to her moped:

> I'm Jewish and I feel very pleased that at last someone has reminded the Germans what they have done. It was perhaps not the ideal phrase he used. But it was just irony. I don't think the prime minister needs to apologise or even explain. If humanity has got over what the Germans did, I am sure the Germans can get over this.

Similar interviews in Berlin found that people regarded Berlusconi's Nazi jibe as 'shameless', 'shocking', 'tasteless'. In Britain, it was referred to as a *Fawlty Towers* gaffe, the reference being to a famous episode in the BBC TV sitcom series (1975 and 1979) where Basil Fawlty (John Cleese), despite his own imprecations to his staff about 'not mentioning the war', offended a party of German guests in his hotel by doing Hitler impersonations and marching the goose-step. The comparison seemed apt, bearing in mind Fawlty's choleric impatience and apparently limitless *faux pas*, but the humour in the sitcom appeared to be acceptable because associated with a comically flawed, homegrown personality whose unacceptable antics served to point up the absurdity of anti-German pre-

judice. It could readily be understood as a satirical assault on such prejudice. In Berlusconi's case, no such interpretative possibility existed. A line
had definitely been crossed. The joke had backfired. His comparison
between a German politician and an SS guard was desperately unfunny.

Humour and offensiveness

The Berlusconi story confirmed the need for a book that would explore
the relations between serious and comic discourse, and more specifically between humour and offensiveness. If it was clear that his
attempted joke had crossed a line, does this mean that there are ethical
limits to humour? The purpose of the book we've subsequently put
together is to explore this question. We all makes jokes, but most of us
are at times uncertain about how to respond when a joke is taken as, or
even suspected of being offensive, either to ourselves or others. We are
uncertain about how to register the offence without seeming to lack a
sense of humour, or without inviting the accusation of being moral-
istic, intolerant or – in what is now an uninspected term of condemnation – 'politically correct' (PC). No one wants to be judged in this way.
To claim that we lack a sense of humour is to launch an assault on our
self-esteem, on an attribute of ourselves that helps define us as an integrated person worthy of being known. It is tantamount to declaring us
deficient as personalities, as being 'literally an incomplete person'
(Wickberg, 1998: 85; and see Lockyer and Pickering, 2001). So how do
we negotiate the perilous terrain that lies between humour and offensiveness, or free speech and cultural respect, in a pluralist society? The
book we have produced is a contribution to the debates that circulate
around this question.

It is an important question because humour is one of the most perva-
sive elements of public culture. It occurs across all contemporary media,
in most of their different institutional formats, as well as being a central
aspect of everyday life and our day-to-day relationships. Humour is not
confined to any particular genre or form of narrative, even though
certain genres and narrative forms are defined by their mode of being
funny, regardless of whether they achieve this. Nor is it by any means
exclusive to conventional occasions or locations. Humour infiltrates
every area of social life and interaction, even rearing its head in situations where it is not normally regarded as appropriate, as is sometimes
the case with 'sick' or 'black' humour. For this reason, humour is not
synonymous with comedy; it extends beyond it and is not exhausted by
its more formal stagings in club venues, broadcasting or film.

It is generally regarded as beneficial to laugh about things, including ourselves; to get problems off our chests and 'see their funny side'; to look back on what was previously regarded as very serious, maybe even tragic, and 'have a good laugh about it'. There are clearly many cases where this is so, but equally there are others when it is inappropriate to laugh, when humour does not sit happily with the general tenor of an event or situation, and when a joke is regarded as overstepping the mark, as being beyond a joke.

The paradox of writing seriously about humour is that humour makes a mockery of seriousness. This is of course why we celebrate it. But there are good reasons for taking humour seriously, even if we risk seeming po-faced or stereotypically donnish in doing so. One of the contributors to this book, Jerry Palmer, has written an engaging study with exactly that purpose (1994; see also Palmer, 1987). Our purpose in this collection of essays is more specific in that we concentrate on the question of offensiveness in humour, but we do so seriously, and without apologies. If a comic assault on someone's sense of themselves as individual subjects, or on the sense of social and cultural identity of a particular social group or category, proves to have seriously damaging results and repercussions, we should take this seriously.

This does not mean that we are somehow opposed to humour or deficient in our sense of it. The contributors to this book have agreed to write about the ethics and aesthetics of humour in their individual chapters because they share in the desire to explore some of the concerns and difficulties raised by humour, to ask where the limits of humour and comedy may be said to lie and how they may be negoti-ated without resort to censorship, which is usually self-defeating. There are certainly cases where censorship is warranted, as for example in protecting children from some forms of sexual humour, but censorship as part of a system of governance or rule is a denial of free speech and deserves to be comically as well as seriously challenged. Free speech entails open debate about the ethics of humour as well as enjoyment of its often anarchic aesthetics, for we're all reduced by attempts to close down such debate rather than pursue the moral and political issues that it necessarily involves.

The ethics of humour raise all sorts of issues, many of which have not been explored to any great degree or in any great depth. We hope at least to make some inroads into these issues and ask why some people are offended by what is, at least ostensibly, intended in fun. How should they deal with the offence? And what kinds of topics, or comic treatments of topics, cause people to take offence? Is it ever legitimate to take offence at an item or instalment of comic discourse? Is it necessarily counter-productive to do so? Should any area of public or private life be taboo so far as humour is concerned? These are the sorts of questions which are high on the agenda when the ethics of humour are being discussed.

Increasing attention is being paid to such questions, particularly when it appears that examples of humour and comedy have hit against a non-negotiable limit. To take two other Third Reich examples, a British video made in 2002 in support of the anti-euro campaign showed comic actor Rik Mayall impersonating Hitler and presenting the euro as a Nazi plot, while more recently Prince Harry, third heir in line to the British throne, donned a Nazi uniform for a fancy-dress party, traditionally a source of comic self-entertainment among invited guests. Both cases were roundly condemned, though Labour MP Kate Hoey, who featured in the video, asserted that anyone who did not laugh at the Hitler spoof 'needs to get a life' (*The Guardian*, 3 July 2002). The British Labour party was also criticised in January 2005 for a campaign poster in which the heads of Michael Howard and Oliver Letwin (the Tory leader and shadow chancellor) were grafted on to the bodies of flying pigs, between which appeared the caption 'The Day The Tory Sums Add Up'. This was considered by some as anti-Semitic because both these politicians are Jewish (ibid., 29 January 2005). Was this a legitimate objection or a species of religious paranoia? Was it malice, insensitivity or thoughtlessness on the part of New Labour and the agency TBWA who produced the poster? (see Byrnes, 2005, and Gibson and Brook, 2005, on TBWA). At the very least, the incident seemed ironic in view of the Labour government's Serious Organised Crime and Police Bill, which went through its second reading just a month before the poster appeared on the Labour party website. This was attacked citing Schedule 10 of the bill which is designed to outlaw a speech, publication or performance that would incite religious or racial hatred. It was considered to be flawed, as for example in its elision of race and religion, and dangerous, as for example in possibly gagging writers, actors and filmmakers in their representations of religious groups or creeds. The government denied this, claiming that the bill would not prevent free speech or religious satire. It was nevertheless strongly opposed by a coalition of politicians, lawyers, academics and comedians, including Rowan Atkinson, star of the BBC TV sitcom series, *Blackadder*, who insisted that 'there should be no subjects about which you cannot make jokes.' He denounced the bill for promoting 'the idea that there should be a right not to be offended ... In my view, the right to offend is far more important than any right not to be offended' (*The Guardian*, 7 December 2004).

This gives some indication of the tension and at times open conflict between those concerned to protect freedom of speech and those concerned to protect minority, oppressed or previously persecuted groups from the public expression of bigotry, misprision, abusive stereotyping, discrimination and hatred. Similar considerations apply to natural disasters and the need to show sympathy and compassion to their victims, for the whole point of 'sick' jokes is that they fly in the face of these feelings. The consequences of such jokes, or even of those judged insensitive and uncaring, can of course be severe. Comic, writer, actor and singer Keith Allen was once physically assaulted by a soldier because of a joke about an IRA bomb (Pickering and Littlewood, 1998: 298). There are also cases when people have been sacked as a result of offensive or tasteless jokes. In the same month as the flying pigs poster appeared, Sky Sports dumped their football pundit Rodney Marsh because of a playground pun he made on the tragedy of the Asian tsunami and the Toon Army, as Newcastle United FC are jocularly known. Sky offered apologies to all 'those who were offended' by this 'inexcusable' joke; Marsh was made to do likewise after Sky edited out and removed his comment from later transmissions of the show in which it had been made. Marsh's position became untenable for what he had said, and while being held to account for what is condemned as 'inexcusable' is usually the cause of dismissal in such cases, there are cases when someone's credentials for satirical comment are undermined by their actions – rather than for what they say – which henceforth place them in a position of hypocrisy or make them vulnerable to the charge of operating with double standards. This was the case with Angus Deayton, chair of a BBC TV news comedy programme, *Have I Got News For You*, cited by Ken Willis in his contribution to this book. Usually, the celebrities involved are expected to stay out of the public eye for a given period of time until they are allowed back into the media fold, their penance apparently completed and their shame apparently expunged.

These two cases may not seem commensurate, so raising questions about the criteria by which they are assessed. Some may feel that, regardless of the insensitivity and tastelessness involved, the official response to Rodney Marsh's 'joke' was excessive, particularly when compared with other offensive jokes. For example, the comedian Mike Read, former star of the BBC TV soap opera *Eastenders*, was said to have made jokes in a stand-up gig at Chatham Central Theatre about

Muslims being made to bungee jump without strings and work as strippers. His performance became subject to a police investigation (*Mail on Sunday*, 27 October 2002). This was one opportunistic incident among many of the anti-Islamic jokes that have circulated since the tragic events of 11 September 2001, but it certainly has implications for the responsibility we have for what we say. Particularly in public, we are held to account as much for what we say as what we do.

Another example discussed by Ken Willis later in the book is the sacking of the Tory MP Ann Winterton from the shadow cabinet, in May 2002, for telling what one Conservative politician described as 'an offensive and sinister joke' at an annual rugby club dinner in the north of England. She wound up her speech by saying 'Let me tell you a story':

An Englishman, a Cuban, a Japanese man and a Pakistani were all on a train. The Cuban threw a fine Havana cigar out of the window. When he was asked why he replied: 'They are 10 a penny in my country'. The Japanese man then threw a Nikon camera out of the carriage, adding: 'These are 10 a penny in my country'. The Englishman then picked up the Pakistani and threw him out of the train window. When all the other travellers asked him to account for his actions, he said: 'They are 10 a penny in my country'.

Despite an apology, Ann Winterton lost her place in the shadow cabinet for what the Tory peer, Lord Taylor, called an 'appalling lack of political judgement' (*The Guardian*, 6 May 2002: 1). Racist jokes and putatively comic references are hardly an anomaly in the Conservative Party – Tory politician Alan Clark once described Africa as 'Bongo-Bongo Land' – and only two years later, Ann Winterton was formally reprimanded again for telling a joke about two sharks going for a Chinese in Morecambe Bay, north-west England, following the tragic deaths in February 2004 of 20 Chinese cocklepickers who had been trapped there by the tide.

Some may see this as tasteless bad timing and others as just a harmless play on words, but it has also to be taken in relation to her racist deprecation of the human worth of the Asian population in Britain, tabloid newspaper hysteria about 'illegal immigrants' and arguably, at least, in relation to the continuing legacy of British imperialism and the hierarchical racial ideology that was a crucial adjunct to it (see Pickering, 2001, ch. 5). Colonial subjects, including indentured Chinese coolies, were widely regarded as '10 a penny' when compared with the white population in the motherland of Empire. The joke entailed a continuity of assessment and regard for ethnic status, and of power differentials and disregard for economic exploitation. The migrant cocklepickers in Morecambe Bay had only recently died, and as migrant workers had been highly vulnerable to exploitation because of British immigration policy. They would not have been deemed a suitable subject for humour if they had been white (Hardy, 2004). Winterton made her Chinese cocklepicker joke in a speech at a dinner for Anglo-Dutch understanding. According to Nick Palmer, Labour MP for Broxtowe, who was present at the dinner: 'Everyone was completely embarrassed and stared at their plates' (*Guardian*, 26 February 2005). Winterton's joke went beyond the English proclivity for a pun since it was demonstrably based on the view that the ethnicity of the cocklepickers made it acceptable. It was this view which made the joke racist. As Simon Hoggart (2004) pointed out, if there had just been a ferry disaster off Denmark, with many people drowned, would she have made a joke about two sharks saying: 'I feel peckish. Fancy a Danish?' And if the Danish people present had not laughed, would they have been deficient in their sense of humour?

When a Muslim or Jewish person takes offence at a racist joke made by a white Christian, this does not mean that they lack a sense of humour, and cannot laugh at themselves or their own culture. Stand-up comic, actor and film director, Woody Allen once made the joke: 'If only God would give me some clear sign! Like making a large deposit in my name at a Swiss bank.' The humour in this derives from the contrastive descent from fervent spiritual aspiration to unrestrained material avarice. In the mouth of someone else, it could have been interpreted as pandering to the long-established anti-Semitic stereotype of a 'sleuth-hound instinct for gain' (Russell and Lewis, 1900: 5), the stereotype which is sent up so tellingly by Eddie Waters in Trevor Griffith's play *Comedians*. In drawing on this stereotype, the joke would then have to be read in the light not only of the mid-twentieth century persecution and murder of Jewish people in Nazi Germany but also of the commonplace antipathy to Jews in Britain in the same historical period (e.g. Goldhagen, 1997; and Garfield, 2004). Stereotypes, whether in comic or other forms of discourse, do not simply derive their ideological currency from a contemporary context. They often trail a legacy of meanings and associations that extend a good way back into the past (see Pickering, 2001).

There is however nothing fixed about the fixities in which stereotypes trade. Identity and application are of direct significance. Who is comically treated by whom and with what consequences are crucial factors that can determine the outcome of a joke and whether or not it is regarded as offensive. For example, the female Muslim comic Shazia Mirza, who we interview later in the book, has included the following tale in her stand-up routine:

> Last year, I went to Mecca to repent my sins, and I had to walk around the Black Stone. All the women were dressed in black, you could only see their eyes. And I felt a hand touch my bottom. I ignored it. I thought: 'I'm in Mecca, it must be the hand of God.' But then it happened again. I didn't complain. Clearly, my prayers had been answered.

Imagine this comic anecdote told by stand-up comedians Mike Read, Jim Davidson or Bernard Manning, with of course the appropriate transpositions of gender and pronoun. It would shift from being a joke at the teller's own expense to a joke told at someone else's. It wouldn't show someone sending up their own religion and culture, but someone mocking the religion and culture of other people. It is in this difference that the potential for comic offensiveness can arise.

The various examples we have given so far should have made one feature of humour quite clear. This is that jokes are not automatically funny. There are things that seem to make us laugh spontaneously, impulsively, without demur. It may be an example of slapstick, an inadvertent malapropism, an off-the-cuff dash of wit. These things may seem to be automatically funny. But in many instances what is accepted as a joke, and so funny on that account, has first to be negotiated as a joke. Its meaning has to be accepted as comic, either in intention or consequence, and then evaluated as comic, for there are definite cases when we say, for whatever reason, 'that's not funny' or 'I know you're trying to wind me up'. Sometimes we are uncertain, as an utterance rides a cliff-edge of ambiguous meaning and interpretation. Comic meaning is also dependent on the settings and contexts in which a joke is told, the competence of its delivery, the identity of the teller, and the recipients of the joke (see Palmer, 1994, ch. 13). What is funny at one time is not funny at another. Humour is a volatile substance. It can explode in a bright, sensational light or simply fizzle out with only the slightest wisp of smoke. This is what makes it such a fascinating phenomenon.

Just one short, single event may be seen in quite different ways. It 'can be given both a tragic and a comic, a serious and a humorous significance, depending on the kind of interpretative work carried out by different participants' (Mulkay, 1988: 54–5). This is difficult to foresee, as satirical writer Richard Ingrams once observed: 'Sometimes what you think will cause offence doesn't. And sometimes what you think is a joke, causes great offence' (Haines and Donnelly, 1986: 76). The joke can go either way because, as comedian and actress Maureen Lipman has observed, 'there's a fine line between the humorous and the offensive' (2000: 216). Treading the line and deciding between the two sides requires an immediate response. To ponder it would kill the joke at a stroke.

Often enough the interpretative work involved occurs within the very glide of what is happening. The process of joke negotiation is usually accomplished at considerable speed, whether the humour involved is on stage or screen or occurs at home with family or friends. Though difficulties of interpretation may be handled within the heat of an exchange, and ambiguities given an initial recognition, what has been involved in negotiating a joke or funny story becomes complicated only when you stop to think about it, or think about it in retrospect, especially where quite subtle, nuanced shadings of meaning and significance are involved.

The purpose of this book is to invite you to stop and think. Most of the time we don't think about how humour and comedy work or what they may entail, and we wouldn't be much good as makers or audiences of jokes or other forms of humour and comedy if we did sit and ponder in that way. But there are times when we should do this. There is every point in stopping and thinking when questions of offensiveness are raised by humour. We have put this book together in order to address such questions, and consider how they may be approached. Here we can identify two clearly defined and opposing sides to the issue of offensiveness in humour (as well as various positions between them). There are those like Rowan Atkinson, who believe that jokes can be made about anything, and that the right to offend is paramount. This means that there can be no limit-cases in humour, even when scurrilous jokes may be directed towards the advocates of no-holds-barred approaches to humour and comedy, involving, say, assertions about their sexuality or the sexual perversions of their mothers or daughters. These must be taken in good part, for the right to offend cannot be compromised.

The defence of this right in the face of those he disparagingly calls 'healers and badge wearers' is the purpose of Howard Jacobson's knockabout, defiantly anti-PC book *Seriously Funny*. His argument is 'that there can be no drawing of lines within comedy' (1997: 37–8). We shouldn't fear derision, mockery or coarse laughter at our expense because it is this which 'makes our hearts strong' (ibid.). This doesn't seem to take us very far. It could be taken not as a robust defence of the antic spirit of humour but as an unwitting endorsement of persecution, never mind plain ridicule. Hearts are only ever made strong by self-belief, and derision or mockery can seriously diminish that or even, over time, rob people of their birthright to it. Whatever goes by the name of humour would then be seriously unfunny.

Some of Jabobson's book is little more than vented spleen, as for instance when he opines: 'a humourless little shit will always be a humourless little shit' (ibid: 15). Elsewhere he does raise some significant points. Two of these are indicative. First, he finds those who take offence at a joke, and who on that account are deemed to be lacking in a sense of humour, as unable to distinguish between 'make-believe rudeness and the real thing' (ibid: 34). This may or may not be the case. There are certainly some who, when implicated in a joke, fly off the handle at the slightest negative reference to their gender or ethnicity, their achievements or personality. These would be the humourless little shits Jacobson finds so unremittingly indefensible. Fortunately, they are few and far between. But can we always be sure that we have understood the distinction between make-believe and the real thing? Can it not be said that the purpose and power of make-believe is, at least in certain cases, precisely that – to *make* us believe, and so accept its representation as believably 'the real thing'?

The controversy over Chris Morris's Channel 4 *Brass Eye* television programmes, which mocked the documentary television genre, played exactly on the difficulty we sometimes have in distinguishing between documentary and spoof. Much of the humour of *The Office*, the BBC sitcom dealt with in the book by Frances Gray, was associated with the cross-over between the two. When we suspend our disbelief, there is both pleasure and danger – pleasure in the make-believe, danger in taking it as 'the real thing'. Our own chapter on Ali G and Mrs Merton deals with the forms of humour that arise out of the ambiguities of comic impersonation and the ethical implications for 'the real thing' that these may be said to carry. There is in any case considerable haziness in the distinction between make-believe or what is said in jest, and real insults or what is meant in earnest. Criticism of this plank in Jabobson's argument cannot be made by advocating attempts to dispel the haziness, to insist on a hard-and-fast line between make-believe and 'the real thing'. That would sound a death-knell for humour. We do want to argue, though, for a clearer understanding of how the distinction operates, how relations between its two dimensions of meaning and reference are negotiated, and how movement between them becomes a source both of the ethics and aesthetics of humour and comedy.

A second interesting point made by Jabobson arises from his claim that if you 'jettison the cargo of offence ... you jettison the joke' (ibid: 37). There are examples illustrating this later in the book, but the one cited by Jabobson backs up his claim well enough. It comes from a spoof act based on an imagined PC version of Bernard Manning: 'There's a black feller ... a Pakistani ... and a Jew ... in a nightclub ... having a drink ... What a fine example of an integrated community!' The joke itself derives from the preposterousness of the failed joke within it, for the punchline completely lacks in punch and trips ignominiously over its own well-meaning intentions. One of the features of humour we explore in this book is how humour at once permits, legitimates and exonerates an insult, whether this is through comic parody, impersonation or two-way badinage. The joke or comic discourse allows the contraband cargo of the offence to be smuggled aboard. The cases we examine certainly support the claim made by Jacobson. At the same time, the claim is too simple. It lumps together all sorts of joke and wit indiscriminately, without distinction or qualification. Racist or sexist jokes become at one with light-hearted banter. The politics and ethics of humour and comedy are swept aside, for if you raise the question of offensiveness then you have made the fatal wrong-step in Jacobson's eyes. You have become anti-humour. This is misleading, in part because registering offence and lacking in humour are not necessary corollaries of each other, and in part because a joke is not simply like a ship that is filled up with a cargo of offence and so by this fact made to sail upright across the seas of humour. Maybe we should jettison the metaphor instead. We want to move beyond such quick-fire formulas as that offered by Jacobson and start exploring in greater detail how humour works in the complexities of our manifold experiences of it, which include the dynamic relations between its aesthetics and its ethics.

A significant aspect of these relations involves identifying the line in the sand between offensiveness and humour. Jerry Palmer put this well when he wrote: 'excessive contentiousness produces offence instead of humour, [and] excessive politeness produces boredom; one of the arts demanded of the comedian is the ability to tread this dividing line' (1987: 175). It is an art because the line is drawn in sand; the wind can erase it and waters wash over it. There is in any case no absolute agreement as to where it lies, for it changes over time and how it is perceived varies according to person and context. The distinction between contentiousness and boredom is clear enough, but the boundary between humour and offence is elusive. This is at least true some of the time, which is why we say there is no absolute agreement about it, but at other times it isn't elusive, and Michael Billig, Dennis Howitt and Kwame Owusu-Bempah deal in their chapters with cases where the boundary becomes abundantly clear. When jokes involve violent racism to the point where, either implicitly or explicitly, they advocate and enjoy physical violence committed against another ethnic group, the ethics of humour are relatively straightforward, for these are by any standard repellent and pernicious forms of non-humour masquerading as jokes. But, *pace* Jacobson, even where the ethics are not so straightforward, we still have to negotiate a line, somewhere or other, between humour and offensiveness. Here we agree with Gary Younge when he wrote that the 'idea that we should never draw an ethical line between what is acceptable and what is offensive when it comes to comedy is as disingenuous as it is bankrupt' (Younge, 2000: 3). This is the other clearly defined side of the debate about offensiveness in humour.

It is true that this ethical line is difficult to negotiate, not least because it is blurred and keeps moving, and because who 'we' might be is heavily burdened with political as well as moral issues. These difficulties may tempt us into drawing a different line, along with Jacobson, between the make-believe of comedy and the 'real world' as quite divorced from that, but the aesthetics of comedy, even if conceived only in terms of its intrinsic formal dynamics, cannot be cleaved off in that way from moral, ethical and political considerations associated with the 'real world'. Comic discourse obviously operates in ways which are distinct from other forms of discourse, and it would be foolish to try to reduce it, or make it conform, to the conventions and values of those other forms. At the same time, it doesn't operate in a completely separate realm, a parallel world without connection to the one we routinely inhabit. It accompanies us all along the way within this everyday world, whether in conversations with friends or in responses to the media. We should therefore make distinctions between serious and comic forms of utterance and dialogue, but not conceive of them as, or allow them to develop into, rigid compartmental divisions. Their interrelations should in themselves be celebrated, for when the aesthetics and ethics of humour and comedy openly interrogate each other, this encourages cultural reflexivity and integration and is to their mutual benefit. Experiencing them in active conjunction with each other is to realise and heighten their value for each other.

It remains the case that while many people expect comedians to push at the accepted boundaries, take risks, attempt to shock us and shatter our illusions, they do not concede that this means comedians can do or say whatever they like, or that certain ethical lines should never be drawn, even if this is confined to individual choice or small-group consensus. Thinking about such ethical lines seems necessary because it is important for public representations and public discourse. If we accept that we should never draw an ethical line between what is acceptable and what is offensive, then we accept that anyone can say anything about other people, however malicious or laden with bigotry, and that they may do so with impunity. There is no general acceptance of this even in contemporary Western societies where standards of acceptance in comedy are broader and more liberal than they have been for at least a couple of centuries.

Along with this welcome expansion of tolerance, societies in the West have become increasingly heterogeneous and diverse, or in a word, multicultural. The key test of this new tolerance is not whether people can say 'fuck' on stage or on television after the 9 p.m. watershed, for that is a fairly trivial matter. The test is whether tolerance can extend across all different social, ethnic and religious groups at least to the extent that they show equal respect for each other's beliefs, practices and traditions. Over the past ten years or so, this test has been failed, as it probably will in the future, but reducing the number of such failures, and trying to further the cause of social and ethical tolerance as part of the way we celebrate multiculturalism, requires a renegotiation of the ways in which 'we' is conceived, both in relation to the sources of laughter and the rationale of ethical values and principles. The tension between them is one reason why the test of tolerance is failed. One of the aims of this book is to explore this tension and the question as to where the limits of humour might lie in order that 'we', in the multicultural sense of the word, may come to laugh together on a much wider basis and without the unexamined prejudice that allows for humour calculated to do little else than cause deep offence in others.

Paradoxically, making offensive jokes about others with total impunity would mean that there are no boundaries to push at any more. This would lead to the defeat of humour, which is subject to our ability to choose. Humour is only possible because certain boundaries, rules and taboos exist in the first place. Their existence, along with the satisfaction and sense of agency gained in overcoming them, are equally vital to why we laugh. Humour goes against the grain, or at least does so in its more liberating moments, but it cannot be pinned down to any specific purpose or significance in any of its manifestations. It may disturb conventional vision and help us see things in alternative ways, or confirm such vision and drive us deeper into our prejudices. It may teach us to delight in contrarieties, in the confrontation of opposing values, in setting ambiguity against certainty, but the exact opposite to these consequences may be its achievement in any actual case or context. The ethics of humour and comedy are inextricably entwined with their aesthetics, which is why we need to keep the lines of dialogue between them open and active. In doing so we need to recognise that no singular or absolute evaluative template can be established for humour and comedy, and perhaps all we can say in the end is that we laugh because we are human, flawed, frail and imperfect. We may all have our own conception of paradise, but we should always remember that inside the Garden of Eden there was no laughter at all.

Outline of the book

The contributors to the book take up the issues we have raised, and introduce others that are specific to their chosen areas of enquiry. These deal with such varied aspects of humour as racist jokes and the comic celebration of racist violence; the ethical discourse of political humour; the relationship between laughter, embarrassment and power in the British TV sitcom; Bakhtin and the ethics of comic parody; the articulation of social anxieties about sexual morality and singlehood in popular film and television; humour competence and its relation to the social distribution of power; and the ethics of comic transgression involving impersonation via different kinds of television personae. The menu is a rich one, and we hope it will sharpen people's appetite for the dialogue between the aesthetics and ethics of humour that is central to the book as a whole.

We have brought the contributors together to write within a single volume because of their different intellectual backgrounds and interests, and the different views and approaches they take to considering the cultural dynamics and ethical implications of humour and comedy. We have also tried to ensure variety and diversity by including interviews with two contemporary stand-up comedians, Omid Djalili and Shazia Mirza, who discuss the ethics of humour and comedy from a practitioner point of view. Despite the broad range of

material covered, with varying perspectives being adopted and alternative views being aired, the underlying intention of everyone whose
voice is heard here is similar. This is to explore, in an open-minded but
avowedly serious way, the book's twin themes: the question of humour
and offensiveness, and how this relates to social divisions and structures of power in society.

We begin the book with an exploration of what is, by most people's
standards, an extremely virulent form of racist humour. This form of
humour, if the term is indeed in any way befitting, involves laughing
at comic representations of violence to certain ethnic groups. Unlike
other forms of racist humour, it doesn't necessarily rely on stereotyping. In violent racist jokes the humour derives from the idea of violence being perpetrated against victims who are identified by race or
ethnicity. Michael Billig outlines the defining characteristics of the
violent racist joke, referring not only to the features of the joke but
also to the wider context in which the joke is told. He analyses the joke
pages of websites supporting the Ku Klux Klan. A significant minority
of the jokes on these websites are violent racist jokes and his chapter
shows how they depict different types of violence. As with his recent
book on humour, *Laughter and Ridicule*, Billig's chapter challenges the
commonly held assumption that humour is necessarily a human good
that should be automatically cherished and celebrated. Comic ridicule
may act in various ways as a form of social regulation, but the examples discussed by Billig operate at the outer limits of humour and call
into question the supposed benison of humour in people's lives. What
then, at these limits, is its value and virtue? Laughter in these cases can
hardly be said to have any positive or beneficial consequences. The
very opposite is true, for violent racist jokes support what is ethically
obnoxious and (without using the word merely for rhetorical effect)
profoundly uncivilised. In Billig's view, the violent jokes he discusses
are so far beyond a joke that they are deadly serious. They are so in virtually every way that seriousness can be taken.

Billig's chapter contains offensive racist words and references. These
occur, though generally to a lesser extent, elsewhere in the book. We
have retained them as a matter of editorial policy because we do not
regard it as right to artificially hide the terms and manifestations of
racism or other morally offensive forms of bigotry. This policy does,
of course, carry the danger of recuperation, of bringing such terms and
manifestations back into circulation. In other words, even their critique may be said to allow them another lease of life. This is what, in
our chapter, we call the Alf Garnett syndrome, through which what is

being satirised becomes a source of celebration among at least a section of the audience. The syndrome is touched on by various authors in the book – and of course it occurred in the United States as well with Archie Bunker, Alf Garnett's North American counterpart – and the danger it raises is that of turning a racist figure into a role model, the butt of the humour into the cause of the celebration. We recognise this danger, but don't believe it helps to soften or alleviate the way certain forms of bigotry or hatred are expressed, in humour or any other area of social encounter and interchange. What counts – as Billig emphasises – is the context of their reproduction. In the context of this book, the reproduction of offensive comedic material is analytical, for we seek to reveal how such material works and to show that what is comically done can also be critically undone.

Racist humour can be viewed in two ways, for the pleasures of humour may not only be pernicious. What is pernicious may also be pleasurable. Again, this depends crucially upon context. Nothing is inherently funny or unfunny. This is decided according to the social conventions operative in any social setting or circumstance. The interplay between humour and social conventions – which determines whether certain jokes are funny or unfunny – applies equally to the joking relationship. This is conventionally established, just as the jokes within it are conventionally negotiated as appropriate or inappropriate. Dennis Howitt and Kwame Owusu-Bempah sketch this process in terms of particular joke maxims. These inform their ensuing discussion of racist jokes and the social and cultural contexts which make them racist. In underpinning racial ideology, such jokes are neither value-neutral nor separable from the consequences of racism, whether these are social, economic or political. In their view, racist jokes are a highly effective propaganda vehicle for racial stereotypes, not least because the apparent humour camouflages their racist import. The many examples Howitt and Owusu-Bempah cite to illustrate this inevitably raises the issue of how power differentials are implicated in the production of racism in popular humour. This may be given a quick and easy reckoning: think of the number of jokes in Britain directed negatively at the Irish or those of African-Caribbean descent, and the number of jokes which are similarly derogatory about white British people. The disparity speaks volumes about whose cultural values predominate, how power is unequally spread across different social and cultural institutions, why power relates to ideas about social superiority, and how whiteness escapes attention or even becomes invisible as an ethnic category in racist humour. The situation can be turned around and looked at in a more positive way. Since ethics are about appropriate standards of behaviour, the absence of a repertoire of jokes which highlight and are appreciative of the richness of cultural diversity is significant. What Howitt and Owusu-Bempah's chapter clearly suggests is that it is high time we began to address the various questions raised by this absence.

The ethical concern with appropriate standards of behaviour is central to the relationship between politics and humour. From Jonathan Swift's 'Modest Proposal' of 1729 to today's stand-up comedy about Tony Blair and George Bush, political humorists have evaluated the conduct of political leaders and ministers, and questioned the moral basis of their policies, decisions, administration and action. In his chapter, John Morreall explores the ways in which humour promotes critical thinking in political life, and examines the ethical implications of political humour. He reviews different approaches to ethics and humour, leading to the key question: does humour about politics do benefit or harm? Morreall suggestively combines incongruity theory with the aesthetics of playful comic experience in order to focus in on the ethical ramifications of humour about politics. To use a metaphor from grammar, in such humour comic ideas or points are presented in the subjunctive rather than the indicative mood, for unlike, say, legal testimony, humour is not a set of bona fide assertions to be proved or disproved. To claim otherwise would be to ignore the imaginative dimension in humour that is central to its aesthetics.

Drawing on his own earlier work, Morreall shows how humorous amusement and negative emotions can displace one another. In his view, a humorous message is able to make people more flexible mentally than an emotional message. It is more likely to make us ask questions, think critically, see new possibilities, and be open to change (Morreall 1983b, 1987a, 1997 and 1999b). This is to point up the ways in which humour, including political humour, encourages audiences to think rather than feel about the issues, and think more subtly and creatively, but the playful, non-bona fide status of humorous messages also carries dangers, as for example with the racist jokes discussed by Billig, Howitt and Owusu-Bempah, or with cruel jokes that jump in to displace feelings of sympathy or compassion, as with those in popular circulation following the Hillsborough football stadium disaster of 1989 and during the hunt for the serial murderer, Peter Sutcliffe (Pickering and Littlewood, 1998: 292). The subjunctive character of comic discourse means it can move in the direction of either benefit or harm. Humour often exaggerates, and so can provide imaginative ballast for stereotypes and the reinforcement of xenophobic constructions of the Other, but in delighting in incongruities, it can expose delusions, pretensions, duplicities and hypocrisies, not least among those in authority and positions of power.

Morreall takes in both the negative and positive aspects of the ethics of humour, and relates these to humour used by politicians, which is usually objectionable, and humour about politicians, which is often commendable. As he makes clear, the humour of politicians is generally instrumental and manipulative, despite their attempts to dissemble on this front. Their masquerade runs against the grain of the playful aesthetics of humour and so becomes, in itself, an unethical use of humour. It is fundamentally dishonest, and contrasts with the use of humour to counteract 'groupthink', bring out the viewpoints of women and marginalised groups, and cut through pomposity, lies, deceit and doublespeak. Although most of Morreall's examples are taken from US politics, the points he makes are applicable elsewhere. With politicians hiring more and more advertising experts and spin doctors, on both sides of the Atlantic, the need to ensure space for the clearheaded, critical voices of political humorists as our watchdogs of democracy becomes ever more imperative.

Parody is an important part of political humour, as it is of other targets of comedic address, but how does it work and what happens when it is judged to have failed? Humour can be rejected for either ethical or aesthetic reasons, but in either case permission to engage in comic ridicule has been withdrawn or rejected. It is judged to be unfunny, or to have crossed a boundary. Jerry Palmer starts his chapter with these negative judgements of parodic comedy. It is because ethics and aesthetics may collide in parody that he revives the neo-classical concept of decorum, which entails public judgements about appropriate or inappropriate forms of expression for any particular theme or setting. In approaching parody in this way, he offers a critique of the theory of parody, which generally sees it as a secondary, derivative phenomenon whose existence is parasitic upon a primary text. Its secondary nature frequently, but not universally, derives from the attempt to use the parodic process in a humorous attack upon either the text parodied, or some social phenomenon of which the text in question is a part, though it may also have a non-humorous function, as in literature and the fine arts, where foregrounded intertextual reference becomes integral to the aesthetic construction of meaning.

Palmer examines the social basis of parody by asking what sorts of text are *permissibly* parodied, under what circumstances and for what purposes, in different social formations. This involves him in a reconsideration of the dialogic and ludic elements in the celebrated theory of parody and carnival advanced by the Russian literary theorist, Mikhail Bakhtin (1895–1975). Parodic mockery doesn't work today in the same ways in which it did in the pre-modern world. Its licence is usually confined to the arts and the realm of aesthetics, and so kept separate from the realm of ethics. When the aesthetic form which is subversively parodied assaults key public symbols or values, it is often regarded as having breached standards of decorum and so become ethically impermissible. It then risks condemnation, censorship, even legal prosecution, though this depends on the degree of consensus about the offensiveness of the parody and may involve power relationships between antagonistic sources of evaluation. Palmer cites war memorials as a form of public commemoration which cannot be constructed in a parodic style, for this would be judged as directly offensive on a number of counts. Decorum is then the public form through which ethical and aesthetic distinctions are standardised and maintained. Palmer's revival of the concept is an important counter to cavalier uses of the notion of carnivalesque parody in relation to the cultural forms of modernity, for such uses often betray a lack of historical understanding or play fast and loose with how categories are historically located and historically meaningful.

Deliciously sandwiched in the middle of the book, are two interviews with contemporary stand-up comedians who come from ethnic minority groups in Britain. Both Omid Djalili and Shazia Mirza challenge the aesthetic conventions of comedy while also remaining sensitive to the ethical issues that concern us in the book. They bring refreshing new voices to the comedy circuit. More significantly they retain the opposition to racism and sexism of the alternative comedy scene of the 1980s, but obviously move beyond the white-male dominance of that scene. As a supplement to analytical concerns raised elsewhere in the book, we explore with Omid and Shazia the actual ethical difficulties and aesthetic triumphs of stand-up comedy on the front line.

Both Shazia and Omid are keenly aware that what can be achieved in comedy is relative to the context and the comedian, but the problem with analytical models of humour is that they attempt to subsume all forms of humour under one single paradigm. This cannot be done. In writing about the execution and display of competence in humour, Ken Willis in his chapter is rightly suspicious of models and theories which strive for universality. His attention instead is focused on localised forms of communicative interaction in humour, and on the relationship between differential humour competence and social power.

The former is significant as it deals with how people respond to humorous discourse, and the latter is relevant as power plays a vital role in, for example, determining whether or not something is to be seen as offensive rather than amusing. Models which consider humour competence to be simply a universal cognitive skill fail to recognise the social and political aspects of texts, responses to which display a differential competence, and not simply a shared competence. Given these differences, those jokes which Freud called tendentious give rise to contested interpretations, and it is usually those with most power in any situation or institution who determine which interpretation shall dominate.

While eschewing any claim to general applicability, Willis draws on different theorists of humour in order to achieve a detailed, bottom-up assessment of the joking relationship involving a dynamic, shifting balance between addresser, addressee and comic butt, and between understanding, appreciation and agreement. These relate to what Willis outlines as humour networks, which are especially important in the negotiation and evaluation of tendentious jokes. He illustrates his approach with close readings of two jokes involving Tory politicians, one as teller and one as butt, the former involving Ann Winterton and the jokes we have already introduced. In contravening private/public boundaries, Winterton on both occasions committed a breach of decorum and was appropriately penalised. Though hardly examples of instrumental or manipulative jokes in the way Morreall refers to them, they offer abundant evidence of the objectionable use of humour by a politician and show her incompetence in judging the broad public nature of the humour networks in which her comic offences were committed and through which they were communicated.

The absence of jokes which affirm as well as send up the benefits of multiculturalism may be lamented, but as we noted in the previous section, it is at least notable that ethical safeguards against gratuitous racist offence in humour and comedy are higher now than 50, or even 30 years ago. Along with this development, at least in Britain, there is now a new self-consciousness about comic practice. In her chapter on the British sitcom, Frances Gray explores the impact of this awareness of the relationship between laughter and power and the way in which some new comic forms have incorporated it. The most significant of these is the recent television phenomenon: the sitcom as pseudo-documentary. In approaching her discussion of this phenomenon, Gray deftly sketches the trajectory of the sitcom from the early 1960s. In doing so, she focuses on a neglected aspect of this television genre in its comedic uses of embarrassment. She notes how this is a much milder form of emotional response than aggression, hatred, anger or humiliation, all of which seem to call stridently for some form of ethical judgement, but embarrassment is no less real for all those involved in the television experience, and is just as common an element in that experience as are stronger emotions.

Gray traces how the comedic uses of embarrassment in British sitcom gradually changed from the unquestioning affirmation of ethical consensus and a broad community of interests and values, through an accommodation of eccentricity, and a series of innumerable shifts in its construction of the position of women, the family, children and social minorities, to the cultivation of self-consciousness and the advent of embarrassment as central to that self-consciousness, rather than to its absence. The introduction of docusoaps and so-called reality TV was a key component in this transformation, involving people 'acting' themselves and collapsing the forms of documentary and sitcom into each other. These new forms paved the way for the entrance of sitcom as pseudo-documentary, most eminently perhaps in BBC's *The Office*, by Ricky Gervais and Stephen Merchant. The unethical exploitation of embarrassment and power which had become common in reality TV was called into question by the programme's self-conscious foregrounding of the equation of commodified culture and comedified selves. David Brent himself self-consciously (and ridiculously) cultivated his office-boss-cum-entertainer persona for the benefit of the fly-on-the-wall camera and his hoped-for celebrity status, showing himself incompetently preoccupied with political correctness and the ethics of humour as aspects of management style, and as lacking in self-knowledge as he was absorbed by his own ego. When the series came to a close, the laughter at his persona as 'real self' finally spiralled into embarrassment at the emptiness inside his shell. The satirical target of the programme was the television industry itself, and its unethical transformation of people from subjects into objects for the sake of mass entertainment.

Deborah Chambers also deals mainly with sitcoms, but is concerned with their representation of single women since the 1990s. She analyses how comedy programmes like *Friends*, *Absolutely Fabulous* and *Sex and the City* have charted changing attitudes to the independence and sexuality of female singletons on both sides of the Atlantic. A range of comedies about the lives of single people has given expression to anxieties associated with finding a partner, sustaining intimate relationships, disrupting traditional gender roles and identities, and developing new forms of lifestyle. Dating, romantic longing, non-marital sex, single parenthood and cohabitation are key themes in these comedy programmes. The source of comic pleasure for the audience has resided in the problematic nature of single women living and making their way on their own. The appeal of these programmes lies in the ways in which they have explored the moral perturbations and dilemmas of female singlehood in the post-feminist period.

Chambers develops a critical treatment of the comic representation of women alone and questions the ethics of portraying them as both aggressors and victims. She examines the different personae developed for single women in sitcoms, but the most prevalent of these involve their characterisation as unruly and vulnerable. In response to delayed marriage and rising divorce rates, increases in single-person households and professional single women, these comedies tend to undermine rather than affirm the status of female singletons. They are at once objects of desire and convenient scapegoats for the disintegration of family values, cultural fragmentation and rampant individualism. The balance is in favour of traditional normative ethics: women as nurturers and carers within the conventional nuclear family. As Chambers suggests, we may question exactly how far women have come in their struggle for equality and exactly how far representations of single women have progressed from the Victorian stereotype of the socially forlorn or deviant spinster.

In our own chapter, we explore how the ambiguities inherent in impersonation allow and facilitate comic offence, extending the ethical limits within which offensive remarks or statements are made while at the same time exonerating them by highlighting the comic frame in which they are made. It is in the nature of responses made to comic impersonators by both audiences and butts that these limits have continually to be renegotiated. They are open and fluid, for if they were not the comic possibilities of impersonation would be considerably forestalled. The question becomes: how offensive is the comic remark; how comic is the comic offence? The ambivalence of meaning and intention is deliberately exploited, as we show via the two cases we chose to exemplify the process: the comic impersonators, Mrs Merton and Ali G. These examples were chosen initially because they involved cross-generational and cross-ethnic impersonations, but as we explored the aesthetics of their different personae, we found ourselves becoming increasingly drawn into the ethical implications of the regional, gender and ethnic stereotypes on which they draw. The key to the way these implications prove benign or otherwise seems to us to lie in how the ambiguities of comic impersonation are developed and deployed in particular forms of popular entertainment. This is what we hope to have shown in our analysis of these two comedians and the different personae they have assiduously cultivated.

As our outline should have made clear, the range of material covered overall is wide, while also allowing for close readings, and mixed, while also turning around the central aesthetic and ethical themes we have identified. Most books about humour are concerned primarily with their aesthetics, and for some, concern with the ethical issues and implications of humour and comedy will be, almost as a matter of course, a source of derision. It will be dismissed as another misguided example of political correctness. That would be simply a smug excuse for failing to engage with the book and giving detailed attention to what it has to say.

We have tried to move beyond both the self-defeating, regulatory, left-wing arguments associated with political correctness, and the opportunistic, unreflexive, right-wing denunciations of its practice. PC polemics effectively close down debate. We want to open it up again around an ethical confrontation between the real hurts and injuries of racism and other forms of oppression, and what has been called 'the dissonant modalities of popular culture confronted by contemporary cultural critics' (Shohat and Stam, 1994: 341). This means asking 'who is producing and consuming what, for what purposes, in what situation, for whom, and by what means – always with an eye on the power constellations and the emancipatory projects at stake' (ibid.).

We hope to have kept an eye on the issues of both power and freedom throughout each of the succeeding chapters, yet in writing about humour and comedy, this is not always easy. Power and freedom are deeply serious issues, while the very spirit of humour is such that it often involves attempts to subvert or explode the intentions or consequences of seriousness. The balance is cast in favour of the aesthetics rather than the ethics. This should be recognised, but not bemoaned. Though we defend the need to engage seriously with what is commonly regarded as antithetical to seriousness, we celebrate humour as a counter to seriousness, and especially to over-seriousness as a besetting academic vice. In view of this, since this is a book about jokes, it seems appropriate to round off our introduction with a joke about books. The joke may serve as advice to our readers. It's by the inimitable Groucho Marx: 'Outside a dog, a book is man's best friend. Inside a dog, it's too dark to read.'

1
Comic Racism and Violence

Michael Billig

Freud, in his book *Jokes and their Relation to the Unconscious* (1905/1960), argued that we constantly deceive ourselves about the reasons why we laugh. We like to believe that we laugh at the clever wittiness of jokes, but, as Freud argued, our pleasure may derive from less creditable sources that we do not care to acknowledge. Otherwise why should there be so many sexual and aggressive jokes? If, as Freud supposed, an element of self-deception surrounds much humour, then this would be especially true of racist humour today. The category 'racist humour' is itself contested. Because the prevailing standards condemn prejudice, people will like to believe that their behaviour, including their taste in humour, does not offend those standards. Those who laugh at ethnic jokes are likely to deny that their humour is racist. They will typically claim that they are 'just joking', defending themselves with a phrase that Goffman described as being one of the most commonly used in the English language (Goffman, 1974). As will be seen, there are academic versions of this position, defending the status of 'ethnic humour' from the criticism of being racist. On the other hand, the term 'racist humour' can create problems for those who criticise the telling of racist jokes. For them, the problem does not arise from the 'racist' part of the phrase 'racist humour'. It derives from admitting that racist humour belongs to the category of 'humour'. Generally, humour is acknowledged to be something good. In the present era, possessing a sense of humour is seen as a self-evidently desirable virtue (Wickberg, 1998). Psychologists and sociologists have also argued that humour possesses positive functions (see Billig, 2005, for a critical discussion of this tendency). Racist humour, then, cannot be humour because it is neither funny nor does it serve positive functions.

However, that is too simple a reaction. The category of 'humour' contains disturbing instances. Even racist and non-racist humour are not sharply distinguished as if they are totally different phenomena, sharing no common intrinsic properties. Indeed, the same basic joke can have racist and non-racist variants. Simon Critchley, in his book *On Humour*, gives an example of a joke that possesses a critical function because it mocks the pretensions of those in power:

> How many men does it take to tile a bathroom?
> I don't know. It depends how thinly you slice them.
>
> (Critchley, 2002: 11)

Critchley classifies this joke as 'true humour' for it 'changes the situation, tells us something about who we are and the sort of place we live in, and perhaps indicates to us how it might be changed' (ibid.). Such a joke plays with accepted forms, and thus makes the accepted structures of society unreal. Critchley goes on to acknowledge that much humour is not of this type, but is reactionary and reinforces social consensus. Instances of such reactionary humour are jokes that laugh at the supposed stupidity of outsiders. Critchley specifically cites ethnic humour: 'the British laugh at the Irish, the Canadians laugh at the Newfies, the Americans laugh at the Poles ...' (ibid:12.). His list does not include whites laughing at blacks. Nor does he mention that the target of the 'true' joke is substitutable. Instead of it being about men tiling a bathroom, it can be about Irish, Newfies or Poles. Or, as will be seen in the contexts of deepest racism, it can be 'niggers'. The disturbing fact is that one word changes a joke from being 'true' humour to the most bigoted humour. To use Freud's terminology, the 'joke-work' is identical. And if the joke is clever 'true' humour in the one form, why, with one different word, does it suddenly become reprehensibly unfunny? Any theory of racist humour must confront this problem.

This chapter looks at the sort of unambiguously racist humour represented by the racist version of the tiling joke. This is a type of humour that analysts, including both Critchley and Freud, have tended to overlook. In order to avoid misunderstanding, the issue of terminology must be discussed. The chapter looks at racist jokes taken from Websites that support the Ku Klux Klan. Such jokes include offensively racist terminology. The analyst is faced with a dilemma: whether to quote the terminology of the original or to replace offensive words by dashes or asterisks. There is no completely satisfactory solution to the dilemma for the arguments in favour of retention and replacement both have validity. The argument for replacement is based on the assumption that some racist terminology is so offensive that it should never be reproduced. Even if terms are being quoted, the mere fact of reproduction threatens taboos against their usage, thereby contributing to the perpetuation of a vocabulary that should never be employed. The argument for reproduction stresses the context of reproduction. In the course of an analysis of racism, the offensive words are not being used in a simple sense. They have become the topic of analysis. It is not possible to analyse racism without looking at its vocabulary, in the same way as a historian of Nazi ideology must quote from offensive texts such as *Mein Kampf*. Indeed, the bowdlerisation of the phenomenon itself is dangerous, for it might soften the full ferocity of extreme racism and bigotry.

A decision, nevertheless, has to be taken by anyone writing on these issues. Accordingly, I shall reproduce the racist material as it is found, without substituting the offensive terms (see Billig, 2001a, for a further justification of this strategy). Because the arguments for and against this strategy both have validity, it should be stressed that the decision is not an easy one. The argument has an extra dimension in the context of racist humour. Sometimes it is said that racist jokes are not serious because they are jokes. That is an argument that will be criticised later and is based on a misunderstanding of the nature of racist humour. It has been claimed that the portrayal of fictional characters uttering racist remarks or jokes can be humorous, because the audience is laughing at such characters. That was the justification for the racist remarks made by characters such as Alf Garnett in the BBC sitcom *Till Death Us Do Part* or Archie Bunker in the US sitcom *All in the Family*. Again, the reproduction of racist terminology for comedic purposes is deeply problematic. The context of reproduction is all important. The present context is that of analysis, not entertainment. It is not expected that any readers will laugh at the jokes. Rather it is expected they will be horrified that anyone might find such material humorous. In this regard, the terminology is certainly not retained for comedic purposes – quite the contrary, it is retained to expose for serious analytic purposes the unfunny aspects of so-called humour.

This leads to the problem of the word 'humour'. Often when writers or speakers call a joke 'humorous' or classify it as an example of 'humour', they are indicating their own stance towards the funniness of the material. The word 'humour' is not being used in this sense.

Humour is the object of analysis, not the judgement of the analyst. There is a case for saying that the concept of humour needs to be critically questioned, in order to understand the social biases of humorous material. Such a critique cannot assume the funniness, or worse still, the moral goodness, of what is described as 'humour' practices (see Billig, 2005, for a discussion of the need for a critical approach to humour). Accordingly, the word 'humour' will not be put into protective apostrophes. Treating racist jokes as jokes does not mean that the analyst finds such jokes funny. As noted above, it is presumed that no reader of this chapter will laugh at any of the examples of racist humour. Nevertheless such jokes are examples of humour, for they are treated as being humour in the contexts in which they are produced. The bathroom-tiling joke does not analytically cease to be a joke when its target is racial and that target is identified by an explicitly insulting epithet. Accordingly, the category of 'humour' is being treated as an analytic category, not as a sign that the analyst personally derives amusement from what is being labelled as 'humour'.

This position is part of a wider critical view of humour which has been elaborated elsewhere (Billig, 2005). This approach seeks to analyse critically views that celebrate humour and downplay humour's cruelties. Such views, it is argued, overlook the central role of ridicule in maintaining social order. Humour fulfils this universal social function because social actors wish to avoid the possibility of ridicule (see also Billig, 2001b). All cultures may use humour to maintain social codes, but there are no universal social codes and so no universal humour. This is not just a matter of differences between cultures. Within all cultures, there will be debates and conflicts about what constitutes appropriate behaviour. Accordingly, there will be debates about the appropriateness, morality and funniness of humour. Thus, humour is a matter of moral, political and aesthetic debate.

The present critical approach draws upon the theories of Freud and also of Bergson, both of whom stressed the role of cruelty in humour (Billig, 2005). For them, cruelty and aggression were not peripheral features that might occur in some unfortunate examples of humour, but were central to the social and psychological functions of humour. Consequently, the present analysis does not seek to protect the category of 'humour' from discreditable instances, as if cruel and immoral jokes could not possibly be humour, or at least 'true' humour. For this reason, racist humour will be treated as a type of humour, but not, of course, as humorous.

Ethnic humour and racism

If racist humour is to be considered as an example of humour – and to be analysed as such – then it must be conceded that racists may possess a sense of humour. This assumption is likely to be contested or, at least, found to be disturbing, given that possessing a sense of humour is often taken as a mark of a desirable well-rounded personality. It is easier to imagine racists as being humourless individuals, with their racism representing a psychological deficit. Certainly psychological theories of bigotry encourage such an assumption. The authoritarian bigot has been characterised as the sort of person who likes clear-cut rules and is unable to appreciate the ambiguities of jokes (e.g., Adorno et al., 1950; Altemeyer, 1988). It may be reassuring to believe that prejudiced people lack humour but there is little evidence to confirm the assumption. Extreme right-wing speakers use irony, sarcasm and humour as much, if not more, than mainstream speakers, and fascist propaganda frequently includes material that is humorous in its intent (see Billig, 2001a, for further discussion). Sartre (1948), in his analysis of anti-Semitism, argued that extreme bigots constantly mock liberalism's standards of rationality. They do not necessarily believe in the outlandish exaggerations of their own beliefs. Sartre's point is a disturbing one: there might be an intrinsic connnection, not a complete disjunction, between humour and prejudice. This possibility needs to be explored. The first requisite for such an exploration is not to be over-protective about the category of 'humour'.

There is a further reason for countenancing a link between prejudice and humour. The 'just joking' defence of ethnic or racial joke-telling often rests on an assumption that because a remark is spoken as humour, it cannot be genuinely racist. Genuine racism, on this account, is serious. There is a notable academic version of this defence and its underlying assumption. Christie Davies (1990), in his major work on ethnic humour, classifies ethnic jokes according to the stereo-types they express. He analyses jokes that depict groups as stupid, dirty, mean, canny, cowardly or militaristic and he argues that there is no link between prejudice and the enjoyment of such jokes (see also Davies, 1988). According to Davies, those who tell ethnic jokes do not necessarily believe that ethnic group members really possess the stereo-types depicted in the jokes. Davies suggests that Jewish jokes, using stereotypes about money, are not necessarily anti-Semitic, for anti-Semites use devices other than jokes to express their animosity. He writes that 'even today, when direct expressions of anti-Semitism rightly provoke criticism, anti-Semites have other preferred disguises than humour with which to cloak their animosity' (1990: 125). In arguing against those who view ethnic jokes as a sign of prejudice, Davies asserts: 'let us not also forget that jokes are first and foremost jokes' (ibid: 119). Thus, ethnic jokes are primarily 'just jokes' and racists are 'just racists', who would not waste their time telling jokes. As will be seen, Davies avoids examining unambiguously racist, or anti-Semitic, humour. Other analysts have taken protective stances towards ethnic humour. Often this can involve pointing out that two groups may equally joke about each other in seemingly benign and mutual ways. Gundelach (2000), analysing the jokes that Norwegians, Swedes and Danes tell about each other, suggests that ethnic joking can produce 'joking relationships' between groups, thereby reducing inter-group tensions. These jokes trade on well-known stereotypes that each group holds about the other.

Critics of ethnic humour, on the other hand, deny that jokes using unflattering ethnic stereotypes are harmless. According to Husband (1988), the repetition of such jokes serves to sediment stereotypes in the public mind, thereby perpetuating prejudice and racism (see also de Sousa, 1987). Boskin (1987) advances a similar argument in relation to white jokes about blacks in the United States. He links 'Sambo' jokes, in which blacks are depicted as childlike, superstitious figures, to the history of racism. Significantly, Davies hardly discusses these jokes in his survey of ethnic joking, just as Critchley omitted such jokes in his admittedly brief list of jokes that mock outsiders. Freud, too, did not discuss anti-Semitic jokes in *Jokes and their Relation to the Unconscious* (see Billig, 2005, for details). It is as if there is a long history of analysts who wish to celebrate the virtues of humour while not looking directly at humour's unambiguously racist forms.

Two features can be mentioned about the debate whether ethnic jokes are 'just jokes' or whether they validate prejudices. First, the issues often seem to revolve around the role of stereotyping. Davies (1990) depicts stereotyping as constituting the basis of ethnic jokes: 'The general theme of these jokes is the pinning of some undesirable quality on a particular ethnic group in a comic way or to a ludicrous extent' (ibid: 4). The debate about the morality of ethnic joke-telling often focuses upon whether joke-tellers believe in the stereotypes expressed within the jokes and whether the telling of such jokes has the effect of perpetuating stereotypes as harmful representations. Davies, by claiming that the joke attributes the stereotype in a ludicrous manner, implies that there is no literal belief in the stereotyping and, because the stereotyping is acknowledged to be humorous, not serious, there is no lasting ill-effect.

A second point is that the debate often assumes that it is possible to determine whether a joke is prejudiced or unprejudiced by examining its content in the abstract, rather than studying the social contexts in which a particular joke is told. For instance, Oshima (2000), in a survey of ethnic joking in Hawaii, distinguishes between healthy and unhealthy ethnic jokes. The implication is that healthiness is a property of the joke itself and can be ascertained by its content. Similarly, Davies (1990) notes in defence of telling jokes about Jews being money-conscious that Jews often tell the same jokes about themselves as do non-Jews. If Jews tell such jokes then the implication is that the jokes cannot be anti-Semitic.

However, this sort of argument presumes that the meaning of a joke is contained within its explicit formal content. Thus, one can determine whether a joke is or is not racist by examining that content in the abstract. However, if joke-telling is a social phenomenon then the meaning of a joke can be affected by the context of its telling (Fine, 1983; Mulkay, 1988; Norrick, 1993 and 2003). As discourse analysts have stressed, the meaning of utterances must be understood in relation to the context of their utterance (Edwards, 1997; Edwards and Potter, 1993; Potter and Wetherell, 1987). People do things with talk and what they are doing cannot be understood if the text of the talk is examined purely in terms of formal semantic meanings. For example, the meaning of ethnic epithets can change depending on context. The term 'nigger' will have a different meaning if it is used as a form of address by young black American males amongst themselves than if shouted by a Ku Klux Klan member from a passing car at a black pedestrian in the southern United States. If ethnic words can change their meaning depending on context, then so possibly can ethnic jokes, especially those that use terms such as 'nigger'. Therefore, the context of joke-telling is crucial for understanding the meaning of jokes.

In an analysis of an actual episode of joke-telling, Sacks (1992) showed how the joke's meaning was discussed and contested by the participants themselves (see also Mulkay, 1988; Hay, 2000; Norrick, 2003). It is possible – indeed it is likely – that the telling of an ethnic joke by members of the ethnic group will differ from its telling by outsiders. Insiders, who tell ethnic jokes about themselves, will acknowledge that there are limits within which the joke is being told. Sometimes when an insider tells a joke that repeats conventional stereotypes, the joke can be understood and enjoyed as mocking stereotyping and prejudice, as Don Kulick (2000) has argued with respect to gay jokes. In this sense the target of the joke can be ambiguous. For instance, Freud analysed Jewish *schnorrer* (beggar) jokes as mocking the traditional religious codes that required the rich patron to give to the beggar. In this interpretation, Freud was putting himself in the position of the patron. The same jokes can also be enjoyed as a triumph of the impoverished beggar over his wealthy patron (Billig, 2005). If the joke is told by a beggar to an audience of beggars, the meaning of the laughter is likely to differ than if told by a wealthy patron to a wealthy audience. As a general rule, therefore, it is necessary to understand the context in which a joke is told and not just determine its meaning in the abstract.

Meaning and context of racist jokes

To move forward debates about ethnic humour, a particular type of unambiguously racist joke will be analysed. As has been mentioned, an important part of the debate has been whether the stereotypes in ethnic jokes should be taken seriously or not – or whether even a joke qua joke can provide ethnic and racist stereotyping with implicit validation. However, by no means all racist jokes trade on stereotypes. The bathroom tiling joke, in its racist form, mentions no stereotype. It represents a type of joke that has been largely ignored by analysts of racist humour.

To understand the meaning of jokes – even unambiguously racist jokes – the context of the joke must be considered. Context does not necessarily refer to the immediate person-to-person context in which a joke is told. It can also refer to a more general ideological or political context that can affect the meaning and understanding of a joke. The role of the more distal context in affecting a joke's meaning can be illustrated in relation to Freud's distinction between the joke-work of a joke and the tendentious purpose behind the joke. The joke-work refers to the technical properties of the joke and the devices it uses to produce the humorous effect. The tendentious purpose refers to the emotional impulse that the joke might express. As Freud argued, the force of a joke frequently derives from its tendentious purpose. Most typically, according to Freud, the tendentious purpose is to express a forbidden desire, principally an aggressive or sexual impulse. We laugh more at tendentious jokes than we do at non-tendentious ones, but we convince ourselves that we are laughing at the cleverness of the joke-work. In this we deceive ourselves, for it is the tendentiousness that provides the greater impulse to laughter. There is, in fact, experimental evidence that people are affected by the choice of targets of aggressive jokes, but are convinced that their enjoyment derives from the joke's technique not choice of target (Zillman, 1983).

Because joking occurs in a social context, then the recipients of a joke by their laughter validate the expression of the forbidden feeling. Freud's insights can easily be applied to racist jokes. Joke-tellers convince themselves that they are 'only joking' and that their jokes do not express real prejudices. Under the cover of the joking situation, prejudiced thoughts can be expressed and socially enjoyed. In this way, the downgrading of outsiders escapes the censure that would inevitably accompany the expression of 'serious' prejudice in many contemporary discursive situations. The joking context creates a temporary situation which seems to permit laughter at exaggeratedly stereotyped unreal members of the outgroup, as jokers celebrate the funniness of their joking and deny their own racism.

The importance of context for understanding the meaning of jokes that express aggression against a target group can be illustrated by considering a joke that Veatch (1998) cites to illustrate his theory of humour. Veatch's theory stresses how humour sets up expectancies of normality and then violates these expectancies. It is basically a variant of the incongruity theory, that looks at the semantic incongruities that structure jokes (see, for example, Giora, 1991, for an excellent analysis of this type of semantic analysis). In Freudian terms, these are theories that examine in detail the joke-work, rather than the underlying tendentious impulses. Veatch suggests that jokes sometimes present the violation before the 'normal' explanation of the violation. He offers an example:

Q: What do you call 1000 lawyers chained to a rock at the bottom of the ocean?
A: A good start!

Veatch suggests that in this case the joke works because the violation, which is a description of mass murder, precedes a 'normal' explanation – and it is incongruous to explain an abnormal event with a 'normal' explanation. Irritation with lawyers is a familiar feature of contemporary society, so the unusual event, suggested by the joke's question, is being explained by something disproportionately banal. One might note that the joke does not attribute any particular stereotype to lawyers but it assumes that recipients will hold negative stereotypes.

Veatch might have added that the joke uses what Freud called the technique of 'exaggeration'. Part of the humour is derived from the sug-

gestion that mass murder might be an appropriate response for the irritation caused by lawyers. Since the sort of person who might tell the
joke will probably encounter lawyers in handling divorces, wills and
house-sales, the murderous response is knowingly out of proportion to
the shared irritation one might have about lawyers. No-one, including
joke-teller and recipients, is seriously advocating the mass murder of
lawyers. That is the point of the joke. Indeed, it is possible for lawyers to
tell the joke among themselves, as they confidently laugh at the low
esteem with which they might be held by their clients. The telling of
the joke amongst lawyers would assume that none of the auditors genuinely feared that they might be murdered by their clients.

One can imagine the joke being told in a very different context,
which would alter its meaning. For instance, there might be a totalitarian state, in which the so-called enemies of the state are regularly prosecuted and executed by the political authorities. Lawyers may act in
defence but the state authorities may frequently judge the lawyers to
be equally as culpable as their clients, because they are committing the
crime of defending the state's enemies. In consequence, the authorities
often execute lawyers for their 'crimes'. One might imagine 'the lawyers at the bottom of the ocean' joke being told in this state among the
supporters of the regime. Then, the humour would not derive from
exaggeration, for the joke is hardly exaggerating anything. Because the
murder of lawyers is actually taking place, the joke would be urging
extension of something that is occurring, rather than fantasising about
something unreal. The basic joke-work would be similar in the two versions. However, the morality of the two tellings would be very different, as would be the tendentious force of any resulting enjoyment.

The 'good start' joke also has a racist version. It is not lawyers who
are chained to the bottom of the sea, but black people. When this
version is told by white people, then its tendentious force is likely to
resemble the totalitarian version of the lawyer version, because racist
murders of black people have taken place and continue to take place.
The similarity to the totalitarian version would be even more un-
ambiguous if the tellers of the 'black' version were members of a white
racist organisation that has a history of violence, including murder,
against black persons. It would be a celebration of the idea of racist
murder in a context in which actual racist violence takes place. Such a
telling would be on a par with an anti-Semite joking that the Holocaust was a good start. In this sense, the humour of irritation and the
humour of hatred might use the same joke forms, but the tendentious
force behind the similar joke-work has a very different meaning.

Ku Klux Klan joke sites

The racist version of the 'good start' joke expresses violence without stereotyping. As such, it does not fit the category of ethnic jokes that, according to Davies, attribute unfavourable characteristics to others. It represents a type of racist joke that has been little explored by analysts. A corpus of racist jokes will be examined. These come from the unambiguously racist context of a Ku Klux Klan supporting Website which offers jokes. Such sites are not officially sponsored by Ku Klux Klan groups but their KKK sympathies are evident (for more details of such Websites and their links, see Billig, 2001a). I have previously focused on the 'metadiscourse' of such humour, examining the discursive meaning of disclaimers that the material was 'just a joke'. I argued that the KKK humour is never 'just a joke', for, amongst other things, it presents and celebrates a racist view of the world that was being taken seriously. The material itself often claimed to be more than a joke, as its authors indicated that a stereotype of blacks was, indeed, 'no joke' but was based on 'fact'. This earlier analysis did not examine jokes qua jokes, but concentrated on the more politically based material of humour, such as parodies of other formats, including dictionary entries, board games and advertisements.

The jokes studied here are taken from a Website entitled 'Nigger Joke Central' (NJC), produced by Whitepower.com. This site specialises in jokes sent in by readers, thus providing an archive of contemporary extreme racist materials. The index page displays the White Power symbol and a Ku Klux Klan motif. By clicking on the KKK motif (which bears the legend 'My Brothers – the Klan'), the site provides a direct link to a Ku Klux Klan Webpage Index. This in turn gives links to individual Klan organisations. NJC, as is to be expected given its title, does not hide its racism. The site has an index page of 'Racist Jokes' that provides entries to 14 types of jokes; that is, 'Faggot Jokes', 'Hispanic Jokes' and 'Yo Mama Jokes'. The pages which are studied here are the 'Nigger Jokes' (NJ), 'More Nigger' (MN) and 'More Nigger Jokes' (MNJ). The very name of the site and its pages establishes the unambiguously racist context of the joke material.

Many of the jokes to be found in these pages can also be found on the various 'sick joke' Websites, and thus they have a wider circulation than the circles of the extreme right and its sympathisers. Some analysts of sick jokes have stressed that the primary motive of sick jokes is to shock and to break taboos and, in consequence, any sensitive topic is liable to attract bad-taste jokes (Dundes, 1987). It might be argued that the tendentious motivation behind sick ethnic jokes, such as Holocaust jokes and also violent racist jokes, lies not in racism *per se* but in the desire to outrage decency. This might explain why such jokes appeal particularly to adolescent boys. Treating ethnic jokes in this way, of course, would fit the arguments of those who wish to divorce ethnic joking from prejudice.

It is at this point that context becomes crucial. It is hard to make the argument that such joking is not racist when the jokes are being transmitted in an explicitly racist context. The sites in question specifically promote the jokes as racist humour and the continual use of the word 'nigger' in this context unambiguously links the jokes to a racist perspective. These are not jokes that happen to be told by Ku Klux Klan supporters. The joke-tellers, in sending their jokes to the Website, have specifically wished to see these jokes portrayed as racist jokes in a context that supports the Ku Klux Klan. In transmitting these jokes the tellers are demonstrating their political loyalties and their racist hatred. If this joke-telling is not racist, then it would be hard to know what would qualify for that label.

Characteristics of violent racist jokes

The first step is to identify the defining characteristics of a violent racist joke, so that it will be possible to distinguish between this type of joke and the sort of stereotyping ethnic joke that is more frequently studied by humour researchers.

The 'good start' joke can be considered as a violent racist joke when its target is blacks or any other ethnic group. Details of the joke can vary without necessarily affecting its status as a violent racist joke. The number of victims is not essential, nor is the chaining. On NJ the question in the joke takes the form: 'What do you call 50,000 blacks in the bottom of the sea?' MNJ uses a different wording: 'What do you call 15 niggers chained together at the bottom of the sea?' The punch-line is identical: 'A good start'. The choice of epithet used to describe the victims is not essential: the joke does not cease to be racist or violent if 'black' is used rather than 'nigger'.

The variants of the joke contain four basic features that will be used as defining characteristics of the violent racist joke:

1 *Racial/ethnic victim and context.* The joke has a victim or victims who are identified by their race or ethnicity, and the joke is told either in an immediate or more general context of prejudice, discrimination and violence against that group.

2 *No stereotyping.* The joke contains no stereotyping of the ethnic or racial group; the victims of the joke are not said to possess a particular characteristic that has led them to be victimised.
3 *Passive racial/ethnic victim.* The victim of the joke is not depicted as an actor in the joke's action, but is merely the recipient of violence on account of membership of a racial or ethnic group.
4 *Racist violence as humorous.* The punch-line presents the idea of racist violence and this violence is the point of the joke. The violence, therefore, is not incidental to the joke, but is integral to its point.

The racist 'good start' joke qualifies on all four criteria. The joke contains no descriptions of the characteristics of the victims who themselves only appear in the joke as victims. The punch-line introduces the idea of deliberate violence and the joke celebrates the death of the victims because they are blacks.

None of the four criteria mentioned above refer specifically to the joke-work or to the formal properties of a joke that mark it out as a joke. Consequently, it is expected that violent racist jokes will use joke-work to be found in other jokes, rather than employ joke techniques that have been specifically created for this type of humour. The 'good start' joke uses the techniques of normalisation and violation identified by Veatch (1998). Its switch from apparently asking about tragedy to exulting in violence is an example of what Raskin (1985) describes as a joke's text employing two semantic scripts of interpretation (see also Giora, 1991). Because the violent racist joke does not employ a specific form of joke technique, it is possible for the same joke-type, and thus the same joke-work, to be found in variants that are not specifically racist jokes. The lawyer version does not have a racist/ethnic victim and the joke is not being told within an ideological tradition of violent prejudice against the victim of the joke. The 'black' KKK version has a direct linkage to an ideological tradition of violence. The joke is not playing with an exaggeration of response but is suggesting that the actuality of racist violence is a matter of fun.

Frequency of violent racist jokes

The number of jokes possessing all four defining characteristics of the violent racist joke was computed for each of the three KKK joke pages. Table 1 presents the total number of jokes on each page and the number of violent racist jokes.

Table 1 Number of violent racist jokes per KKK Webpage

Page	Violent Racist Jokes	Total Number of Jokes	Percentage of Violent Jokes
NJ	16	135	11.85
MN	6	39	15.38
MNJ	25	210	11.90
Total	47	384	12.24

It can be seen from Table 1 that over 12 per cent of the total number of jokes were violent racist jokes. These results suggest that a consistent and substantial minority of extreme racist jokes are violent racist jokes. It should be mentioned that the total number of violent jokes does not constitute 47 different jokes. Many of the jokes, whether violent or stereotyping, appear on more than one page. For example, the 'good start' joke, as has been mentioned, appears on two pages. Moreover, the same basic joke, whether violent or not, can appear in different versions both within and across pages.

The definition of the violent racist joke is strict, in that it was formulated to distinguish the violent joke from the sort of ethnic/racial joke that plays with stereotypes. The type of joke, which is here being recorded as a violent racist joke, is a *purely* violent joke, deriving its whole humour from the notion of racist violence and depicting the victim purely as victim. Jokes about racist violence, which also use racist stereotypes, are not included in this count. For this reason, it would be wrong to conclude that over 80 per cent of the KKK anti-black jokes contain no violent themes. In fact, racist aggression is common throughout the corpus. The point has been to identify a type of racist violent joke that does not contain stereotypes.

Types of joked-about violence

Although violent racist jokes might possess common characteristics, they do not all joke about precisely the same sorts of violence. Distinctions can be made between Fantasy Racist Violence, Political/ Historical Racist Violence and Banal Racist Violence. Examples of each will be given.

Fantasy racist violence. In some of the jokes, the violence appears as mythical, unreal or unlikely to occur in actual life. One joke on both the NJ and MNJ pages is a modern version of the pied-piper story. The joke tells of a man buying a brass sculpture of a rat in an antique store.

When he takes the sculpture out, he notices that rats start to run after his car. The man drives his car towards the river and jumps out at the last moment. The rats follow the car into the river and drown. So the man returns to the antique store to ask the seller whether he had any brass statues of blacks.

The violence might be unreal, for the events depicted in the joke are not expected to occur. However, the joke depends for its effect on the recipient finding enjoyable the idea of someone wishing to kill blacks. Thus, the joke represents a fantasy of unreal violence, but it assumes the psychological reality that the fantasy will be shared by recipients of the joke.

In some instances the recipient of the joke is enrolled into the fantasy by the syntax of the joke. This is clear in the racist version of the joke that Critchley (2002) identifies as 'true' humour:

How many niggers does it take to roof a building?
Ten if you slice them thin enough.

(NJ; variant about wallpaper on MNJ)

Again the violence takes a fantasy form. No violent racist is actually going to cut black people into slices in order to make roof-tiles or bathroom tiles. Although the violence is fantasy, the context of the joke and its telling is marked by actual racist violence. This distinguishes the racist version of the tiling joke from the radical feminist version, admired by Critchley. Feminist politics has no political heritage of lynching, burning or murdering males. The joke of the feminist variant is that women might wish they engaged in such things, but they do not. Racists joke about violence, knowing that racist violence has been and continues to be perpetrated. The joke is part of a political context that almost certainly will perpetrate further acts in the future.

The joke uses the pronoun 'you' to indicate the perpetrator of the fantasised violence: 'if *you* slice them thin enough'. 'You' as a deictic pronoun is ambiguous (Mühlhäusler and Harré, 1990). It indicates the specific person or persons being addressed; at the same time it refers to people in general, or what Perelman and Olbrechts-Tyteca (1971) called 'the universal audience'. In this way, the specific addressee is made to stand for people in general. In the case of the roof joke and other such racist jokes, this universal audience is assumed to be racially circumscribed. 'You', by assuming its audience to be white, excludes blacks from the universal audience. Moreover, the 'you' takes it for granted that the universal audience will wish violence upon blacks. In this way, the wish for racist violence is treated as something that the universal audience would universally and normally wish for. Thus, the joke rhetorically enrols the recipient into the racist community, which is presented as if it were the universal community. Although the violence might be fantasised, the existence of racists, who might celebrate such violence, is assumed by the joke to be real and to be normal.

Historical/political racist violence.   In some of the KKK jokes the form of violence alludes to the types of violence that have been practised historically against blacks in the United States. Such jokes can be analogous to the sick Holocaust jokes described by Dundes (1987), in that they make the serious topics of racist violence into a joke. As in the Holocaust jokes, the violence can be attributed to other racist actors, rather than the joke directly enrolling recipient and teller in the idea of perpetrating violence:

> What's black and white and red all over?
> A Ku Klux Klan house-warming party!
>
> (NJ and MNJ)

Again, the context of the telling is important. In some contexts, the joke might appear primarily as a joke about the Ku Klux Klan, who might be considered distanced from teller and recipient, rather as many Holocaust jokes are about German Nazi actions. On the KKK supporting Websites, however, there can be no presumption of distance. The Ku Klux Klan is 'us' not 'them'. In this context, the joke shares the ideological heritage of the perpetrator, and thus it shares the violence of that heritage.

Some of the jokes use 'you' to enrol the recipient in the historically perpetrated racist violence of the Ku Klux Klan:

> How do you keep niggers out of your back yard?
> Hang one in the front.
>
> (NJ, MN and MNJ)

The joke does not ask how a racist third party would keep blacks out of their backyard. It directly addresses the recipient, asking how they would do so, while simultaneously universalising the recipient as a general 'you'. 'You' is not necessary for such a joke to express a shared presumption of the desirability of violence:

What do niggers and apples have in common?
They both look good hanging from trees.

(MNJ)

In these jokes, the teller is not conjuring a fantastic image of racist violence, as in the pied-piper joke. It is no coincidence that the jokes refer to 'hanging' rather than any other form of murder. The jokes, especially when told in the context of the KKK, implicitly refer to the historical tradition of lynching: the tellers are positioning themselves and their recipients within that historical tradition. On other pages of the KKK joke Websites, actual lynchings are celebrated as objects of mirth, illustrated by actual photographs of black victims (Billig, 2001a). The jokes that enrol the recipient perform a similar function. They are not merely breaking taboos by joking about a topic that should not be joked about, as do many Holocaust jokes (Dundes, 1987). These jokes are more directly associating themselves with violent actions: they celebrate past historical racist violence, while fantasising its present and future recurrence.

Banal racist violence.   There is a range of jokes whose violence is neither fantasised nor a reference to the ideological tradition of the KKK, but refers to the sort of accidental violence that might be encountered in ordinary contemporary life. In the main these are jokes about road deaths. The joke-work involves a sudden shift of semantic structure. An event is presented as a tragic accident, but to understand the punch-line the recipient has to reinterpret the tragedy as a deliberate act of violence because of the racial identity of the victim:

What's the difference between a dead dog in the road and a dead nigger in the road?
Skid marks in front of the dog.

(NJ, MN and MNJ)

What's the difference between a pothole and a nigger?
You'd swerve to avoid a pothole, wouldn't you?.

(NJ)

What do you do if you run over a nigger?
Reverse.

(MNJ)

The latter two variants use 'you' as a form of rhetorical enrolment. The second emphasises the enrolment of the recipient by the addition of 'wouldn't you?', as if the joke is alluding to a natural, expected reaction that 'anyone' would have. Once again, the whiteness and racism of the 'universal audience' are assumed. Such jokes depict a world in which any white would wish to run over and kill a black person should the opportunity present itself. As in all these jokes, the word 'nigger' serves to identify the teller with this depicted world of racist hatred.

Concluding remarks

This analysis of extreme racist humour contains implications both for theoretical debates about the nature of humour and also for wider debates about the inappropriateness of certain forms of humour. Theorists, who have sought to justify ethnic humour as playful and essentially innocent, have tended to overlook the nature of violent racist humour. Their analyses have often concentrated on the use of stereotypes in jokes and they have suggested that jokingly exaggerated stereotypes are not to be confused with 'real' stereotyping. Such arguments tend to give ethnic humour a clean, or almost clean, bill of health. However, this is achieved by ignoring the sort of violent jokes that are based on aggression, not stereotyping. One might suggest that the strategy of defending ethnic joking by concentrating on stereotyping depends upon a form of avoidance: the blatantly cruel and bigoted aspects of humour are ignored. This sort of avoidance is not peculiar to analysts of ethnic humour. The phenomenon is much wider. Today, there is a general cultural climate that looks favourably upon humour. Social scientists have contributed to this climate by producing theories that tend to sentimentalise humour and avoid examining its more problematic and crueller aspects. In this context a critical approach to humour is called for (see Billig, 2005, for more details). Certainly, it is possible to claim that defenders of ethnic humour downplay the social importance and problematic nature of humour when they imply that a joke is 'just a joke'. This is where the material discussed in this chapter can act as a reminder. It is hard to look at the extremes of racist humour and conclude that these are 'just jokes', as if 'just joking' excuses, or even explains away, the phenomenon.

It might be argued that the extremes of racist hatred comprise something separate from the general category of ethnic humour, and thus what has been discussed here is far removed from other, more 'respectable' forms of ethnic joking. It would be wrong, however, to conclude that violent racist jokes stand apart from stereotyping jokes and that the latter represent more 'moderate', and thereby more 'acceptable' forms of joke. As has been mentioned, many of the jokes on the KKK Webpages are stereotyping jokes. The jokers make no distinction between the two types of joke, grouping them both under the label of 'racist jokes' and 'nigger jokes'. The fact that 'nigger', a term of extreme racist abuse, is used in both forms of joke indicates that both are used to derogate their victims and to celebrate a racist perspective. Moreover, the violent jokes are not rendered any less violent should they employ less offensive terminology to describe the ethnicity of their butts. An invitation to enjoy imagined violence is offered regardless of the epithets employed. In Freudian terms, the tendentious nature of the joke does not depend on the offensive nature of the terminology. It might be enhanced by the presence of knowingly offensive epithets, but it is not diminished by their absence.

The violent racist joke, especially one that is told in an overt racist context, represents an unambiguously racist form of humour. Its existence should act as a caution to any theoretical attempt to oversentimentalise humour. The question is not whether humour is in itself desirable or undesirable: what matters is the nature of the humour and the purposes that it serves. In the current cultural climate, which overvalues humour as being intrinsically desirable, critics of various forms of humour, including racist humour, can find themselves at a disadvantage when they contest the morality of certain examples of humour. They can be accused of lacking a 'sense of humour', whose desirability is taken for granted. The charge is easily made. However, the continuing existence of unambiguously violent racist humour illustrates that a so-called 'sense of humour' does not exist in the abstract. Different people – different ideologies – may find different things funny. The morality or immorality does not lie in the fact that people may be prepared to joke and laugh. The morality lies in the nature of the humour. So, when the charge of 'lacking a sense of humour' is made, the critic can reply that there exists a body of joking to which the appropriately moral response is not laughter, but outrage – and that such humour has no place within a moral society. On that basis, the critic can then proceed to debate the undesirability of other forms of racist, sexist or violent humour, that seem more ambiguous.

Certainly, the material that has been presented here can be used to question an assumption that is easy to make: namely that tolerance is on the side of humour and that bigotry knows no laughter. Psychological theories, as well as common stereotypes, lend themselves to depicting the bigot as stern-faced and lacking all sense of enjoyment. It is a dangerous assumption: the bigot, in effect, can say 'Look, I can enjoy a joke and therefore I cannot be a genuine bigot'. However, bigotry is not without its own enjoyments, as Blee (2003) has shown in her analysis of the world of the Ku Klux Klan. This raises Sartre's neglected and disturbing idea that there may be an integral connection between bigotry and humour. The bigot derives pleasure from being outrageous, enjoying the freedom from the constraints of liberal rationality and truth. In this respect, bigotry is itself a form of mockery – indeed, for the bigot it becomes a form of fun.

If these notions are taken seriously, then this would entail re-evaluating many assumptions about the psychology of bigotry (Billig, 2001a and 2002b). Much previous work has portrayed the bigot as too emotionally fragile, too inhibited and too cognitively rigid to enjoy the pleasures of humour. The temptations of bigotry may include pleasurable temptations, and this may help to explain the persistence of bigotry. In this respect, racist jokes are not, and never can be, 'just jokes'. In addition to being jokes they are racist. And as such, they are serious. And as the tendentiously violent history of racism suggests, the racist joke can be more than 'just serious' – it can literally be deadly serious.

2
Race and Ethnicity in Popular Humour

Dennis Howitt and Kwame Owusu-Bempah

Both racism and jokes are social and cultural products. The ideology of racism holds that humankind comprises different races which vary in their worth. Racism dictates, explains and justifies who does what to whom, where, when, why and how. Caucasians claim the right to treat other 'races' in whatever manner they see fit, including disparagement in the form of jokes. Black people are commonly patronised or insulted under the pretext of humour. Here is an example. A few years ago, a black person was inside a local shop when a man covered in coal dust entered and placed his hand next to the black person's. He then chanted 'I wanna be like you, black like you ...'. This was objected to on the grounds that, unlike the 'joker', he was black and not dirty. Those in the shop joined in the denial of racism: 'it's only a joke', they said, almost in unison. One of them actually counselled him (the victim) to cultivate a sense of humour in order to 'get on in this world'. This is not a hypothetical example. The incident involved one of the authors of this chapter.

What does it tell us? Clearly, pointing to the underlying assumptions in the 'joke' caused conversational difficulties for the white people in the shop. Despite these difficulties, they shared the message of the joke and expected the victim to do so as well. The problem is, of course, that the word 'black' has major negative connotations, and in jokes it is frequently used as an evaluative rather than a descriptive term, simultaneously invoking evil, badness, filth and unacceptability, as in phrases such as 'as black as sin'. Such evaluative terms are integral to racist discourse and its hierarchical division of humankind into different races, some of which are regarded as inferior to others. The anecdote shows that racism is a social and cultural product, not the product of individual psychology; racist humour is an aspect of racist society

45

and not just an idiosyncratic feature of a particular individual or group. There is a strong temptation to see it in this way when racism is re-termed 'racial hatred'. 'Racial hatred' implies that intense negative emotion, such as anger or loathing, is a characteristic of racism. It is not. Not all racists harbour racial hatred (McCullough, 1988). Much racism is perpetrated as a routine and even casual activity – sometimes by individuals who regard their actions as well-meaning – and forgetting this can distract attention from subtler and perhaps more dangerous forms of racism (e.g., Howitt and Owusu-Bempah, 1990, 1994; Owusu-Bempah, 1994, 2003; Owusu-Bempah and Howitt, 1999). This particular joke incident is one such case of everyday racism.

The incident shows that jokes are bounded by social rules which, when not followed, can cause problematic social exchanges. Challenging the assumptions underlying racist jokes is a refusal to follow these rules. 'Only joking' is the rhetorical device frequently used in efforts to neutralise such a challenge. The phrase 'only joking' presumes that words can be used without serious intent, and that they are not intended to cause offence. It is a device by which the teller of the joke essentially refuses to change the message, and instead passes the responsibility for the conversational difficulty to the challenger – for not having a sense of humour. Thus it effectively releases the joke-teller from an obligation to consider the offensive nature of their 'jokes'. If the man in the shop had said 'you are a dirty nigger', then a challenge would, perhaps, have been socially acceptable. The difference between the joke and the insult for some is clearly great, yet the assumptions of the joke better indicate the racist inclinations of the joke's teller and listeners than their rejection of the insult would.

Joke maxims

Some jokes arise spontaneously in conversation, but many are recognisable set-pieces which have a familiar structure and often contain common phrases. 'What is the difference between a ...?' 'What do you call a ...?' 'Have you heard the one about ...?' and 'There was an Englishman, an Irishman and a Scotsman ...' are all indicative of the start of set-piece jokes. There are acceptable ways of responding to jokes which might be described as maxims since they are general principles of good conduct. This may appear odd given that jokes allow the teller to flout social conventions (for instance, not talking about bodily functions in inappropriate circumstances). Some of the maxims seem prosaic but this is indicative of their ordinariness to everyday conversationalists and, hence, their power. Here are some examples which may be helpful in discussing racist jokes:

Maxim 1. Jokes should be signalled as jokes such as by using a standard format or formula which identifies the start of the joke. Jokes not clearly signalled cause conversational difficulties because the listener fails to understand and respond appropriately to the joke. Failure to signal a joke properly may lead to embarrassment while participants struggle to make sense of the exchange.

Maxim 2. Jokes should be responded to appropriately by the hearer. There is no single appropriate response to all jokes, though to fail to recognise the joke can be conversationally problematic. The appropriate response typically may be a smile or laughter, but alternatively an affected groan may be a deserved or playful response to a particularly bad joke or one suffering from over-repetition. There are inappropriate responses to jokes – for example, failing to recognise the joke as a joke or criticising the teller for, say, sexism.

Maxim 3. The listener should speedily indicate that they have 'got the joke'. Often, listeners appear to actively seek to get the joke as quickly as possible; they may even indicate (false) appreciation, especially in the presence of others. Silence between the end of the joke and indications of its appreciation may cause embarrassment. Indeed listeners will often provide early signals before the joke is completed.

Maxim 4. Jokers are not held responsible for the joke's content. Indeed, to hold them responsible may cause conversational discomfort. As we have seen, 'It was only a joke' is held to be an appropriate apology or excuse when a listener protests in some way that the limits of this licence have been breached. Failure to accept this 'apology' results in the butt of the joke being seen as unreasonable or maybe 'having a chip on his/her shoulder'.

Thus joker and listener both have active roles in making the joke work – to raise laughter. Racist jokes from this perspective should be regarded as essentially social acts involving interacting participants. In many ways, they can only be understood by reference to the cultural conventions of joking, the social characteristics of the participants in the joke and, to a lesser degree, the individual psychological characteristics of participants.

The following has many characteristics of racist jokes. A specific national group is identified and attributed negative characteristics:

Q: How can you tell when a plane load of English have landed in Sydney?

A: The engines have stopped but you can still hear the whining.

(www.headspace)

As racist jokes go, this seems to be relatively benign. The butt of the joke is the English, hardly defenceless victims of pervading racist attacks. So, in a sense, one major argument against racist jokes is not appropriate in this case. The joke hardly helps perpetuate the racist oppression of the English. But the joke's very acceptability is problematic. For many readers, the joke ought to be largely meaningless, as stereotypes of the English would not include whining. Indeed, the stereotype of the English stiff upper lip negates that employed by the joke. Australian readers, on the other hand, may have a different view which includes whinging 'poms'. Essentially what the joke does is to present whining as if it were a stereotype, and consequently it reinforces the stereotype. Even those ignorant of the stereotype can decipher the joke as reflecting a stereotype. In other words, the joke builds the stereotype, the stereotype does not make the joke. The stereotype is firmly established by the joke despite its unfamiliarity to the listener.

The maxims outlined above come into play with this joke. The joke begins with a question which strongly signals the joke, the listener is eager to recognise the joke and signal understanding of the joke, so much so that they may laugh at a stereotype with which they are unfamiliar, and finally they do not protest the stereotype which makes the joke. The joke has its effect not simply through its content but because of the requirements of social interactions involving jokes.

Understanding racist jokes

The use of jokes to disparage other groups is as ancient as contact between groups (Apte, 1985). The question posed, however, is why do people laugh at or tell jokes with racial content, no matter how rudimentary? Following Freud (1905/1960) one suggestion is that humour allows individuals to gratify their repressed or socially sanctioned needs, to rationalise the prejudice or hostility felt towards other ethnic groups; it reinforces one's superior position; and it enhances and affirms one's social membership. However, there is little to be gained by conceiving the racist jokes as manifestations of repressed psychological needs. Laughing at such jokes requires much more than that; in fact, psychological repression itself is not a requirement. To understand a racist joke entails understanding the culture producing the joke. All members of a culture have this understanding. Jokes, in general, do not begin and end with individuals, they are transmitted socially, changed and embellished (Heider, 1958). Jokes are communicative acts which play a significant role in social exchanges – a medium through which society disseminates and generationally transmits its dominant attitudes towards outgroups. Racist jokes, therefore, act as propaganda in support of racist ideology. It is noteworthy that one extreme right-wing Internet Website sells packs of leaflets of racist jokes for distribution (http://www.tightrope.cc/catalog/product_info.php? products _id=107). This is akin to the publication of a political manifesto.

Two important historical figures in social psychology, Lewin (1933) and Heider (1958), saw both action and interaction as the basis for meaning making and hence representation. The environment, Lewin believed, is constructed in terms of personal meanings – that is, in terms of the actions it is seen to invite, repel, permit or prohibit, given an individual's or a group's current goals and their behavioural repertoire. Partly for this reason, attempts to marginalise racism by defining it in terms of specific characteristics or associating it with specific sections of society are unhelpful. Dummett (1984) and Cashmore (1987) questioned the tendency to marginalise racism by equating it with the extreme and violent racism characteristic of the far right such as the British National Party and the Ku Klux Klan. Most people probably have little truck with the racism of such groups. Consequently, the racism of everyday interaction (for example such as takes place in the pub, the social worker's office or the police canteen) is both more difficult to identify and to deal with than the racism of extreme right groups. Nevertheless it is possible to identify racism in sectors of society professing to abhor the racism of the far right. For example, because of the power that professionals yield, their racism is especially pernicious (Howitt and Owusu-Bempah, 1990; Owusu-Bempah, 1994; Owusu-Bempah and Howitt, 1999, 2000). Who, for example, is likely to do the most harm? The teacher who believes that African-Caribbean children just excel at sports, the British National Party member who believes that black kids are stupid, or the educational psychologist who recommends that:

> We ... need to think in terms of planning, for the children ... the type
> of curriculum which would aim at exploiting their particular interests,
> with emphasis on ... woodwork, metalwork, handicraft, art ... For this
> group particularly we would need a reorganization of the traditional
> remedial class within the school, if we hope to sustain their interest in
> class, and reduce the degree of difficult behaviour seen at school.
>
> (Dwivedi and Varma, 1996, p. 47)

While racialised superiority/inferiority is construed in a variety of
forms which differ across time and place, the common thread running
through racist humour is some sort of violence against other ethnic
groups and their cultures. It is essential to serve this ideology of racial
hierarchy with notions, ideas and myths masquerading as 'facts'. The
function of racist jokes is to reinforce the presumed superiority of one
racial or ethnic group over another. Examine a joke for this message
and it is not difficult to detect its racial violence.

Remarkably, it requires little intellectual effort to create racist jokes.
Many are 'jokes' simply because they take a familiar joke form. There
are numerous examples of such racist jokes which simply reiterate the
belief that black people are worthless:

Q: What's the difference between a nigger and a bucket of shit?
A: The bucket.

(http://www.racist-jokes.com/)

It is hard to detect even the semblance of humour, let alone creativity
in this 'joke'. When one finds page after page of virtually identical
jokes which repetitively equate black people with muck, it becomes
apparent that the jokes are not jokes at all, but rather plain verbal
assaults on black people's humanity and dignity. Why endlessly repeat
such so-called jokes? Their endless repetition only makes sense if the
jokes are understood as propaganda to reify or buttress a belief in the
worthlessness of 'niggers'.

The same may be said of the racism of the notorious British comedian Bernard Manning's stage performances. It is worth noting the following incident, given the lack of ethnographic documentation of
racist jokes. The context is important. The events took place in front of
an audience of 300 police officers attending a fund-raising charity
event. According to press reports, his audience did more than laugh
when he launched the following barrage of obscenity upon the one
black police officer present:

Where is he? How are you, baby? Having a night out with nice people? Isn't this better than swinging from the fucking trees? – You're black, I'm white. Do you think colour makes a difference? You bet your fucking bollocks it does!
They actually think they're English because they are born here. That means if a dog's born in a stable, it is a horse.

The white audience cheered. There was more but the gist is contained in the above. One must construe Manning's attack as social, emotional and psychological violence against the vulnerable since immediate retaliation from the black police officer was simply not possible (see Pickering and Littlewood, 1998: 299–300).

Humour establishes a light-hearted context, which invites laughter in others. This discourages others from inferring racism since anger, for example, is an inappropriate response to a joke. Any response from the victim, the black officer, would have been, by implication, against his colleagues who were more than silently complicit in the verbal onslaught. Figuratively, the man's colleagues held him down while Manning 'mugged' and robbed him of his humanity and dignity. Nevertheless, the sequence is more calculatedly matter-of-fact than emotional in tone. One would have to stretch definitions alarmingly to find emotive hatred in this onslaught. Manning's comments simply expressed many of the fundamental principles of racism in a graphic form. Taken in turn, these are that black people are not part of 'decent' society; that black people are just animals; that race is fundamental; and that black people are biologically inferior to whites. In the sequence of four jokes, not once did Manning need to make reference to any stereotypes. Each joke had obviously been rehearsed and calcu-lated to be an unmistakably direct expression of brazen racist ideology. Whether or not Manning was aware of this, he was virtually parroting Francis Galton (1822–1911) who claimed that black people as a race are grossly inferior even to the lowest of any white people (see Howitt and Owusu-Bempah, 1994; http://www.goacom.com/overseas-digest/History/whattheysaid.html). That the sequence is cognitive rather than emo-tional is probably indicative of its ideological rather than psychological basis.

Jokes built on stereotypes are perhaps more difficult to deal with. These are actually many and varied but amount to part of the system of ideas which supports the political ideology of racism. Devine (1989) and Owusu-Bempah (1994) have demonstrated a number of important things. The first is the ease with which people can evoke lists of racial stereotypes. Thus racial stereotypes are very familiar in Western communities. These would include stereotypes of criminality, intellectual inferiority, laziness, sexual prowess, sporting prowess, and the innate rhythm of black people. The second is that, in emotive or ambiguous situations, people tend to resort to stereotypical ideas irrespective of their measured racial attitudes. In contrast, when aware that a situation allows for the expression of racist ideas, the actual expression of these ideas is related to measured racial attitudes. In other words, all people, off-guard, are vulnerable to acting on racial or ethnic stereotypes, irrespective of their repugnance or proclivity towards racist views. It is not simply a matter of some individuals having racist stereotypes and acting on them; we all harbour ethnic stereotypes, and cannot always successfully censor them.

As a consequence, it can be argued that racial stereotypes are probably a key weapon in the armoury of racism. Reading through numerous anti-black jokes, Devine's (1989) view that racial stereotypes are part of the common currency of Western cognitions is amply illustrated. Indeed, without knowledge of the stereotypes, the jokes are largely meaningless. The following combines two racist stereotypes for contrastive effect:

> A woman meets a black guy and invites him back to her place. She handcuffs herself to the bed and screams, 'Do what you black men do best!'. The nigger grabs the TV and runs!
>
> (http://www.racist-jokes.com/)

Both stereotypes – those of black men's sexual prowess and the criminality of black people – are deeply ingrained. Of the two, that of black criminality has the most tangible manifestations in the form of prison statistics (Hudson, 1996; NACRO, 1986; Quillian and Pager, 2001). The arguments are complex, but there is good reason to believe that black people are imprisoned in disproportionately large numbers as the result of, and not the cause of, this stereotype. Crime statistics are part of a long social process which involves discretion and thus vulnerability to the effects of racial stereotypes at a number of stages. Discussions of this are to be found in Maxwell, Robinson and Post (2003) for example. The cheering of his police audience at Bernard Manning's racism cannot be regarded neutrally. It was indicative of their acceptance of racist ideas. There is only a small step from this to the discriminatory policing in which race is at the heart of numerous incidents of harassment and worse.

Taking this argument further, many racist jokes give expression to the belief that black family life is pathological. The following joke was submitted to a site specialising in racist jokes:

Q: What's the definition of Mass Confusion?
A: Fathers day in Harlem!

(http://www.racist-jokes.com/)

Of course, most, if not all, readers will instantly recognise the stereotype which is the nub of the joke. That stereotype basically suggests that black families are characterised by father absence and multiple fathers siring children by one mother. The idea of black family pathology has been academically and professionally reified and nourished by a whole sequence of psychiatrists and others. Consider the following quotations (they aren't joke jokes!):

> The father in the West Indian culture is not the central, stable, providing person that he is in the Asian or European cultures. The loss of African child-rearing practices and their inadequate replacement by European practices are ascribed by most observers to the destructive effect of slavery.
>
> (Lobo, 1978: 37)

A few years later, Brian and Martin (1983/1987) put the finishing touches on this portrait:

> [West Indian children] find a great deal of choice bewildering, as they are not encouraged to be self-regulating at home. Strict discipline and ... corporal punishment at home can mean that softly-spoken restraints and explanations about behaviour limitations go unheeded at nursery ... Their responsiveness to music makes it almost impossible for them to remain still when music is being played.
>
> (Ibid: 246-7)

These depictions of the black family must not be dismissed as history; they still occur in textbooks for childcare professionals (e.g., Dwivedi and Varma, 1996). The notion of black family pathology serves racist ends. Its purpose is not to help black families, black children, or anything like that, but rather to hold the family responsible for its condition and not society. This is pernicious since the family constitutes a keystone of any culture. The joke lamely, but tersely, expresses the same sentiment. The

joker and the 'expert' are doing exactly the same ideological work of reinforcing the putative inferiority of black people. Supporters of the view try
to justify their damaging assumptions about the black family on biolo-
gical, cultural or historical grounds (e.g., Coleman, 1994; Lobo, 1978).
Notice how easily one could transform the racist joke into a non-joke:

In Harlem on Father's day the mass of people are confused.

One consequence of removing the conventional joke structure is that
the statement becomes harder to interpret, it does not conform to 'the
rules of the game'; it does not fit into the system of cultural, social or
personal meanings. Expressing the stereotype using a common joke
structure actually facilitates the recognition of the message!

The stereotypes incorporated into racist jokes should not be regarded
as trivial matters. Indeed, they often reflect some of the major fronts in
the subjugation, discrimination, oppression and exploitation of black
people. Such jokes frequently employ the very stereotypes which
underlie some of the major controversies over 'race' in the last hundred years (see Pickering, 2001) – such as the question of the educabil-
ity of black children (e.g., Eysenck, 1971; Jensen, 1969). The arguments
have been long and many. Nevertheless, they all have much the same
effect – they excuse and justify educational systems which have consistently failed to enable black children to reach their full educational
potential (e.g., Coard, 1971; Owusu-Bempah, 2001). Examples of jokes
employing this view of racial inferiority are as follows:

Q: What do you call a black man in high school?
A: Janitor.
Q: Why can't Ray Charles or Stevie Wonder read?
A: They're niggers!

(http://www.racist-jokes.com/)

Virtually every racial stereotype is represented in racist jokes – there are
numerous jokes about the laziness of black people, for example. However, exceptions do occur. In particular, very few racist jokes make reference to the stereotype of the athleticism of black people. This stereotype
can contribute to how black children are dealt with in the educational
system (Cashmore, 1982). In essence, black youngsters are 'valued' for
their physical ability and steered away from academic endeavour.
Possibly because athleticism is generally regarded nowadays as a positive
attribute, its application to a disparaged minority may seem 'acceptable'.
Exceptions may be dependent not on the athleticism-stereotype, but on
other stereotypes such as that of black criminality in the joke:

Q: Why are all the niggers fast runners?
A: All the slow ones are in jail.

(http://www.racist-jokes.com/)

The damaging effect of this racist joke transcends the problematic nature of athleticism in disparaging racist discourse.

By their very nature, the use of stereotypes can introduce negative connotations to what otherwise are valued attributes. For example, attributes such as being careful with money are lauded as a good thing: 'take care of the pennies and the pounds will take care of themselves'. Conversely, wasting money is not a positively valued activity. Yet in jokes these positive values take on negative connotations because the very structures of racist jokes explicitly carry the implication that the minority group is being disparaged – that actually they are 'other' in that they do not share the values of the majority. So, there is a long tradition of attributing to minorities the characteristics of 'stinginess' and 'tightness' with money. Scottish people and Jewish people are typical recipients of such attributions:

Q: What's the difference between a Jew and a Canoe?
A: A canoe tips.

(http://www.racist-jokes.com/)

There are many such jokes just as there are others specifically aimed at other minority groups (the Irish and black people) which take the opposite tack. Surely this is one of the dangers of racist jokes? To explain, it would be conversationally problematic to introduce the ideas underlying racist jokes so repeatedly in normal conversation. For example, the idea that the Irish are stupid and deposit their wages in pubs is the theme of virtually all jokes about Irish people. Conversationally though, without Irish jokes, this idea could not be introduced into conversation so repeatedly. One can imagine the flow of conversation if it were:

I think the Irish are stupid.
Oh do you?
Yes.
Why?
I don't know – people just tell me they are.

It is not simply that jokes give the teller a degree of licence to express such views but, provided that the teller has a repertoire of such jokes, it allows prolonged repetition of basic themes which would tax conversation otherwise.

References to racial stereotypes are NOT the defining feature of racist jokes. Racial stereotypes, although integral, are not the essence of racist ideology. For example, the stereotype of Jewish people as gifted academics lacks the suggestion of their inferiority which would be required by racist ideology. However, the stereotype does the work of all stereotypes by suggesting that all members of a group can be characterised by the putative characteristics of a small number of that group. This simply amounts to a denial of the individuality of the butts of the stereotype. The group targeted is established as socially and culturally Other (Pickering, 2004). It is hard to imagine jokes which are built on the assumption that minority group members are 'the same as us'.

Some racist jokes contain no recognizable stereotype which requires adjustments to the Freudian view that racist jokes deal in stereotypes (e.g., Billig, 2002a). One joke which has taken on a special analytic role in analysis of racist jokes is the following:

Q: What do you call three blacks at the bottom of a river?
A: A good start.

The implication of this joke is, of course, that the death of black people is a good thing , and so perhaps a small step from lynching and genocide. It also contains the essence of racist thought – black people's worthlessness. However, it is incorrect to assume that this joke works merely because it directly reflects the racist ideology of the teller and hearer. Or, alternatively, that, in some way, laughing at the joke is indicative of racial hatred. The inadequacy of either of these analyses can readily be illustrated by a theoretical exercise in which we vary the subject of the joke. The joke is, in structure, like a good many: 'What do you call an elephant that can't do sums? Dumbo.' The 'bottom of a river' joke works by creating a social group against which a callous attitude can be expressed and the social milieu for its expression. The punch-line of the joke, in itself, is relatively witty compared to that of many racist jokes – 'A good start'. Indeed the joke works even when other social groups are substituted for 'blacks' (see pp. 33–4).

These alternative social groups do not have to be the ones against which the teller and hearer of the joke have negative feelings. Exactly this same joke is heard made about, for example, banjo players or drummers. Most of us would laugh at these alternative versions: What do you call three drummers at the bottom of a river? A good start. It is the fact that such jokes create, through their very structure, a group of 'others' which allows the joke to work. Quite evidently tapping directly into deep-seated animosity is not essential. The joke creates 'others'; it does much more than simply reflect the tellers' and listeners' feelings. To understand the joke the hearer has to perceive and understand the disparaged nature of banjo players or drummers in the eyes of the joke teller (c.f. Heider, 1958; Lewin, 1933). The interplay between the joke structure and the joke content is bounded by distinct limits. Try turning this joke into one about 'new-born babies', 'people' or 'old fridges', for example, and the listener will probably be caused some consternation if it were introduced into a conversation:

Q: What do you call three new-born babies at the bottom of a river?
A: A good start.

Beyond certain limits, then, the joke becomes meaningless and falls flat. While not relying on hostility, as such, it does depend on cultural knowledge of antagonisms which can also be inferred from the fact that a group has been made the subject of disparagement. The same joke may be quite readily accepted by the butt of the joke sometimes. For example, jokes about banjo players circulate readily around banjo clubs and societies. The same would be true of situations in which Bernard Manning's audience were predominantly black (Jaret, 1999).

So jokes do more than merely reflect prejudices. They are active in the process of the construction of the meaning of 'otherness' and inferiority of social groups. Indeed, jokes can be just as effective when there is no stereotype and hostility prior to hearing the joke. The 'blacks' version of the joke is, of course, not entirely equivalent to the 'banjo' version since it taps the historically and socially deeper repertoire of racism. Nevertheless, clearly racist jokes do not work (i.e., evoke/create laughter) by allowing public expression of repressed hatred and anger of particular ethnic groups. Some racists may have definable emotional responses to members of other races – contempt, disgust or anger – but we know of no evidence to suggest that such emotions are typical of racists. Racist acts are often perpetrated by those who claim positive feelings towards minorities. There are numerous occasions when one hears people trying to exonerate themselves from racism with such proclamations as: 'My best friend is black!' No man could seriously exonerate himself from sexism simply because his wife is female.

Are there acceptable ethnic jokes?

Some jokes refer to a specific racial or ethnic group but do not appear to incorporate the racist element of racial superiority. They may be jokes which require a sophisticated understanding of that ethnic culture in order to understand them. There are numerous examples of jokes which are idiosyncratic to an ethnic group which circulate within that community – some Jewish jokes are examples. Nevertheless, the constant reference in these jokes to racial or ethnic minorities elevates race and ethnicity to a dominant position in conversation. That is, they define race and ethnicity as an important part of the social agenda. Individually, such jokes do not appear to be significantly harmful:

> A Jewish man was praying at the Wailing Wall in Jerusalem crying out repeatedly 'Lord I want to be where my people are'. A tourist walks over to him and says 'But you are where your people are – this is the Holy Land'. The Jewish man retorts 'Mine are in California.'

However, simply because one can find relatively innocuous examples is insufficient to establish that the entire genre is benign.

The following joke is examined in some detail since there is no dominant group which is patently disparaging a minority group. Indeed, the joke appears to involve two separate ethnic groups in the form of a Jewish rabbi and a Muslim Mullah:

Rabbi Goldberg and Mullah Nasruddin have the following conversation:

Rabbi: I don't like Muslims.
Mullah: Why not?
Rabbi: You brought down the twin towers, that's why!
Mullah: Every single Muslim can't be blamed.
Rabbi: Syrian, Libyan, Palestinian, Tunisian, Moroccan, doesn't matter, you're all the same.
Mullah: Well I don't like Jews!
Rabbi: Why not?
Mullah: Jews sank the Titanic that's why!
Rabbi: Jews didn't sink the Titanic you idiot, it was an iceberg!
Mullah: Iceberg, Goldberg, Greenberg, Rosenberg, doesn't matter, you're all the same.

                                        (http://www.sharif.org.uk/humour.htm)

To understand the 'joke' (whether or not it is seen as funny) requires a sophisticated appreciation of race, racism, race categories and so forth. The 'joke' may be read at a number of different levels – there are discourses of racism ('you're all the same'), for example. Nevertheless, overall the effect is confusing read from a traditional anti-racism perspective and the joke may well amuse those who typically find racist jokes offensive. The Mullah triumphs intellectually over the Rabbi. Muslims are presented as quick-witted whereas Jewish people lose out in the exchange and are prone to racial stereotyping since the Rabbi makes inappropriate generalisations about an ethnic group – which is the reason why the joke can work in the first place. Partly we understand the joke because we know the thought processes behind it. But is this the sort of joke that we should condemn? Overall, it can be read as disparagement of a minority group (Jews) by comparison with Muslims. Even though it initially represents Muslims as terrorists, the joke works to negate this. The joke depends also on the tension produced by reference to the 9/11 terrorist acts in the United States, for this sets the listener on guard to expect possibly 'sick' commentary on the events at the twin towers. There is relief that the 'joke' does not step on those sensibilities. If the Rabbi had said instead "Your suicide bombers attack Israel, that's why!" then the 'joke' no longer seems to work at any level.

Given the complexities inherent in this 'joke' (and how rapidly it reveals things which we would not wish to reveal about ourselves), dealing with it is not easy. So, the need for a failsafe response when doing race can readily be understood. Dealing with the threat of the joke is a complex microcosm of the problems of doing race, of shunning or challenging the racist use of racial categories. From any modern anti-racism perspective, the only workable advice is to reject all such jokes. Racist jokes are simply not made against any racial group. In Britain, for example, there are few (if any) jokes about English people in general in which white English people are derided. In contrast there are countless numbers of angry, hostile, crude, crass, obscene and offensive jokes about black people. Take any of the latter 'jokes' and try to turn them into anti-English jokes, and you are very likely to cause only puzzlement. There is no longer a 'joke' at all apparent.

Anti-racist jokes

If jokes serve racist ideology, a corollary would be that they can also serve anti-racist ideology. This, theoretically, we would accept as possible at a superficial level of analysis, but for a joke to work listeners must understand something of that which the joke is conveying. However, anti-racism is not routinised in our thoughts to the degree that racist ideas are. One can find attempts at anti-racist jokes on the Internet but here is one we cobbled together ourselves to make a point:

Q: What do you call an empty seat on a coach full of racists going over a cliff?
A: A crying shame.

More or less, this is the same as the 'in the river' joke. But it simply does not work since anti-racism lacks the divisive structure of racism. Anti-racism is about valuing peoples and cultures, not disparaging them. Although racists may be disliked by anti-racists with a vehemence matching that of some racists against their targets, since anti-racism is not the reverse of racism but different from racism, racist thoughts cannot be transposed to it. Another example:

Q: What are the best four years of a racist's life?
A: Year 6.

(http://www.effect.net.au/lukastan/humour/Jokes/Racist.htm)

For all intents and purposes, this joke is an exercise in insulting the intellect of a racist. Again it is problematic for that very reason.

The following joke turns out to be ambivalent in terms of meaning:

I like black people ... I used to have some black friends 'till my dad sold them!

(http://www.racist-jokes.com/)

Initially it appears non-racist because it starts 'I like black people ...'. Indeed, the joke does not refer to 'blacks' but what we would see as an acceptable phrasing and one that we use in our writings – black people. This term grants them humanity because it fully acknowledges their status as humans (people). Then it appears to go on to poke fun at white racists. In this respect it can be seen as an anti-racist joke – to have friends who are your father's slaves is incongruous to say the least. However, the joke was found on a self-proclaimed racist joke site so presumably the reference to slavery is regarded by the racist reader as sufficient derogation of black people. Nevertheless, in many respects it seems to be an example of that much self-lauded and much-criticised genre – anti-racist racism – which was exemplified many years ago by television series with notoriously bigoted characters (Alf Garnet in the

BBC sitcom *Till Death Us Do Part* and Archie Bunker in the US sitcom *All In The Family*). The argument being that by vilifying the character by ridicule, the nature of racism (and other forms of bigotry) is exposed for what it is. Research has revealed this to have no substance. Bigots appreciate the rantings of the bigoted characters as the truth, whereas non-bigots see them as bigotry.

To bring the argument up to date, Jaret (1999) examined the American public's attitudes about racial-ethnic humour, especially that which demeans a particular group. The findings challenge the common excuse that one can negate racism with racism. Jaret was motivated by an incident in a popular club in New York. An actor, Ted Danson, took the stage wearing "blackface" make-up and delivered a litany of obscene, explicit jokes and vulgar stereotypical imagery of a racist nature in which black people and women (especially black women) were demeaned. Public objections to this performance were dismissed by Danson and his acolytes on the grounds that the "humour" satirised anti-black images and ridiculed racism. The results of the study showed that the public was not convinced by his argument:

- A majority disagreed that anti-black jokes were worse than derogatory jokes about other groups. Most people believed that jokes about other groups were equally offensive as jokes about black people.
- The vast majority believed that it is always unacceptable to tell demeaning or insulting jokes about African-Americans.
- The majority of respondents found Danson's jokes offensive and ignorant.

Although Danson argued that racist stereotypes were being lampooned by him, this in itself involves exaggerating an already distorted characteristic. Consequently, the effect is to keep demeaning racial-ethnic images alive. The difficulty of the anti-racist joke is that it is forced to take much the same structure as a racist joke so it tries to right one wrong with another wrong. However, by doing so, one is assuming that anti-racism is merely the reverse of racism – that is, the group attacked is racist rather than a racial minority.

Conclusion

The following is a joke circulating recently:

> Shamus shyly asks his black friend Leroy: 'Can you tell me how to get a big penis like yours?'

Leroy smiles and replies that it was easy. Simply tie a piece of string around a house brick and then tie it to the end of your willy for two or three weeks.

A few days later Leroy bumps into Shamus in the bar. 'Thanks for your advice – it's working?' says Shamus. 'How come?' asks Leroy. 'Well', says Shamus, 'my willy has turned black already.'

Quite clearly this joke uses a variety of racial and ethnic categories in problematic ways which tell us a great deal about the cultural context of racism. At the point of its creation, this joke requires such a fundamental knowledge of racial stereotypes that the very existence of the joke is dependent on ours being a racist culture. Furthermore, listening to the joke would be a meaningless exercise without the listener sharing that fundamental racial stereotype with the teller. The existence of jokes about racial categories is testament to the importance of these categories. It requires little knowledge of the history of racism to realise the joke's deep-seated racist ideas. We need little else to conclude that the existence of racist jokes simply reinforces racial categories which do not serve the interests of black people.

Not only do racist jokes provide ready opportunities to give expression to ideas of 'racial' superiority of one group to another, but they continually reinforce the use of race categories in our thinking. Ethnic jokes are conceptually more confusing in that often they are promulgated almost as if they were an opportunity to rejoice in the culture of an ethnic group. After all, should we take the jokes made by Jewish people about Jewish life as a means of gaining insight into that community? There may be instances of this but we believe that the dangers of these are greater than any potential benefits. For example, just what do jokes made about Jewish mothers by Jewish comedians do to promote an appreciation of Jewish culture? Do they not provide an opportunity to deride that culture in the minds of those who would put no effort at all into trying to appreciate Jewish culture otherwise? We have argued at some length about the problematic nature of professionals working with a wide variety of cultures (Owusu-Bempah and Howitt, 2000). Even the best intentioned professional will have the greatest difficulty in working effectively with members of the range of cultures to be found in Western communities because of each culture's sheer complexity (ibid.). In many ways, the ethnic jokes reduce cultures to the trivial, to be laughed at and not something to be valued. Given this, it is extremely difficult to see how even ethnic jokes contribute positively to the development of understanding relevant to multicultural society or globalisation.

3
Humour and the Conduct of Politics

John Morreall

Introduction

Humour has been intertwined with politics since ancient times, when the pharoahs in Egypt and emperors in China first appointed court jesters. In ancient Athens, democracy was born alongside comedy in the fifth century. Aristophanes's *Lysistrata* was the first in a long line of anti-war comedies. In his handbook *On the Orator*, Cicero offered tips to politicians on when and how to use humour in speeches. He advised them not to make jokes about tyrants, for example, since the audience will expect something stronger. Political cartoons have been part of newspapers almost as long as there have been newspapers, and the rise of democracy in the eighteenth and nineteenth centuries was correlated with the rise of sophisticated political cartooning in the hands of Gillray, Rowlandson, Daumier and Nast. Around the world, political jokes are a standard part of conversation. In the United States, political jokes on television are monitored by politicians to gauge the success or failure of their campaigns.

Scholars from many disciplines have studied humour in politics. The *International Society of Humor Studies* has held forums to examine political humour from linguistic, rhetorical and cultural perspectives. A few years before the collapse of the Soviet Union, the Society hosted a group of Soviet humorists, including cartoonists from *Krokodil*, a humour magazine which had a larger circulation than any magazine in the West.

Because this is a book on the ethics of humour, I will be concentrating on ethical issues. But doing that requires some background on ethics and on the nature of humour. So the next section of this chapter will present some approaches to ethics, singling out one as the most promising in exploring the ethics of political humour. Section 3 will present a version of the incongruity theory of humour and Section 4 will relate humour to aesthetic experience and to play. The last three sections will establish some general ethical principles about humour, and apply them to politics. Because I am more familiar with American politics than British politics, most of my examples will be from the USA.

Approaches to ethics

There have been many ethical systems in Western culture. The oldest is 'royal command' ethics, in which morality is obedience to a ruler, and what is right or wrong is what rulers command their subjects to do or not do. This is the kind of ethics that dominates the Biblical religions, with God as the ruler issuing commandments.

A second ethical system in the ancient world was based not on obeying a ruler, but on fulfilling the potential found in human nature. This was the 'virtue ethics' of Greek philosophers like Aristotle. In this approach, there are certain actions such as caring for one's friends which bring out the natural abilities of human beings and thus promote human flourishing. Dispositions to act in those ways are virtues, and they bring happiness; while vices are dispositions which frustrate the exercise of human abilities, bringing unhappiness.

With the Enlightenment came two more ethical systems, the duty ethics of Immanuel Kant, and the utilitarianism of Jeremy Bentham and John Stuart Mill. According to Kant, all human beings naturally feel bound by two principles. The first is to act only in a way that one could recommend that everyone act. And the second is to always treat persons as valuable in themselves, never merely as a means to one's own ends. Together these principles constitute what Kant calls the Categorical Imperative.

Utilitarianism, the newest major ethical system, was created in nineteenth-century Britain, largely as a way to decide issues of public policy. In its simplest form, it says that what is right is what produces the greatest happiness for the greatest number of people.

Of these four ethical theories, utilitarianism seems the most useful for discussing humour in politics, and so that is the approach I will take. In what ways, I will ask, does humour in politics contribute to or reduce people's happiness. More simply, in what ways does humour in politics benefit or harm people?

The nature of humour

Exploring the ethics of humour is a tricky business, because there is no consensus on the nature of humour. Just what is happening when people are amused by something? What are they doing when they share jokes? In order to articulate my views about the ethics of humour, I need to answer such basic questions.

Over more than two millennia, there have been three main theories of laughter and humour: the Superiority Theory, the Relief Theory, and the Incongruity Theory. In 'Humour and Emotion' (Morreall, 1983a), I examined each in detail; here I will show the inadequacy of the Superiority Theory, the promise of the Incongruity Theory, and the compatibility of the Relief Theory with the Incongruity Theory.

The Superiority Theory began with the ancient Greeks. It views laughter as expressing our feelings of superiority over someone else, or over a former state of ourselves. The classic version of this theory was presented by Thomas Hobbes (in Morreall, 1987b: ch.4), who said that laughter was caused by 'sudden glory'.

While this account of laughter dominated from the time of Plato to the eighteenth century, it does not seem to account for all laughter and humour, nor to explain the object of humorous amusement. If the Superiority Theory is true, then whenever we are amused, two conditions must be met. First, we compare ourselves with someone – either another person or a former state of ourselves. And second, in that comparison we find ourselves superior. But there are counter-examples to both conditions. Sometimes we laugh without comparing ourselves to anyone. In an experiment by Deckers (1993), for example, subjects are told to pick up a series of apparently identical metal bars. The first several bars are of a uniform weight, but then subjects pick up a bar which is much lighter or heavier. Most people laugh as they pick up the anomalous bar, but not because they feel superior to anyone. Similarly, when we are hundreds of miles from home and happen to meet our next-door neighbour, we may find that funny even though we do not compare ourselves with the neighbour or with anyone else.

Even when we laugh while comparing ourselves with others, we do not have to find ourselves superior. When my son was 7 years old, I agreed to attend a gymnastics show at his school, expecting to see only somersaults. When one of the children executed a flawless standing back flip, I laughed heartily. I saw clearly that she had much more gymnastic skill than I had, so whatever caused my laughter, it was not feelings of superiority.

Not only are feelings of superiority not necessary for humour; they are not sufficient either. If I pass a group of beggars, I may well be struck by how much better off I am, but my feelings are hardly humour. Even if I am in Hobbesian competition with someone, mere victory is not humour. If I win a game of tennis or chess, for example, and feel that I performed much better than my opponent, that by itself is not humour.

In the mid-eighteenth century, thinkers like Francis Hutcheson (in Morreall, 1987b: ch. 6) began pointing out flaws like these in the Superiority Theory. What soon came to compete with that theory were two quite different accounts of laughter and humour, the Incongruity Theory and the Relief Theory. The latter attempts to explain the physiology of laughter, why amusement issues in the bodily movements of laughter. The Incongruity Theory explains not the physiology of laughter but its psychology. I will leave the Relief Theory aside for the moment, and focus on the Incongruity Theory, which is today the most widely accepted theory of humour.

To understand the Incongruity Theory, we can think again of the tennis match or chess game in which we beat our opponent handsomely. That is not enough, I said, for humour. What, then, has to be added to create humour? Well, suppose that the opponent in the tennis match has his legs too far apart, slips and does the splits. That might be funny. Or if the opponent in chess gets so flustered over her poor opening that she accidentally knocks over her own king, that could be funny. What makes such situations – or any situation – humorous, according to the Incongruity Theory, is that there is something odd, abnormal or out of place, which we enjoy in some way. In its simplest form, the theory says that humorous amusement is the enjoyment of incongruity.

The Incongruity Theory does not deny that when we laugh at vanquished opponents, we may be enjoying feelings of superiority. But it does say that enjoying feelings of superiority is neither necessary nor sufficient for humorous amusement, while the enjoyment of incongruity is both necessary and sufficient for humorous amusement. In fact, we can subsume the examples cited by proponents of the Superiority Theory under the Incongruity Theory, so the latter is more comprehensive than the former. It is also more accurate, its proponents argue, in specifying what makes things funny.

In this chapter, I want to combine the theory that humorous amusement is the enjoyment of incongruity, with insights into the playful social nature of humour, to explore the ethical ramifications of humour in politics.

Ethics is about how people treat one another, and humour is usually a social phenomenon. As many researchers have noted, people laugh far more often in groups than when alone. Robert Provine (2001) speculates that laughter evolved in early humans as a social signal to the group that they could relax. Early humans lived in tribes, often with predators and dangerous neighbours close by. When a tribe was aroused to confront some danger, but members noticed that the danger had passed, or that things were not as dangerous as they appeared, they laughed as a signal to the others that they need not be concerned. This account can be accommodated to the Incongruity Theory by saying that in early humour situations, the incongruity was between a perception of danger and an actual lack of danger. The awareness of this incongruity was naturally gratifying, and so laughter was pleasurable for the group.

If Provine's hypothesis is on the right track, it helps explain why shared humour creates or reinforces a social bond so quickly, as when politicians make funny comments to create rapport with an audience. This social bonding seems to work especially well when the humour is based on either some strength in the group or some shortcoming in opponents of the group. Provine's hypothesis would also explain why what is funny for one group is not funny for their enemies. Imagine a battle between tribe A and tribe B, in which tribe B is about to launch a volley of flaming arrows. Tribe A is initially struck with fear, but then shifting winds cause some of the B warriors to accidentally ignite their own clothing, and they run away screaming. So tribe A easily routs tribe B. Tribe A might well laugh at this unexpected turn of events, their laughter signalling that the danger is passed. But tribe B would not be laughing; for them the incongruity of their burning clothing and their loss is anything but enjoyable. They cannot relax, but must struggle to escape with their lives.

In *On Aggression*, the ethologist Konrad Lorenz (1963: 284) speculated that laughter produces 'a strong fellow feeling among participants and joint aggressiveness against outsiders. Laughter forms a bond and simultaneously draws a line. If you cannot laugh with the others, you feel an outsider even if the laughter is in no way directed against yourself or indeed against anything at all.'

The third theory of humour mentioned above, the Relief Theory, says that laughter is the release of energy in the nervous system which has been suddenly rendered unnecessary. I am not going to examine this theory, but the scenario above shows how it may be linked with the Incongruity Theory, as well as with the Superiority Theory. The laughter of tribe A on seeing their enemies running away with their clothing aflame could be seen as the nervous energy of their previous fear dissipating as it was suddenly rendered unnecessary.

Humour as aesthetic experience and as play

Humour has come a long way since our Paleolithic ancestors first laughed, of course. Today we laugh at wordplay, at the antics of babies, at odd coincidences, and at absurd humour. We even laugh sometimes when the incongruity is our own failure. Our ability to enjoy the violation of our expectations and our conceptual schemes, I have argued elsewhere (Morreall, 1983b: ch. 10; 1989), developed as part of human rationality, and it involves thinking in a way that frees us from practical concern over what is happening to ourselves and to others.

In advanced humour, practical disengagement is coupled with cognitive disengagement, that is, a lack of concern with knowledge or truth. Amusement is evoked by fantasies as easily as by real events. In order to laugh at a cartoon or a film comedy, we do not have to believe that the story is true or even that it could be true. Indeed, a lot of humour involves enjoying impossible events for their impossibility – consider the characters in violent cartoons who are crushed by 10-ton weights and then immediately recover.

If we take the idea that humour is the enjoyment of something experienced, and add to that idea practical disengagement and cognitive disengagement, we have a characterisation of humour that matches the traditional concept of aesthetic experience (Morreall, 1981; 1983b: ch. 7). Laughing at the sudden twist in a joke is like enjoying the dynamic lines in a painting or the resolution of chords in a symphony: we are not trying to accomplish anything or learn anything, but are simply enjoying the experience of something.

Understood more generally, humour is an activity engaged in for its own sake rather than to reach a goal. It is a kind of play, and that makes humour different from most human activities. When we are being funny, the usual intentions, presuppositions and consequences of what we say and do are not in force. We do not assume sincerity on anyone's part. To use a term from Victor Raskin (1985), humour is a non-bona-fide mode of behaviour.

Because of the play element in humour, no analysis of a humorous message which reduces it to assertions, questions, imperatives or other serious speech acts will be adequate. Many humorous messages involve exaggeration, for example, intended not to inform or to deceive listeners, but to entertain them. If in conversation you tell us that your dog just graduated from obedience school at the top of her class, someone might say, 'Next, she'll be applying to graduate schools'. A comment like this is not meant to convey information or to open a discussion about possible future events. It's a playful move in the conversation, introducing a piece of fantasy for the group to enjoy and expand upon.

A humorous message has a different status than the same message would have ordinarily, in a way similar to the contrast between what grammarians call the indicative mood and the subjunctive mood. The speaker is putting ideas into listeners' heads not to cause belief or action, but for the pleasure that entertaining those ideas will bring. Listeners process those ideas in a 'What if?' way, not to reach the truth about anything or to figure out the next step to take, but for fun. Put in philosophical terms, humorous messages are aimed more at the imagination than at speculative reason or practical reason.

If a friend of ours has been dreading her upcoming fiftieth birthday, we might hold a surprise party for her, presenting her with a walking cane and a card that says 'Happy 80th Birthday'. Normally, to give someone a cane presupposes that you think that person needs help to walk. And giving someone a 'Happy 80th Birthday' card presupposes that you believe that that person is turning 80. But here we are playing with both these ideas, putting them into people's heads so that they will enjoy the clash between those ideas and reality. If all goes well, the birthday celebrant will laugh along with us at the fantasy that she is old and infirm.

The general ethics of humour

I would like now to sketch some general ethical principles about humour, which we can then apply to politics. The first is that if humour is the enjoyment of incongruity, there is nothing intrinsically morally objectionable about it. Enjoyment or pleasure, considered in itself, is good. Indeed, aesthetic experiences are among our most valuable. Where a case of humour is morally objectionable, then, the fault must lie in something other than the pleasure. Usually that is some harmful effect which the enjoyment of incongruity has, either on the person laughing or on others. Humour can also be morally praiseworthy, and that is usually because of some beneficial effect which the enjoyment of incongruity has. Our general approach to the ethics of humour, therefore, will be utilitarian: we will ask what effects, good and bad, enjoying incongruity might have.

As we investigate this question, the playful, non-practical, non-cognitive orientation in humour takes centre stage. In finding something funny, we are for the moment not concerned about truth or about consequences. The ethical ramifications of practical disengagement and of cognitive disengagement can be considered one at a time.

In amusement, as in aesthetic experience generally, action is not called for, nothing is urgent. Like art lovers strolling through a gallery or music lovers listening to a concert, humour lovers overlook the practical needs of themselves and others. This practical disengagement in humour shows in the natural opposition between amusement and negative emotions. To face a situation with practical concern is to be emotionally involved in it. If the situation is not going as we want, then it is natural to feel emotions such as fear, anger or hatred if we are focused on ourselves; and pity or compassion, if it is someone else suffering the setback. As Henri Bergson (1911: 150) said, 'Laughter is incompatible with emotion. Depict some fault, however trifling, in such as way as to arouse sympathy, fear, or pity; the mischief is done, it is impossible for us to laugh.'

It is because of the practical disengagement in humour that someone who is practically engaged with a situation naturally resents anyone who is laughing about it. To laugh about something is not to take it seriously, and for you not to take seriously what I take seriously is for you not to take *me* seriously.

Humour, as we said, involves not just practical disengagement but cognitive disengagement. As long as something is funny, we are for the moment not concerned with whether it is real or fictional, true or false. This is why we give considerable leeway to people telling funny anecdotes. If they are getting extra laughs by exaggerating the absurdity of a situation or even by making up a few details, we are happy to grant them comic licence, a kind of poetic licence. Indeed, someone listening to a funny anecdote who tries to correct the teller – 'No, he didn't spill the spaghetti on the keyboard and the monitor, just on the keyboard' – will probably be told by the other listeners to shut up. As we have said, the creator of humour is putting ideas into people's heads for the pleasure those ideas will bring, not to provide accurate information.

When we evaluate humour morally, we usually focus on its practical disengagement, cognitive disengagement, or both. Humour can be irresponsible, for example, by supplanting some action which we should have taken to remedy a serious problem. Suppose that I have diabetes and my physician tells me that I must follow a special low-carbohydrate diet or risk blindness and early death. If I laugh off the problem with a quip that the physician is fatter than I am, and I ignore the diet, then my joking has supported my failure to treat my disease. Or suppose that a friend needs me to help him control his alcoholism. If the next time he gets drunk, instead of giving him disciplined support, I laugh at his antics, then my humour may prolong his problem.

Even when it does not block actions to remedy a problem, humour can be objectionable by showing insensitivity or cruelty toward a person who is suffering from a problem. In some situations corrective action may not be possible, but compassion may still be called for. As a social species, we depend on each other for emotional support even when, or especially when, little can be done to eliminate our problems. Displays of solidarity and compassion may be as important as reducing physical pain, for suffering is often at least as much psychological as physiological. Compassion by itself helps reduce our suffering, and *not* showing compassion can itself harm us.

Perhaps the most generally accepted moral principle is this: Do not cause unnecessary suffering. From that it follows that we should not laugh at someone's problem when compassion is called for.

An egregious example of humour involving a lack of compassion was the cover of the American humour magazine *National Lampoon* in July 1974. At that time a famine was raging in Biafra in Nigeria. Tens of thousands of Biafrans had starved to death, and pictures of emaciated children were common in the news media. During the famine *National Lampoon* published its 'Food Issue'. On the cover was a chocolate model of a starving Biafran child with part of the head bitten off.

Even worse than such cruel humour are cases in which those laughing cause suffering in order to then enjoy it. There are many historical examples of amusement motivating the infliction of suffering. In 106 CE the Roman emperor Trajan celebrated a military victory by having 5000 pairs of gladiators fight to the death. Ugandan dictator Idi Amin is said to have cut off one of his wives' limbs and sewn it on to the opposite side of her body, for his own amusement. In seventeenth-century France, taunting the inmates of insane asylums provided entertainment for the upper classes. In Britain, bear-baiting – having dogs tear chained bears to pieces – was a popular form of entertainment from the twelfth century until the early nineteenth century. For a special royal bear-baiting attended by Elizabeth I in 1575, 13 bears were provided. A recent example of cruel humour is the humiliation and torture of prisoners by Americans in Abu Ghraib prison in Iraq. When asked why they made prisoners pile on top of one another naked, for example, some soldiers said that they did it as a kind of practical joke, 'just for the fun of it'.

From considering such cases of irresponsible and cruel humour, I propose a general ethical principle: Do not promote a lack of concern for something about which people should be concerned.

Having seen some kinds of harm resulting from the practical disengagement of humour, let us turn to cognitive disengagement. When we are joking, as I said, we are presenting ideas to delight people, not to give them information. Like literature, humour is addressed to the imagination more than the intellect. The lack of commitment to truth is obvious in the comic technique of exaggeration. One harm that can come from this cognitive disengagement is that ideas presented to entertain can shape and reinforce harmful beliefs, most notably the beliefs we call stereotypes. In ethnic jokes, for example, a group such as the Jews, the blacks or the Pakistanis are presented as greedy, oversexed and lazy. While most people who trade in such jokes will say that of course real Jews, blacks or Pakistanis are not as bad as those in the jokes, they do associate those negative features with those groups. For at least some such joke-tellers, the humour lies in the exaggerated representation of the negative features, not in the association of those features with those groups. So each time they share those jokes, they reinforce the stereotypes in their minds. That is how racist jokes promote racism.

For centuries, too, humour promoted sexism by entertaining men with stories about fictional women who were manipulative, stupid, fickle and irresponsible with money. Sexist jokes may not have led anyone to believe that real women were as bad as the fictional women, but they kept alive the association of those negative traits with real women. That is why such jokes have been steadily declining as feminism has gained in popularity.

While the cases of humour we have been considering involve harm, the ethics of humour are not all negative, for there are also ways in which humour can be beneficial. One is by promoting critical thinking. The humorous mind looks for incongruity, and that is frequently a discrepancy between what people should be and what they are. From the days of the ancient Greeks, comedy has focused on self-deception, pretence, and hypocrisy. In looking for the comic in society, we look beneath appearances and do not take what people say at face value. We are not as likely, therefore, to blindly follow leaders, or to do what everyone else is doing merely because 'we've always done it this way'. The humorous person may be irreverent and even disrespectful toward those in authority, but that can be beneficial, especially if leaders are misusing their power and deceiving people.

It is useful for even honest, well-intentioned leaders to have people ask challenging questions and think for themselves. That prevents 'Groupthink' (Janus, 1972). Spurring critical thinking through humour was part of the traditional job of court jester. A contemporary example comes from the Canadian Imperial Bank of Commerce, which, like many corporations, produces a monthly video watched by employees. On most corporate videos, leaders present themselves as omniscient and infallible, but on the CIBC videos, a wise-cracking hand puppet shows up to ask the CEO tough questions about recent decisions and policies. Employees love this segment, because the humour relaxes everyone to be able to talk about issues in an open, even playful way. That not only makes them feel empowered, but leads to a wider range of ideas than would be forthcoming under Groupthink.

Humour can also foster an open, constructive attitude toward mistakes. As John Cleese, comedian and the world's largest producer of training films, has said, when we laugh about a mistake, we get the perspective we need to learn from it and move beyond it. Usually when we make a small mistake, and often when we make a big mistake, laughing it off can be more beneficial than reviewing the error again and again, to sink into self-blame or depression. If practical concern will not help us deal with a mistake now and will not improve our behaviour in the future, then practical concern is counter-productive, and practical disengagement prudent.

Life is full of potentially stressful situations, and in many of them, negative emotions such as fear and anger do more harm than good. Because humour blocks or displaces such stress emotions, it can be beneficial (Morreall, 1997: ch. 4). Stress is measured by four chemicals in the blood. While all four increase in stress, they decrease in humorous amusement. While stress suppresses the immune system, humour boosts it. Because of the opposition between humour and stress, over 100 hospitals have created humour rooms or comedy carts (with funny audio, video and printed materials) to relax patients and their families, and to promote healing. There is even an Association of Applied and Therapeutic Humour. Physicians themselves engage in humour to block negative emotions and keep their cool, and so to operate at the peak of their skill.

War is another setting where humour can decrease stress. During the Blitzkrieg over England in World War II, for example, one shop was heavily damaged. The owner placed a sign in the window, 'OPEN AS

USUAL'. When a second night of bombing destroyed the roof, he replaced that sign with another, 'MORE OPEN THAN USUAL'. By doing so, he helped keep his own spirits up, and those of his fellow citizens.

Humour can also be beneficial in restoring personal relationships after a rift, by reducing or blocking negative emotions. If I have done something to hurt a friend, I should admit the wrong, apologise, ask for forgiveness and try to make amends. But once I have done all that, then we should get beyond the problem and restore our relationship. Dwelling on the offence is likely to slow down the process. Forgiving includes the willingness to put the offence out of mind, and one of the most effective ways we show people that we have forgiven and forgotten is by joking with them. Indeed, we would not believe a friend who said she had forgiven us, but then was unwilling for weeks to joke with us in conversation.

Humour used by politicians

As we turn now to examine the ethics of humour in politics, we need to distinguish between humour *used by* politicians and humour created by non-politicians *about* politicians. The former, I will argue, is usually objectionable, while the latter is often commendable. Let us begin with humour used by politicians. In analysing humour as the enjoyment of incongruity, and in citing examples of friends' joking, I have been considering an ideal type of humour which is engaged in merely for pleasure. We can call it aesthetic humour. Almost no humour used by politicians is like this, however, though most of it is made to emulate aesthetic humour. A political advertisement, for instance, is not a communication between friends, and if there is humour in it, that humour is not created merely to delight people. Like humour in any other advertising, it is created to get people to do something – here to vote in a certain way. In contrast with aesthetic humour, we can call this instrumental humour.

Three common uses of humour by politicians are to reduce the harshness of bad news, to defuse criticisms made against them, and to make opponents seem foolish. When Winston Churchill went on BBC radio to announce that Italy had entered World War II on the Nazi side, he said: 'Today the Italians have announced that they are joining the war on the side of the Germans. I think that's only fair – we had to take them the last time.' With this joke, Churchill made the bad news more bearable.

Second, humour can reduce the sting of a criticism, or even get people to overlook it. That makes humour useful in what is now called damage control. In the debates between Abraham Lincoln and Stephen Douglas in the 1850s, Douglas accused Lincoln of being two-faced. Lincoln turned to the audience and said, 'Ladies and gentlemen, I leave it to you. If I had two faces, would I be wearing this one?' The criticism evaporated. A century later John Kennedy faced criticism for using his father's wealth to finance his campaign for the presidency. And so at a large gathering he held up a piece of paper, saying, 'I have just received this telegram from my generous daddy. It says, "Jack, don't buy a single vote more than is necessary. I'll be damned if I pay for a land-slide."' Again, the issue was not raised after that.

Third, humour can be used to make an opponent's statements or actions seem stupid or foolish. An example combining this use with the second use occurred in the 1984 US presidential campaign between Ronald Reagan and Walter Mondale. In their first television debate, Reagan had seemed uninformed and confused. Critics pointed out that he was an old man; some suggested he might be suffering from Alzheimer's disease. So Reagan's speechwriters prepared two sentences for the second debate. When someone asked about the 'age issue', Reagan said, 'I will not make age an issue in this election. I will not exploit for political gain my opponent's youth and inexperience.' That made Mondale rather than Reagan look foolish, and for the rest of the campaign the age issue was dead.

These and other uses of humour by politicians have a paradoxical feature – the more obvious it is that humour is being used to accom-plish a goal, the less likely the humour is to be successful. Instrumental humour works best when it hides its purpose, and looks relaxed, playful, spontaneous – like the aesthetic humour that friends engage in. If it is obvious that someone is trying to amuse us only in order to get something from us, we are likely to feel manipulated and so are less likely to be amused. No one wants to be manipulated, especially with something like humour that is so often based on friendship. So in pol-itics there is an odd masquerade of instrumental humour emulating aesthetic humour.

This masquerade is fundamentally dishonest much as humour in commercial advertising is dishonest. Comparable to the creators of a funny political advertisement are the creators of an advertisement for a brand of cigarettes who use humour to get people to relax, laugh, like the advert and so feel favorable toward the cigarettes. Neither team of advertisers is interested in persons and their happiness, as friends engaging in funny banter are. Amusement is merely a means to an end – the purchase of the cigarettes or the votes for their candidate.

To make matters worse, humour is often used in political advertisements and speeches to block legitimate practical concerns and cognitive concerns about politicians and their policies. Its purpose is to belittle or trivialise an issue which should command our attention, so that we will not think about it and act upon it. When Ronald Reagan's speechwriters created the quip about 'the age issue' for the 1984 debates, for example, they got Americans to dismiss some important and potentially disturbing facts: that Reagan was 73 years old, that he often quickly forgot information he had been given in Cabinet meetings, and that on several occasions he had confused events in his movies with reality. Such facts should have been taken seriously, but the funny line about the age issue swept them out of political discussions and American voters re-elected a man in the early stages of Alzheimer's disease.

A more recent example of humour used to block legitimate concerns emerged in the Abu Ghraib prison scandal. In spring 2004, as more and more information and pictures became public about the abuse of Iraqi prisoners by Americans, a common line in speeches by officials was that 'thousands of people are involved in handling Iraqi prisoners and they're not all Boy Scouts'. Phrases like this were created to get voters who had moral objections to the abuse to 'lighten up', laugh and forget the issue.

Around the same time, President Bush used humour in a similar way to try to defuse the criticism that no weapons of mass destruction had been found in Iraq, even though he said he invaded Iraq to eliminate its weapons of mass destruction. Standing in his office, Bush looked under his desk and behind a chair. With a smirk, he quipped that he had looked everywhere but hadn't been able to find the weapons of mass destruction. This attempt at trivialising an important issue failed, as even some of Bush's supporters said that he should have answered the questions rather than joke around for the TV cameras.

In cases like these, humour blocks careful thinking, moral investigation, acknowledgment of wrongdoing, apology and correction of serious problems. Humour has also been used in more heinous ways to promote xenophobic stereotypes and even genocide. In their anti-Semitic propaganda, for example, the Nazis created dozens of cartoons of Jews with distorted features stealing money from Aryan Germans, and plotting with Communists against Germany. The purpose of the humour was to block careful thought about whether the stereotypes were accurate, and to get people to relax, laugh and accept the Nazi ideology.

A milder example of humour used to get the public to swallow a stereotype came up in the 2004 US presidential campaign. Early on, Bush's strategists created the theme that his opponent, John Kerry, was a coward unfit to command the armed forces. Kerry's military record and numerous endorsements from military leaders belied that idea; so much of the 'Kerry is a coward' rhetoric was light on evidence and heavy on assertion. Humour was often used to make the assertion palatable and the stereotype stick. When Senator Zell Miller pushed the 'Kerry is a coward' message on the television programme *Hardball*, he said, 'Senator Kerry expects our soldiers to fight with spitballs.' The host of the programme, Chris Matthews, saw instantly that Miller was trying to get the audience to accept a questionable characterisation of John Kerry by expressing it with humorous exaggeration. Rather than playing along, he treated Miller's line as a direct assertion, and said, 'No, he doesn't!' Miller got indignant, saying that he had not come on the programme to be insulted, but what he was really angry about was that Matthews had thwarted his attempt to get the audience to swallow a false depiction of Kerry. His line that Kerry expects soldiers to fight with spitballs was a direct attack masquerading as playful humour in friendly conversation.

Humour about politicians

While examples like those above violate the ethical principle proposed earlier – Do not promote a lack of concern for something about which people should be concerned – not all political humour is like that. Churchill's humour in announcing that Italy had entered the war, for example, was beneficial in reducing the anxiety of the public and bolstering their courage. And at the beginning of the chapter, I cited many historical examples of humour *about* politicians, rather than *by* them, which can be beneficial in promoting critical thinking.

Germany in the 1930s provided many more examples. Among the first to criticise the Nazis publicly were cabaret comedians. In the ghettos, Hitler's masterpiece was known as *Mein Krampf* (My Cramp). Such humour promoted not only critical thinking but opposition to the diabolical Groupthink sweeping across Germany. There was even anti-Nazi humour in the concentration camps which strengthened inmates' courage and resistance (Lipman, 1991; Morreall, 1999a). In

Dachau, a play satirising the Nazis was performed for six weeks in 1943.

Today the easiest place to see such beneficial political humour is on television programmes such as *The Daily Show with Jon Stewart* in the United States. Made to look like a news programme, *The Daily Show* is mostly political satire. Video clips of speeches by George Bush, Tony Blair and others are followed by earlier speeches of theirs that belie the later ones. One recurring segment on the war in Iraq is entitled 'Mess'o'potamia'. During the scandal over the abuse of Iraqi prisoners at the Abu Ghraib prison, President Bush was shown saying that he was not going to ask for the resignation of Defence Secretary Rumsfeld, who, he said, was 'doing a superb job'. Jon Stewart simply asked what a less-than-superb job would look like.

If humour can be misused to get voters to overlook serious problems, it can also be used to reveal those problems and the trickery that covered them up. If politicians sometimes use humour in propaganda, comedians also undermine that propaganda. Speaking negatively, then, the ideal kind of humour in politics would seem to be humour that is not used as a trick, to trivialise something important, or to get people to swallow vicious beliefs and attitudes. Speaking positively, the ideal political humour would emerge as playful moments in honest discussions between people who care about one another, like the humour in conversations between friends. What we need is more of the humour court jesters offered, to benefit their monarchs and their countries. Here it is encouraging to note an advertisement in *The Times* in August 2004, placed by English Heritage, for someone to be Britain's first court jester since 1649. Job qualifications: 'Must be mirthful and prepared to work summer weekends in 2005. Must have own outfit (with bells). Bladder on stick provided if required.'

4
Parody and Decorum: Permission to Mock

Jerry Palmer

Introduction

The central character of the Monty Python comedy *Life of Brian* is a carpenter from Nazareth at the time of the New Testament events, who is mistaken for the Messiah. The biblical reference is obvious, and the story contains clear allusions to events recorded in the Testaments, such as the Sermon on the Mount, as well as the Crucifixion itself. On its release the film was accused of blasphemous parody by Christian and Jewish organisations; in the UK, various local authorities banned the film on the grounds that it was offensive (*Guardian*, 2003). Salman Rushdie's *Satanic Verses* (Rushdie, 1988) received essentially the same judgement from Muslim organisations: as is well known, the Ayatollah Khomeini, the then religious leader of Iran, issued a *fatwa* in 1989 condemning Rushdie to death for blasphemy. The novel was seen as a 'blasphemous parody of Islam' by the Iranian religious leaders (Beaver, 2003) or as a 'simple-minded parody of Islam' (Samuel, 1989), it was 'a serious parody of militant Islam' (Calico, 2004), criticised in so far as it 'paints nauseous grotesque absurd accounts of incoherent events, mostly with cartoons and caricatures' (Roy, 2002).[1] Similarly, when punk rock band, the Sex Pistols, released a record entitled 'God Save the Queen' to coincide with the Royal Jubilee in 1977, the song was banned from various forms of performance, the record company's workers refused temporarily to press it or its cover because of the content; various stores refused to stock it, and the band were attacked in the street by a group shouting 'We love our queen, you bastards' (but it rose to second place in the Hit Parade) (Savage, 1991: 347–9, 365).

In these cases we see clear examples of a boundary beyond which parody ceases to be a legitimate artistic device for humour and/or social criticism, and becomes unacceptable, to some group of people. This chapter examines the implications of recognising the existence of this boundary.

Ever since Mary Douglas's seminal article, it has been axiomatic that humour needs to be both understood *and permitted* in order to be a joke (Douglas, 1968), albeit that the question of whose permission is necessary is left unsettled in her account (Palmer, 1996: 24–8). Both incomprehension and ethical refusal threaten humour's communicative success, as does aesthetic refusal, where humour is rejected on the grounds that it is boring, stupid or childish. In the case that parodies such as *Life of Brian* or *The Satanic Verses* are judged by some to be blasphemous rather than amusing, we see that permission for humour and/or mockery has been withheld by some portion of the public, whereas another portion has registered its approval by giving commercial success to the works in question. Once such a disagreement has occurred, it is largely a question of power relations: one or other of the groups in question prevails in an interaction whose parameters may vary greatly from case to case.

In parody, some pre-existing discursive entity is both repeated (in part or in whole) and simultaneously transformed, in some measure, commonly for humour and/or ridicule.[2] The purpose may be mockery of the original, mockery of some other associated entity, or mere playful allusion – all of these possibilities are to be found in the literature about parody (see below). Such a repetition/transformation, whether playful or mocking, may or may not cause offence to someone. If a negative judgement is made, it may be on ethical grounds (if we can label the accusation of blasphemy an ethical judgement) or aesthetic or both. I shall propose that the nature of parody is such that the ethical and the aesthetic converge, and that it is appropriate to revive the neo-classical concept of 'decorum' to label the space where this process occurs. Decorum can be defined as a decision about the form of expression which is publicly judged appropriate for a given setting and theme.

As a first stage in the argument, we can turn to recent theorising about parody. We shall see that the theories currently available are ambiguous in some crucial respects: in them, it is unclear to what extent parody is necessarily funny and necessarily critical. As a result, the ethical dimension of parody is difficult to analyse using these theories; however, in one central aspect of parody, recent theory gives us a further line of enquiry, namely the extent to which parody necessarily destabilises textual meaning.

The theory of parody: the destabilisation of meaning through allusion and humour

Modern theories of parody consider it primarily as one form of inter-textuality among others (Genette, 1982; Rose, 1993; Hutcheon, 1985; Dentith, 2000). There is some common ground in these discussions about the extent to which this form of intertextuality has changed its meaning and function through history, while retaining some common features. Debate is driven in part by the fact that the term 'parody' has a significant if somewhat obscure role in ancient Greek poetics, which has given the term both longevity and a certain authority. Specialists give different etymologies, and attach somewhat divergent practices to them, in their analysis of Greek theory and practice (Rose, 1993: 6–20). However, it seems clear that the term passed into the discussions to be found in subsequent periods of history via Aristotle's *Poetics*, where it has equal status in his system of genres with tragedy, comedy and the epic. The system of genres in Aristotle is deductively based on the poss-ible combinations of *a priori* features of texts (Genette, 1986: 95–100). In the case of parody, Aristotle deduces its place in the genre system through the combination of two pairs of *a priori* elements: the actions represented in a work are either more or less elevated than the average level of a culture, that is, basically either 'heroic' or 'vulgar' in relation to a culture,[3] and the actions are either imitated (drama) or narrated by a poet. In combination, these two pairs of elements give four possibil-ities, which constitute the four genres Aristotle recognises:

Level of actions represented	Mode of representation	
	Imitation	Narrative
Above	Tragedy	Epic
Below	Comedy	Parody

The authority given to Aristotle during the Middle Ages ensured the survival of his ideas well beyond the culture within which they were formulated. This is significant because whatever the actual role of par-ody in ancient Greek poetry, the version of it which became influential after the Renaissance was the idea encapsulated in Aristotle's genre system: parody is associated with vulgar actions. Additionally, the ele-ment of vulgarity associated it with humour (it is paired with comedy in this respect) and specialist historians appear to concur that in the ancient world parody was largely considered to be funny (Rose, 1993: 25); arguably, it was the element of comic incongruity in parody which distinguished it from other forms of imitation – allusion and quotation (ibid: 31). How this incongruity arose is far from clear, but one supposition is that it was a mismatch between style and content that constituted it: either a noble action could be represented in debased language, or a vulgar action could be represented in language normally reserved for noble actions (Genette, 1982: 20–3). Genette asserts that it is in this form that parody was understood in the post-Renaissance world, and he gives a revised partial genre classification system based upon post-Renaissance commentaries and artistic practices:

Style	Level of actions represented	
	Noble	Vulgar
Noble	Tragedy, epic	Parody
Vulgar	Pastiche, burlesque	Comedy

Genette reserves the term parody for a practice in which there is minimal alteration of the parodied text and significant 'perversion' of its original meaning (ibid: 33). However, it is clear from his subsequent analyses that he does not consider the distinction between parody, burlesque and travesty to be consistent in practice. In this scheme it can be seen that in the post-Renaissance world parody is not only funny but also critical: the capacity for mockery that has come to typify it may or may not have formed its central feature in antiquity, but there is general agreement that it subsequently did (Brand, 1998; Rose, 1993: 29).

Parody always consists of the imitation (allusion, if not direct quotation or misquotation) of some other text or texts, even if only by using stylistic devices which are typical of the text(s) in question. In the ancient world, it is the element of stylistic imitation which is its primary defining feature (Brand, 1998). The role of imitation means that, from the first, intertextuality is integral to parody. Indeed, Genette's comments on parody are grounded in a generalised theory of literary textuality, where parody is only one form of intertextuality; the two versions of textuality which he considers to be most relevant to parody he calls 'intertextuality' (citation, plagiarism, allusion) and 'hypertextuality', where one text gains meaning by partially copying but also transforming an original text (1982: 7–15).[4] In hypertextuality, as is clear from examples such as Joyce's *Ulysses* and Mann's *Dr Faustus*, neither humour nor polemic are necessary components, and therefore the extent to which this practice should be considered as parody is open to question; however, we shall see that in recent debates, non-humorous 'parody' has become increasingly central. While this can be reduced to a question of terminological consistency and nothing more, the question of humour is central to the ethical question of permission to parody, because of the potential for aggressive mockery. This can be seen in two twentieth-century examples: a well-known parody of the socialist anthem *The Red Flag*, and the closing chapter of David Lodge's *The British Museum is Falling Down*, which parodies the Molly Bloom soliloquy in Joyce's *Ulysses*.

The parody of *The Red Flag* sets mocking words to the tune of the original:

> The working class
> Can lick my arse,
> I've got the foreman's
> Job at last.

Clearly the mockery of the original anthem is also a mockery of one of the central values of socialism: class solidarity. The choice of song is integral to the political purpose of the mockery, and the mockery is aimed at two, associated targets simultaneously: mocking the song is integral to mocking the value. The parody may also be understood in the opposite way, as a socialist attack on those who break solidarity; such shifts in meaning are largely context-dependent (Palmer, 1994: 154, 165). In either case, such mockery may be accepted or rejected by an audience, probably largely on political grounds.

David Lodge's use of the Molly Bloom soliloquy has a very different purpose (Li, 2004). The Joyce original is an affirmation of sensual delight in love, using the repeated refrain 'Yes, yes' as one of its central devices. In the Lodge novel, the hero's wife reflects on her life in a decidedly unsensual way – as a Catholic, sex has led to a large number of children, which her student husband finds difficult to support, and their sensuality is limited by Catholic doctrine on contraception, as they are permanently worried about a new conception. The refrain in her meditation is 'perhaps, perhaps', a decidedly less affirmative message. Yet the intention is less to mock than a wry reflection on the difficulties for young Catholic married couples in their circumstances. It appears, from Lodge's 'Afterword' to the Penguin edition, that no mockery of Joyce is intended (Lodge, 1983: 170–1).

From our point of view what is significant about these two examples is this: in both cases the parody has the potential for transforming our understanding of the original (assuming we recognise the relationship between the two), but whereas in one the question of permission to mock is decidedly controversial, in the other it is arguably not so. In the *Red Flag* parody, the mockery of a central socialist value (or of a failure to live up to it) is – to put it at its mildest – subject to ethical and political evaluation. In the Lodge allusion, reader response to the novel may produce a negative judgement about the aesthetic value of the reference (it is one among many in this novel), but it is highly unlikely that anyone would make the judgement that Lodge was *ethically* wrong to make it, if only because there is no implied mockery of the original; this distinction and relationship between aesthetic and ethical response is one to which we shall return when we consider the value of decorum. To this extent, we may assimilate the intertextual play in the Lodge novel either to the (serious) hypertextuality of Genette's examples, or to what he calls non-aggressive 'pastiche', a playfulness in allusion, an 'exercise in distraction' in intertextual relations, which involves no aggressive intent on the part of the author (1982: 34, 36). However, none of these considerations should be taken to indicate that such judgements are unproblematic, for reasons that we shall turn to below.

The latter version of parody, in which funniness is arguably less important than the capacity to generate meaning through intertextual allusion, appears to dominate recent analysis of parody. For example, Rose outlines a definition of parody which insists on the element of funniness: it is a 'comic refunctioning of preformed linguistic or artistic material' (1993: 52); however, in his analysis of recent theories in Chapter 4, the element of funniness is largely marginalised in favour of the work of transformative allusion in generating meaning, despite foregrounding writers such as Lodge who emphasise the humorous element of parody (ibid: 252–9). According to Hutcheon, parody and self-reference are central to contemporary art practice, where it becomes a major form of 'modern self-reflexivity' (1985: 2–3). Clearly this form of intertextuality is more than imitation, since the allusions invite a response from the reader that is based on the simultaneous presence of two texts and the relationship between them. To this extent the use of the term 'parody' is justified, although it is often replaced in such commentaries by 'meta-fiction'. While it may be the case that such use of intertextual allusion generates meaning in a way that is not otherwise available, there is little doubt that it is publicly accepted as a legitimate artistic device even where aesthetic objections are raised against individual examples.

An example which illustrates the type of practice in question is Cindy Sherman's *Film Stills* series, in which she photographs a model (herself) in poses and against backdrops and lighting that are reminiscent of Hollywood cinematic styles. The result is a set of images in which meaning is generated both by the image in question and its capacity to allude to something which has some air of familiarity about it. No doubt such images *can* be seen as parody in the comic sense, however commentary on them appears to avoid this line, despite the fact that Sherman herself has said that she stopped the series when she 'ran out of clichés', which implies a denunciatory function.[5] Here the question of permission in the ethical sense scarcely arises: the process of intertextual allusion is indeed a central element in modern artistic creation, and – short of outright plagiarism – permission to allude to, or echo, other texts is not ethically controversial.[6]

On the other hand, different artistic movements give different aesthetic values to such a practice. In particular, modern theoretical poetics, informed by post-structuralist debates, attaches great importance to this form of intertextuality as it is held to demonstrate the way in which discursive constructs are built up, thus allowing the audience to disengage from the ideological mechanisms involved: meaning is destabilised in the space between text and audience. This can be seen in Hutcheon's analysis of what she calls 'self-consciously intransitive narrativity': a form of cinematic narrative in which formal devices of various sorts serve to remind the viewer that this is indeed 'only cinema'. These operate to break the spectator's suspension of disbelief which allows identification or empathy with characters and situations (Hutcheon, 1990: 125–6). This is held to break the moment in which ideology 'interpellates' the subject, a process which provides the subject with a sense of wholeness and closure which is constitutive of subjectivity. Parody is a privileged version of this rupture because in it the pretensions to narrative transitivity of the original are clearly foregrounded: she refers to 'the possibilities of the positive oppositional and contestatory nature of parody ... [which begins] a subversion from within'; and later she says that:

> Multiple and overt parody ... can paradoxically foreground social issues by its very baring and challenging of conventions.
>
> (Hutcheon, 1990: 129, 131)

Such parody is not necessarily comic, as Hutcheon's examples show. While mockery may form part of the procedure, it is certainly not a necessary part, and modern aesthetics readily accepts referentiality, reflexivity and critical distance *vis-à-vis* other works: permission to parody, in this sense, is not in doubt.

Parody thus has come to have two somewhat divergent senses: first, imitation for aggressive mockery; second, intertextual reference; a third sense – playful allusion – mixes elements of both. It is not my purpose to assess the descriptive relevance of these senses, but we shall see that approaching the subject from an ethical perspective allows some assessment of their implications.

Destabilisation and ethics: carnival

Modern theories of parody privilege the elements in it which produce a destabilisation of meaning. This destabilisation is ethical in orientation, in so far as the destabilisation of meaning implies the destabilisation of subjectivity, which in its turn involves an element of disalienation, of recovery of something like authenticity, or at least a move away from a position in which authenticity is radically impossible. Our focus till now has been on another ethical dimension of parody, the question of the permission to mock. The two questions are linked because the use of parody to create this destabilisation of meaning involves creating a distance from the source text which can readily be seen as critical of it, or critical of some aspect of its use in the social world. Moreover, the two questions are inextricably linked as soon as one considers the matter from an ethical perspective, since critical parody raises the question of the permission to (ab)use a text in this fashion. We can best approach this matter by considering a theory which suggests that there is a generalised ethical permission under a particular category of social occasion – carnival. It is central to this theory that this category of occasion creates an element of disalienation through a consensual extended licence for humour and mockery; we can use Bakhtin as our entry point into this debate.

The key relevant element in Bakhtin is the relationship between monologic and dialogic discursive and cultural forms. In his theory, these forms are both features of textuality and also elements of cultural formations,[7] and it is the relationship between the two that is the key to understanding Bakhtin's relevance to parody considered in ethical terms.

For Bakhtin, all language, in all societies, is essentially an interacting series of discourses – as opposed to a structure, in the Saussurean sense – a process to which he gives the name dialogism or heteroglossia.[8] In most historical, recorded societies attempts have been made to impose a single unified language and/or culture on to these interacting sets of discourses, from above, usually by Church or State (monologism, in his terms). However, total suppression of heteroglossia is impossible and the multiplicity of discourses continues to exist, if in a form which is marginalised or partially suppressed. Thus heteroglossia represents for Bakhtin the life of the people continuing despite attempts from above to suppress or change central elements of it: if there are attempts to impose a monologic culture, heteroglossia is always subversive. Bakhtin identifies two primary locations of the continued existence of hetero-glossic forms alongside the 'official' culture to which they are meant to be subordinated: one is the novel, the other is popular festivity, or 'carnival'.[9]

Carnival is important because its practices – especially the 'lowest', least respectable ones, such as gluttony, drunkenness, buffoonery – encapsulate an entire philosophy of life, and one which acts as a coun-terweight to the philosophy of life advanced in official culture:

> The feast had always an essential, meaningful philosophical content. No rest period ... can be rendered festive per se; something must be added from the spiritual and ideological dimension. They must be sanctioned ... by the highest aims of human existence. ... Under the feudal regime ... the characteristics of festival, in other words the relationship between festival and the higher purposes of human life ... could only be fully realised ... in carnival ...
>
> (Bakhtin, 1984: 8–9)

And in the following pages Bakhtin repeatedly stresses the relationship of opposition between the official culture of Church and State, and the culture of carnival, all the while insisting on carnival as the incarna-tion of a whole way of life – the 'second life of the people'.

Central to carnival is the parody of elements of the official culture. Bakhtin is at pains to stress that the relationship here between parody and what is parodied is very different from parody in the modern world. This is a point to which we shall return. For the moment it is sufficient to note two things: first, that parody in this context is clearly historically specific (his example is mediaeval Europe), and to that extent loses some of the universality associated with the heteroglossia of which it is a component; second, that the feature of mediaeval parody that distinguishes it is that it is integrated into the 'second life of the people' in such a way that it is only comprehensible in this context. It is therefore important to understand the elements of this 'second life' that are relevant here.

First, carnival is a set of activities which has meaning through uni-versal participation: in the rituals of carnival there is no distinction between performers and spectators, and in the joyous laughter evoked by these rituals – for example, clowning or buffoonish parodies of official ceremonial – the crowd is laughing as much at itself as at something Other; there is no aggressive mockery of something that is cast as outside the group in question. Carnival is in fact a (temporary) way of life, without spatial frontiers within the community celebrating it.

Second, it is in its essence democratic and therefore fully human in that it inverts or disrupts all social distinction through the 'temporary suspension ... of hierarchical rank':

> People were so to speak reborn for new purely human relations with their fellows. *Alienation disappeared, provisionally.* [This] was neither the fruit of the imagination nor of abstract thought, it was effectively brought into being and experienced in this living, material, felt contact. Utopian ideal and reality blended provisionally ...
>
> (Bakhtin, 1970: 19; emphasis added)[10]

Third, as implied above, carnival is essentially a set of activities grounded in laughter. However, this laughter is by no means an individual phenomenon, one person laughing at something they find funny, it is 'the laughter of all the people' (1984: 11), and it is universal – within the time limits of carnival – in that it affects everything: the whole world is turned upside down by it in that the perception of the world that it incarnates is inimical to everything 'that is ready-made and completed, to all pretense at immutability' (ibid: 11). Essentially, the subversion of official, monologic forms produces provisional disalienation.

While this is by no means a full description of what Bakhtin means by the carnivalesque, it allows us to make sense of the role of parody in his thought. From the opening pages of the introduction to the study of Rabelais, Bakhtin insists on the role of parody in the culture he is going to analyse: in his first, partial list of the components of the culture of carnival, parody features twice, along with all the other comic and grotesque manifestations involved (ibid: 5); shortly after he gives a preliminary analysis of the parodic forms he considers relevant (ibid: 13–15). Here we should note the distance that separates Bakhtin from the semiotic tradition: for the latter, parody is a relationship between texts, which participants in a common culture are likely to recognise. While the textual relationship is of course present in Bakhtin's thought, as it must be in order for parody to occur, it is not this relationship that is of primary importance for him: parody is no more important than laughter aroused by any incongruous spectacle. We could say that the intertextuality is necessary for the carnivalesque/ parodic relationship to exist, but that it is only a means towards, or one element in, the carnivalesque, whose value is given by its place in the whole, in the 'second life of the people', which is the essential because it is the ground in which all the different elements are rooted. It is their integration in the social form 'carnival' that gives them their meaning and their value.

Carnival, parody and the other forms of heteroglossia thus share various fundamental features: first, heteroglossia is a universal dimension of human existence as it is the foundation of all discourse; second, in their historically specific forms they incarnate the second life of the people;[11] third, they are in opposition to all monologic attempts to create and impose a unified culture such as the official culture of Church and State.

There is a point of tension in this analysis: the fact of permission for opposition makes the status of such opposition unclear. As Bakhtin himself notes, the forms of carnival were permitted by the very official culture to which they were in opposition, and were permitted because they incarnated something fundamental to the life of the people. However, the passage in which he discusses this has an element of ambiguity in it. Analysing the difference between official festivities and popular festivity in the Middle Ages, he says that the official version was always marked by seriousness, and lacked the comic spirit typical of genuine popular festivity:

> the tone of the official feast was monolithically serious, and ... the element of laughter was alien to it. The true nature of human festivity was betrayed and distorted. But this true festive character was indestructible; it had to be tolerated and even legalised outside the official sphere, and had to be turned over to the popular sphere of the marketplace.
>
> (ibid: 9)[12]

Now, it becomes clear in his discussion of particular festivals – for example, the Feast of Fools (ibid: 72–9) – that they were indeed characterised by the joyous carnival spirit that he identifies with popular festivity. Was the Feast of Fools a genuine incarnation of the indestructible 'human festivity'? Or was it a stultified, permitted version that was not really true to the original? Certainly it was 'tolerated' and 'permitted', terms which suggest restrictions on its validity, but this is the evaluation of the Church authorities, not necessarily the point of view of participants. The question remains unanswered, yet the detailed discussion of the forms of popular festival that fill many pages of the book on Rabelais imply through their enthusiasm that Bakhtin did not consider them to be truncated and inauthentic. Indeed, had he done so, it would have been difficult to make the case about dialogism, carnival and the novel, in which he presents Rabelais as the authentic voice of popular festivity (ibid: 2–3, 61–2).

What is implied in this definitional difficulty is the question of permission. According to Bakhtin, the official culture of the Middle Ages accepted an oppositional culture, to which it accorded a certain licence in the form of carnival and related cultural forms. As Stallybrass and White say, this means that carnival was not truly, fundamentally oppositional: it was a marginalised opposition that was tolerated because it posed no real threat to the social order that tolerated it; indeed, official culture found numerous uses for it (1986: 12–19; cf. Dentith, 2000: 52–4). Yet, on the other hand, we know that the institutions of carnival, and especially the ones which involved direct parody of Church ceremonial, increasingly came under attack in the second half of the Middle Ages and were eventually abolished.[13] Perhaps the resolution to this paradox is to be found in another central element of carnival in Bakhtin's definition.[14] At various points in his analysis of Rabelais he makes the argument that carnival, being a philosophy of life, shows that medieval man effectively lived in two world orders simultaneously:

> Mediaeval man participated on an equal basis in two lives: the official and the carnival life. Two aspects of the world, the serious and the laughing aspect, coexisted in their consciousness, ...
>
> (Bakhtin, 1984: 96)

This is significant because it implies that the mind-set which appreciated carnival in the way he suggests must have been a permanent feature of the medieval way of life. Indeed, this is obviously necessary: how would it be possible for entire populations to suddenly adopt a frame of mind for a few weeks a year which was totally unknown to them for the rest of the year? In one mind-set the world was experienced as it was shown in official culture, ordered and hierarchical, meaningful because ordered – and, Bakhtin insists, highly repressive (1970: 82); in the other, it was experienced in a different way, meaningful because disordered and by the same token subversive. And we should remember that it is this element in carnival that allows for disalienation, according to Bakhtin: 'The individual seemed to acquire a second life ... Alienation disappeared, provisionally' (ibid: 19).

However, he says, the parodies of sacred rituals and texts in no way implied a lack of piety, neither on the part of the author/performer, nor on the part of the audience (ibid: 95). It must be stressed that the parodies were indeed extreme, by the standards of the Church in its official incarnation, as well as by modern standards:

> Priests and clerks may be seen wearing masks and monstrous visages at the hours of office. They dance in the choir dressed as women, panders or minstrels. They sing wanton songs. They eat black puddings at the horn of the altar while the celebrant is saying mass. They play at dice there. They cense with stinking smoke from the soles of old shoes. They run and leap through the Church, without a blush at their own shame. Finally they drive about the town and its theatres in shabby traps and carts; and rouse the laughter of their fellows and the bystanders in infamous performances, with indecent gestures and verses scurrilous and unchaste.
>
> (cited in Palmer, 1994: 46)[15]

The degree of parody in no way implies a lack of piety: integral to carnival is the capacity to both believe in something profoundly and to enjoy parodies of it, without the apparently subversive parody in any way disturbing the belief.[16] It is the capacity to believe in something and its opposite simultaneously, without this experience seeming incoherent. It is this dimension of experience that became suppressed eventually: the level of 'incoherence' must have come to appear intolerable.

By the same token, Bakhtin argues that laughter (and by extension parody) changed their meaning after the birth of the modern world. Carnival laughter, as we have seen, is trans-individual and is an expression of the carnival philosophy of life. In the modern world, on the other hand, laughter is individualised and becomes the mark of negativity:

> The Renaissance attitude towards laughter can be roughly described as follows: laughter has a deep philosophical meaning, it is one of the essential forms of truth concerning the world as a whole, concerning history and man; it is a peculiar point of view relative to the world; the world is seen anew, no less (and perhaps more) profoundly than when seen from the serious standpoint; ...
>
> The attitude toward laughter of the seventeenth century, and of the years that followed, can be characterised thus. Laughter is not a universal philosophical form. It can refer to only individual and individually typical phenomena of social life.
>
> (1984: 66–7)[17]

This argument suggests that for some unspecified reason 'modern man' came to abandon a particular, dual way of looking at and experiencing the world. We know that the carnival institutions were attacked and eventually suppressed – usually on the grounds that they were rowdy and disruptive. However, they had always had those characteristics – something led to a re-evaluation of them. What that might be has often been the subject of speculation and analysis – for example, the classic analysis which links the suppression of all these cultural forms to the imposition of work discipline (Thompson, 1967). For Bakhtin, however, it is the imposition of seriousness (monologism) that is the core of the process.

Carnival, ethics and comic licence

Fortunately it is not necessary for our purposes to fix on an explanation of such far-reaching changes. Nor is it necessary to ask whether there is something in common between the medieval carnival and similar-seeming practices observed elsewhere in the world: we certainly should not assume that there is some generic 'pre-modern' set of meanings to which observation of such rituals gives access. The changes and differences have been noted only for a reason central to our subject: assuming that these changes did indeed occur, that the differences really exist, regardless of the exact nature of the original meanings and the cause of the changes, the implication is that parody fundamentally changes its meaning with the birth of modernity, that parody therefore *cannot* mean the same thing now as it did in the medieval carnival. By the same token, it is not legitimate to argue that the carnivalesque has some generic capacity for disalienation: Bakhtin's thesis about disalienation is sociologically specific.

At this point we can return to the ethical questions with which we started: permission to parody, and the processes involved. The use of Bakhtin has given us an opening into the process: carnival is the classic example of a setting in which what the modern world experiences as parodic mockery is allowed without the mockery being subversive of the established order. It is not subversive of it because it incarnates a parallel order which coexists with it, and it was typical of the population in question that it lived both orders simultaneously without the contradictions between them being experienced as such; they appeared as different dimensions of the same thing. Parody in the modern world has a different status. It may be aggressive or merely playful, and it may destabilise textual meaning; in the latter case, it may be subversive in so far as it destabilises ideology; in this case, destabilisation is less likely – in the period since World War II – to produce shock and ethical condemnation, as was the case with parodies of canonical works such as Manet's *Olympia* (see note 6). However, in neither case can it be described as the incarnation of a second life of the people, precisely in so far as it does not refer to a second, parallel, valorised set of meanings. Indeed, on the occasions when parodic mockery moves in the direction of the real subversion of central symbols and rituals in the modern world, it risks being condemned as offensive and may be prosecuted: permission to mock may well be withdrawn, at least by some section of the population, as we saw in the examples with which this chapter opened.

We are now in a position to consider the question of decorum: the judgement about the appropriateness of expression to themes and settings. For example, it is difficult to imagine permission being given to erect a parody of a war memorial, especially in any location associated with veneration for the war dead. War memorials have a clear stylistic unity: whatever the formal variations (which are quite visible on an international scale), they are always solemn, and use forms which are locally considered appropriate for commemoration: a playful war memorial is a contradiction in terms. By the same token, it is difficult to imagine a set of circumstances in which it would be possible to publicly parody an act of commemoration such as the UK Remembrance Day parade. Although it is not difficult to imagine some members of our society who might want to, it is likely that they would judge it excessively dangerous, such is the public strength of feeling involved; and such would be the institutionally organised pressure brought to bear on the attempt.

The condemnation of the Sex Pistols 'God Save the Queen' is similar in its terms of reference: criticism of the British Royal Family is commonplace, and humorous mockery is common; however, the anthem is not just *their* property, it is the expression of nationhood and citizenship, perhaps of patriotism, and as such the form of expression involved is significant. To evoke it in a musical form which has utterly different aesthetic qualities, and therefore is a different form of expression, is already a breach of decorum; to do so in a song which is also critical adds to the breach – as does the timing of its release, to coincide with the Jubilee.[18] In short, what is 'playful allusion' in – for example – a novel or a photograph may well become anything but playful if it breaches decorum in respect of some deeply held public value by 'playfully alluding' to something associated with it.

These two examples, however, are not entirely homologous: in the case of the Sex Pistols, there was certainly antagonism to the song, yet it was a major commercial success, indicating that antagonism was far from universal. Because it was not prosecuted (and under what law could a prosecution have occurred?), the two antagonistic evaluations played themselves out in the domain of taste, mediated by the market and by institutional relayings of taste (see note 18). The hypothetical example of parodies of commemorations of war dead would be likely to evoke far stronger reactions, and might well be prosecuted, if only under a catch-all offence such as disturbing the peace. The difference lies in the degree of consensus about the undesirability of the parody, and therefore the degree of pressure brought to bear on it. In both cases, there is a power relationship involved, but because of the evaluative differences, the political process would be different in the two cases.

In carnival, it is clear that the rules of decorum did not apply, even in parodies which would otherwise have amounted to blasphemy. This is (according to Bakhtin) because such parodies were part of the second, parallel conception of the world incarnated by carnival taken as an integrated whole. In modernity, we no longer have this dual conception of the world (says Bakhtin). Instead, where parody is concerned, we have the licence given to the arts, which occupy a space defined as aesthetic and freed, at least partially, from the constraints of ethics. Parodies which are held to observe the distinction between the aesthetic and the ethical are not normally considered to be breaching decorum, which only occurs at points of sensitivity where the aesthetic form parodied is closely associated with another value, such as patriotic commemoration. At this point the rules of decorum come into play, because decorum is exactly the form taken by the overlap of the ethical and the aesthetic. The restrictions on modern parody mentioned above show that the freedom is limited, if wide, even if in the recent past aesthetic freedom has been extended beyond the arts considered as a canon of worthwhile creations to virtually any set of representations, as the near-legalisation of pornography suggests. None the less, the examples of blasphemy and the potential for parody of war memorials show that the limits are real, if not necessarily consensual. Once they are non-consensual, then clearly a power relationship is involved in the decision whether or not to pursue the parodier. However, the power relationship is likely to play itself out in different ways according to the ethical/aesthetic status of the artefacts and activities involved in the parody.

The extended permission to parody, in combination with some real restrictions, should be taken into consideration when we consider the thesis that parody destabilises meaning. Of course it is by definition true that any parody potentially destabilises the meaning of the parodied text, on the assumption that the reference is recognised and attended to by the reader. However, the thesis about the destabilisation of meaning is more ambitious than this, for it refers to a thesis about the origin of meaning and subjectivity in ideology: the destabilisation of meaning occurs in the act of interpellation, the act where meaning is transferred in ideology. It operates because the stability of meaning in texts is held to be a position occupied by a subject which finds closure in the act of occupying this subject position.[19] Therefore the destabilisation of meaning is not just a destabilisation of textual meaning, but a destabilisation of subjectivity in the same moment. When Jameson (1984) criticises post-modern art practice (and especially the use of pastiche) on the grounds that it has lost the critical edge typical of modernist art practice, he is arguing from a position that attributes to the arts the capacity to destabilise ideology. The use of Bakhtin's disalienation thesis as a support for a theory of the destabilisation of ideology arguably derives from the same position. However, the ontological analyses are not the same in the two cases, as we have seen, and Bakhtin should not be used for this purpose.

Moreover, the wide permission for aesthetic parody, in combination with real restriction on parody which breaches widely and deeply felt limits of decorum, suggests that any destabilisation of meaning is restricted to the aesthetic realm, or at least to purely individual response: it is for that reason that there is a visible limit around permissible parody, which excludes parody that really does threaten to destabilise publicly important meaning. Permissible parody is part of the generalised licence accorded to the arts in the post-Romantic world. Ironically, the carnivalesque parody which is often cited in commentaries on modern parody is also licensed precisely because it was not subversive, but part of a parallel way of thinking. The meanings which it incarnated, according to Bakhtin, appear to us to be fundamentally subversive because they are close to unthinkable in the modern world, but this is because we no longer inhabit the dual world he analyses.

Notes

1 These quotations are taken out of context, and in some cases are taken from essays that defend Rushdie. The point is only that the writers – whether sympathetic or opposed to Rushdie – see the book as parody.

2 See, e.g., galegroup (n.d.), for a commonplace definition; see also Brand (1998). Some writers insist that the element of polemic is integral to parody (Dentith, 2000: 19–20, 37), others that comedy is essential, as if it is lacking, 'parody' is simply imitation (Russell, 1987). We return to this issue below.

3 Which is assumed to be relatively homogeneous in this respect; the values in question are assumed to be universal or at least potentially so.

4 Genette's terminology gives a more restricted sense to 'intertextuality' than other critics', for whom all textuality includes (among other things) forms of intertextual reference. There is a convenient summary of Genette on parody in Dentith (2000).

5 See for example the Museum of Modern Art comment on the 1997 exhibition of this series: 'Although most of the characters are invented, we sense right away that we already know them. That twinge of instant recognition is what makes the series tick, and it arises from Cindy Sherman's uncanny poise. There is no wink at the viewer, no open irony, no camp. As Warhol said, "She's good enough to be a real actress."' (Galassi, 1996).

6 However, in the past it was. For example, Manet's *Olympia* contains clear references to Titian, and it uses these references in a way that scandalised Manet's contemporaries (Clark, 1980); to what extent the scandal derived from the parody and to what extent it was from the vision of the world that the painting gives is unclear. We return to this issue later.

7 This dual existence leads to a certain amount of terminological inconsistency in his work (Brandist, 2001). Terms normally associated with textual structure are used in analysis of cultural forms, and vice versa.

8 What follows is a summary of elements of two of Bakhtin's works: *The Dialogical Imagination* (1981) and *Rabelais and his World* (1984). I have been helped in my understanding of the relationship between the different elements of Bakhtin's thought by Brandist (2001).

9 For Bakhtin, the relationship between the two is important (Brandist, 2001). In the present context we may ignore it.

10 This passage is my translation from the French edition of Bakhtin's book on Rabelais (Bakhtin, 1970). The English translation omits most of this paragraph (along with other passages); see Bakhtin (1984: 10).

11 The phrase 'second life' is probably misleading, as it could be taken to imply that it is 'second to' the alternative, which in this context would be official culture. However, it is likely that the phrase refers to Aristotle's dictum about political association being a 'second nature', which is in no way inferior to the first nature. Mediaeval apologies for laughter (which was largely condemned in the Christian tradition) refer to it as man's second nature (quoted Bakhtin, 1970: 84–5; see also Palmer, 1994: 44, 57).

12 The French edition says that festivities had to be 'tolerated and partially legalised in the external and official forms of the feast', a formulation which has greater ambiguity than the English translation (Bakhtin, 1970: 18).

13 See Palmer, 1994: 44–50 for details and references to specialist literature on the subject.

14 Stallybrass and White resolve this issue by arguing that carnival had no essence, that it was used (permitted, forbidden, etc.) in different ways at different times by different authorities (1986: 17–19).

15 A personal anecdote to illustrate this point: a few years ago I gave this paper at a symposium on humour in a Catholic university in Europe. The university chaplain was in the audience. He was visibly shocked by this text, to the extent that he refused to accept its authenticity. It is part of a letter from the Faculty of Theology in Paris to the Bishops of France, dated 12 March, 1445.

16 Similarly 'extreme' (from the modern, Western point of view) parodies of ceremonies have been observed in other parts of the world; they are integral parts of the ceremonial; see Palmer, 1994: 13–14, 26–8.

17 In the French edition 'a peculiar point of view' is replaced by 'a particular [or "individual": JP] and a universal' point of view, and it adds, at the end of the passage quoted here, 'phenomena of a negative variety ...' (1970: 76). The point is repeated on p. 108.

18 The lyrics are available at http://www.sing365.com/music/lyric.nsf/GOD-SAVE-THE-QUEEN-lyrics-Sex-Pistols/49061AFE8EB8D78A4825691B000AA568, and in Savage, 1991: 348. The band's original preferred title was 'No Future', but they were persuaded to change it. See Savage (ibid: 314–20, 340–7) for details of the timing of the record's release. At its launch performance, on a boat outside the Houses of Parliament, the police intervened when the boat docked and arrested many of the participants; the myth has grown that the band themselves were arrested (PhatNav, n.d.), but according to the most authoritative account available, they were hustled away to avoid it (Savage, 1991: 362–4). It has also been alleged that the Hit Parade was manipulated to keep the song from being No.1 (Savage, 1991: 364–5).

19 This thesis has its origin in analysis of 'classic Hollywood' film-making done by a group of English film critics in various publications associated with the journal *Screen* in the 1970s (see Easthope, 1988: 51–67). It holds that this is true of texts which are broadly speaking 'realist', not all texts.

5

Breaking the Mould: Conversations with Omid Djalili and Shazia Mirza

Sharon Lockyer and Michael Pickering

Introduction

The British comedy circuit has traditionally been the preserve of white men telling jokes primarily about sex and alcohol. However, in recent years, thanks to comics such as Omid Djalili and Shazia Mirza, jokes not only about acts of terrorism, holy pilgrimages and Orientalist stereotypes, but also humour from an ethnic minority perspective, have been firmly placed on the comedy landscape. Both Omid and Shazia have been described as original and groundbreaking comics, helping to move British comedy forward in innovative and progressive ways.

We bring two interviews with these comics together in the light of what they do and do not share. While both are members of ethnic minorities born and brought up in Britain, Omid Djalili (aged 39) is an established actor and comedian. He is internationally known, with a shining career stretching back over 15 years. Shazia Mirza (aged 27) is an apprentice comedian who is still finding her feet and making a name. This contrast between them was very much in our minds when we paired the two interviews. We wanted to capture the experience of stand-up comedy from an ethnic minority viewpoint, but also compare the ways in which comedians with distinct profiles and reputations see the world of British comedy at quite specific stages in their careers. Significantly as well, Shazia is Muslim while Omid is Baha'i, a religious faith quite different to Islam. This is clear enough in the interviews themselves, though there is still a danger that both our interviewees become stereotyped as 'Middle-East' comedians dealing only with 'Middle-East' issues. That would diminish both of them. Even though they deal with these issues, their acts are about so much more.

Plate 1   Omid Djalili. Photograph by Piers Allardyce.

Omid Djalili has been appearing in comedy clubs for the last ten years. He has been one of the great successes at the Edinburgh Festival. His shows, many of them award winning, include *Short Fat Kebab Shop Owner's Son* (1995), *The Arab & The Jew* (1996), *Omid Djalili is Ethnic* (1997), *Omid Djalili/The Iranian Ceilidh* (1999), *Warm to My Winning Smile* (2000), and *Behind Enemy Lines* (2002). Omid has huge international appeal, and has performed his live shows across Europe, Australia, Canada and the United States. He has appeared on BBC TV's *Jack Dee Live at the Apollo,* and has starred in Channel 4's sitcom *Small Potatoes* and NBC's sitcom *Whoopi.* He has written and presented documentaries, such as Channel 4's *Bloody Foreigners,* which explored the plight of asylum seekers in Britain and was recipient of the One World Media Award 2001. A Perrier Award Nominee, Omid has also received a number of awards including the London Weekend Television Best Stand-Up Award 1996 and the *Time Out* Award for Best Stand-Up Comedian in 2001, and in 2002 the BBC's EMMA Award for Best Stand Up.

Alongside his stand-up performances and many TV appearances, Omid is a successful actor on the big screen. He has appeared in block-busters, such as *The Mummy, Gladiator, The World is Not Enough* and *Spy Game*. He has also appeared in films such as *Mean Machine, Anita & Me, The Calcium Kid* and *Sky Captain & The World Of Tomorrow*. Playing the role of Picasso in *Modigliani* with Andy Garcia, he presented his first lead role, following that with a principal role in Lasse Halstrom's *Casanova*.

Shazia Mirza, born in Birmingham of Pakistani parents, has been per-forming stand-up since September 2000. A former physics teacher, she now writes and performs stand-up full-time. As a practising Muslim, Shazia makes jokes about her experiences of living as a young Asian Muslim in Western culture and uses her comedy to challenge the pre-judices of non-Muslims and the particular conservative views held by Muslims on women and their position and role in society.

In her relatively short career as a stand-up comedian, Shazia has received a number of awards including the 2001 Hackney Empire Best New Act at The London Comedy Festival, the 2001 Young Achiever of the Year Award at the Government's Leadership and Diversity Awards, the 2002 Metro Magazine's People's Choice Best Comic Award (in asso-ciation with Jongleurs Comedy Clubs and The London Comedy Fest-ival) and the 2002 Asian Woman of the Year (Arts and Culture).

Surprisingly, her distinctive deadpan delivery and Brummie accent has successfully crossed national and international barriers. In addition to being a familiar face on the British Comedy circuit, Shazia has per-formed in France, Germany, Denmark, Belgium, Italy, Sweden, Switzer-land, Holland, Canada and the United States. In February 2005 she toured Pakistan – the first-ever comedian to do so. Shazia has written and performed her own monologue in Eve Ensler's *The Vagina Mono-logues* and has written and presented a variety of television programmes including BBC TV's *10 Things You Always Wanted to Know About Islam (But Were Afraid to Ask)* and *Have I Got News For You*. She has also been profiled on American, Danish, French, German and Swedish television networks.

Shazia and her comic material have courted controversy. She has been criticised by those both within and outside her faith. She has re-ceived vicious hate mail and death threats, and whilst performing, has been physically and verbally attacked by Muslim men who believe Muslim women should not appear on stage.

One particular event increased and intensified the attention both Omid and Shazia received from within and outside the comedy circuit.

Plate 2   Shazia Mirza. Photograph by Steve Ullathorne.

The events of 9/11 and their subsequent comedic reactions thrust these two stand-up comedians into the comedy spotlight. In his interview with us, Omid describes his initial apprehension about performing stand-up post 9/11. He explains how he dealt with and incorporated the tragic events into his show, *Behind Enemy Lines*, where he deliberates over the post-9/11 media coverage and other Western reactions. Equally, Shazia reflects on one of her memorable jokes, made after 9/11 and with that event in mind: 'My name is Shazia Mirza. At least, that's what it says on my pilot's licence.' Dealing with 9/11 in their comedy routines were seminal moments in both Omid's and Shazia's comedy careers.

We were delighted when Omid and Shazia agreed to talk to us about their ethical and aesthetic triumphs and tribulations as these have arisen through their efforts to break the comedy mould and push out the boundaries of contemporary stand-up comedy. Here's what they had to say ...

In conversation with Omid Djalili

15 December 2004

OD: Omid Djalili
SL: Sharon Lockyer
MP: Michael Pickering

MP: Can we start by asking what's distinctive about your routine?

OD: I was lucky because in 1995, a Jewish comedian called Ivor Dembina, who's very well known on the circuit, who'd been doing it for 12 years, took me under his wing and we did a show together called 'Arab and the Jew'. At the end of 1995, when Yitzhak Rabin got shot, we decided to do a double act. I saw the humour of this, sort of, Arab character and developed it into what I felt was a more rounded character, though in retrospect it was probably just a re-incarnation of a Johnny Ethnic kind of thing. But I remember thinking people were really laughing a lot, which is what you want but I wasn't 100 per cent sure. It was all just really playing on the stereotype, I don't think it's particularly sophisticated but it did get massive, massive laughs.

Around 1998, I started playing a more heightened version of myself by doing a bit of the Arab character at the beginning and then switching it and saying, 'I don't really talk like that' and I'd pretend to be this management consultant who was the 'just the wackiest' guy at the office kind of thing. And this is all well before *The Office*. I felt I was going towards political commentary but I could never take myself too seriously, so I would always undercut the political commentary with belly dancing and Godzilla impressions just to keep a kind of impish absurdity to what I was doing so people wouldn't say, 'oh he's one of those serious comics'. With the running jokes, the bits of physicality like the belly dancing, the bingo numbers, you keep the laughs all bubbling along with very high energy, I found the political points that I did make were made stronger because the audience really were in effect softened by being in such an entertained state. They would take the political points more.

MP: How did it work like that because some people might say that such tomfoolery would actually undermine the seriousness of the other part of the act, the political import of what you're saying? Why does it actually work to strengthen it?

OD: The whole point of the absurdity is to make me like you so that we will listen to anything you say. When I was on the *Jack Dee Show* on TV the edit was such that they went top-heavy on the tomfoolery. In my live act I take meticulous care for there to be a definite balance and I think whatever you do in comedy, it's all about the night and if you're doing a 45-minute set or an hour set, you piece it together so carefully, it's like a wave. It's a wave and it finishes with a crescendo. But they edited out the extra political dimension of the act so a lot of it was a whole bunch of silliness. I don't really have a problem with that. Not yet anyhow. I don't think it was direct censorship, but this was around the time of the Ken Bigley kidnap. It was a very sensitive time and the BBC was understandably nervous. Every day, they kept moving the broadcast date of my show back, 'can we take this joke out? That joke?' I don't particularly think I'm an offensive act at all. But they cut out the routines I thought would make the most cultural and political impact. I do believe it was a blessing in disguise. When you're talking about mainstream Britain, people can only take so much. I think it's enough that 4 million people tuned into a funny belly-dancing Iranian comedian, rather than a heavy political comic. They have to know you and trust you so much more for that. I would like to think they will get the more 'political' stuff later, when they know me better.

The problem here is the media because the people who are inciting religious hatred are the media. The irresponsible sections of the media that is, the tired lazy ones who have run out of an angle. For sensational stories, they go to nutcases. They don't go to a liberal Middle Eastern person in a suit from a university. They go to nutcases with a hook who will go berserk on camera, on cue. Anyone can mouth off but then if you put it all over the media, then that's inciting racism because everyone has racist thoughts sometimes. I'm saying that, in answer to your question, yes, I think there has to be a real balance, and when you're really being funny and you're hitting all the nerve centres that are at the very root of our humanity and what we're struggling with, it's brilliant comedy. 'Who am I? Why am I here? And where am I going?' It's no good just being a performing monkey. My wife watches me sometimes and she says 'enough with the Godzilla, it's so silly and you're far more serious than what people see when you're up there'. It really is an act. So it's just a question of how to find the right balance – and it's a crucial question.

MP: Do you try and create a balance between the ways you approach different national or ethnic categories?

OD: I think that's something I do very consciously. At the end of the day, I will only talk about something that really makes me laugh, really, really makes me laugh. So in one sense, that's a secondary consideration. You can make fun of religious people, because like everyone they have foibles and that's what makes them human, and humanity is at the centre of all good comedy. So you can make fun of the people, but I would never make fun of the central tenets or the central figures of a religion. I've made fun of fundamentalism with these routines about Al Qaeda and that mentality. But I would never poke fun at Jesus or Mohammed or any other central figure of a religion.

I suppose I'm guided here by my Baha'i background. The Baha'i faith is inclusive. It believes that all religions essentially come from the one God, a different chapter of the same book and that religion is progressive, they come in different parts of the world with the same spiritual message but a different social teaching. As a Baha'i, I believe in Christ, I believe in Mohammed, I believe in Moses. So I would never make fun of Islam, but I would definitely make fun of those aspects of Islamic people which other Muslims find strange, bewildering or abhorrent. I do it with Baha'is, but only to a Baha'i audience (people don't know enough about the Baha'i faith for it to work in the mainstream). I'm not a vicious kind of comedian but I would like to point out any aspects of cultures, be it home or foreign, that other people universally connect with. So if I make fun of Iranians, I would do so in my own personal way, but no, I just think that it's about what makes me laugh and I just don't think I'm the kind of person who is aggressive and nasty.

MP: Because everything has its funny aspects doesn't it?

OD: Yes, there are always these aspects, like for example, one of the first jokes I did ten years ago. My mother would go to Macdonalds, she said 'give me two Big Macs, two chips, two coke, how much?' – '£8.50 please' and my mother said, 'okay, I give you £1'. It was such a basic joke but it's playing on the fact that in the Middle East we haggle over everything. Very basic joke but then, as you get older and more sophisticated, you find other things that irk you but it all depends on your standpoint, if you come from a more positive humanitarian standpoint, I think audiences can feel that and they'll trust you. It really is all about an audience trusting you – you come out with a few jokes, bang, bang, bang, bang, which is who am I and what have I got to say? If you can get that across in your first minute, then people can trust you, like with the first joke I had about a comedy cultural exchange and I'm here and Jim Davidson's being buggered in Baghdad. It usually gets a very big laugh. It's not just the absurdity of Jim Davidson performing to a group of Arabs, it's Jim Davidson being buggered senseless in the Middle East which also means 'I don't like what he stands for (i.e., racism, bigotry) neither do you, I am funny, I will say what I like, so sit back, relax and enjoy the ride.' You've got to come out quickly and set your stall out. In a sense, the subliminal message here is that I am affirming the principle of unity and diversity, which is really what comedy should do. It really should be all-embracing and break down barriers.

MP: Is there any reason why you specifically have become popular? Do you think it's because you've got this sort of niche of British Iranian that no one else is filling or is it more than that?

OD: Firstly, I don't think I'm that popular, and that's not false modesty. I get my fair share of criticism. I like to think that people see something different and right now, still, unfortunately, being a British Iranian is very different for people, especially when you go to Wales and if you go to all these different places. I was joking about … I was saying I went to Wales and I spent the morning with the entire ethnic minority population of Wales, and I can tell you, he's a great bloke – I think that people like that, it's novel for them and then I think there's always a surprise element. I also believe, because there have been so few to precede me, it's kind of expected that you will be a bit crap, so there's obviously a very low expectation – I certainly felt that in the early days. Once I heard an 'Oh God no' from a lady in the audience at the very introduction of my name by an MC at a club (who even got my name wrong). I like to think, especially when I first started touring around and I wasn't selling out and I was getting a half-full audience, a 300-seater theatre and a 150 people show up because they're interested in comedy and think, who's this bloke? I toured a couple of times and I realise they want to see what I say about 9/11 because they've been very affected by 9/11 and they want to see what I've got to say, and when the expectation is low and then pow! it would be a great night. When I was at the Edinburgh Festival and Perrier nominated and had three shows you do as a nominee, the expectations were very high and I found that decidedly more difficult than with the previous 20 shows with an audience who came to just enjoy the night.

That was me growing as a comedian but I like to think there's something more as well. I like to think that the style of stand-up I do is energetic and I like to think that it's my personality too. I would like to think that because there is something in a Middle-Eastern personality where we're just slightly more aware of the showman in us, by doing accents for example and acting things out, so you're not just getting a dry voice. You're getting images, you're getting characters – you feel you can conjure up loads of scenarios. When you listen to someone like Lenny Bruce, I didn't really notice it until I thought, my God, he's actually acting out whole scenarios. He's almost doing a one-man play. Eddie Izzard does that as well, does lots of voices and things, and I like that. So I think that it's a combination of energy, the force of your personality and the fact that people trust you.

SL: Can we talk about the other part of your audience, the other negative reactions that you have had? Do you think you offend many members of your audience, and if so, what type of material did they take offence at?

OD: I hate to hurt anybody. I'm very keen not to offend. If anything I want them to like me, because most comedians have had some kind of lack of love in their lives, a lack of validity and a lack of someone telling them they're okay. I, more than most comedians, have this 'please love me' attitude. I even started joking about it, it was one of my running jokes, 'Do you like me? Please love me'. It was funny because it's a desperate, fat, sweaty man pleading for attention and it was a successful running joke. But I did get taken aside once by a couple of Pakistani Muslims, after a corporate gig in fact, who pointed out that a suicide bombing routine 'could have' caused offence. What they were offended by we talked about in a frank and open discussion and I agreed with them, and I stopped doing it because it wasn't a necessary part of the whole routine. They also were very respectful and I appreciated that and that was probably the main reason I even listened. I can't abide hysterical people. I just cut off and don't listen. I'm always open and I like to feel that I'm open enough for people to come up to me and tell me. Nobody is above criticism. My wife is very good at pointing those things out by saying 'I think that's offensive'. She also very much doesn't like blue humour and doesn't like any unnecessary swearing; she's a very good critic so I mainly listen to her.

You have to understand that I've become a standard-bearer for many groups, not just Iranians, for Baha'is, for Muslims too who see me as someone who's a defender of Islam – in a sense I'm representing all ethnic minorities (or at least those without a strong presence in the world of comedy). I even do a joke about that – even after 9/11, I say if I walk down the street and there would be such a sense of communal injustice and brotherhood that emerged amongst all dark ethnic minorities that even if I passed a Sikh bloke in the street I'd nod at him and say 'hey man', then you'd see an Indian guy walk past and you go, 'hey how's it going?' and he would acknowledge you back, and then you'd see a Chinese bloke who would acknowledge me and say 'hello', and I'd say menacingly 'you what? This has got nothing to do with YOU, what are you looking at? ... Go on, piss off.'

I think I have done stuff that's been disappointing or stuff that wasn't very good, like when the *Whoopi* show opened on NBC and this is huge. America is nearly 280 million people, first-time ever they had an Iranian character on prime time, NBC prime time, Tuesday nights just before Frasier, 8 o'clock and it's huge – we opened to massive ratings (16 million) so it was a super high-profile show. The pilot episode was very heavy on terrorist jokes and they said, look, it's just the pilot episode, and there was one joke I wasn't happy about when we did the pilot. It was my first time doing it and I was very keen to control the jokes I was doing – and there was a joke for my character with me saying, 'it's too bad we're in America and you don't have a secret service because in my country, we just put a bag over him and bash him and put two electrodes on his ...' I remember telling one of the writers I've a bit of problem with this line, because, well, in America, you do have a secret service and it's called the CIA, but I felt it would look like I was a very dumb Iranian who doesn't know. It was implying that I'm stupid and I had a problem with that. I didn't want my character to be the butt of a whole bunch of anti-Middle-Eastern jokes. He goes, 'no, the line is meant to be ironic'. I did it and it got a big laugh on the night but then I was shown the numerous Iranian-American websites saying to me directly, 'you moron, you idiot, they do have a secret service, it's called the CIA!!! Get it, CIA!!! What planet are you from?! Who are you, you're Bush's puppet!!!' and it was really a deluge of reaction. After that, I became very, very tough on the material I did and there were no more complaints and I put a real vice-grip on that and made sure I didn't do anything which my instincts were screaming at me not to do. So naturally after that initial experience I really went with my instincts. So I'm saying that offence is something that's organic and it develops. You're always going to offend; you're always going to do things that upset. But as you grow you realise it not just about being as funny as you can be – as an ethnic minority act, especially belonging to an obscure faith which purports to bring unity to the world, there is a responsibility to be something a bit more than just 'funny'. You have to be entertaining, educating and enlightening.

But causing offence and then dealing with it is all part of a tough process.

I had an experience of that doing sketches at school when I would pick certain people ... there were lots of sketches I did, there's a sketch I used to do about, 'we've made a monster that's so ugly that if you look at it you die'. Kids would then come up on stage and take a look at it from under a blanket and then fake a horrible death and then we'd choose the prettiest teacher, or a teacher that was popular, or a particularly loved or charismatic teacher who then had to come up on stage, look at it and the monster would go 'Aaargh!!!' and drop dead (the implication being because that teacher was so ugly). Doing this sketch over and over again, we invariably picked people who weren't that beautiful, or charismatic, or popular and they would go up on stage and the monster would die and they'd be really offended. So I learned a real tough lesson: know your audience. So from age 13–15 I realised that you can offend through comedy, but the more I grew up the less inclined I was to offend. It was a skill that just developed. But you never stop learning, believe me.

MP: How do you deal with heckling?

OD: I was terrified of it at the beginning because I remember thinking basically it undermines you as a performer. But when I started thinking about it, it's all part of this process of being present in the room together. You don't welcome it but you learn to be much more relaxed about it. I'm so different anyway and usually that stuns people. When I was doing Jongleurs comedy clubs which is usually hen nights, stag nights, pack 'em in nights, they're not really interested in what you have to say, you've got to be big, bold and brash, and usually they wouldn't heckle me because they'd be so stunned that there'd be this Iranian with this accent and they'd just laugh. But then I realised that, if they're so stunned if I'm so different, I have to deal with heckling in a very different way. So what I started doing – 'if you give me aggressive heckling, I'm just going to give you the love of Cliff Richard'. So I sang Cliff Richard songs and that became a big thing where people would heckle and then I'd just cover it by, 'We're all going on a summer holiday' and there'd be 'get off you fat git', I'd say 'Christmas time, mistletoe and wine'. If anybody said something, usually in those clubs they really were quite rowdy, it was a great way to keep things bubbling along and it would kill it really quickly, and it got to a point where people started expecting it. They'd heard about me, 'here's the Cliff Richard singing Arab act', so people came and would heckle and then it got to a point where people started defending me and people said, 'shut up, leave him alone' and someone else said, 'what are you going to do about it?' and they'd say, 'Carrie doesn't live here any more' so they'd start heckling each other in Cliff Richard songs and I remember thinking, this is great but they're so aware of it now I'm going to have to drop it. It was fun while it lasted.

So then I started a therapist viewpoint of doing it and someone would heckle something and I'd say, 'now what I'm hearing is aggression, but what I'm sensing is disconnection from your parents as a child'. The more loose you get, and the more you realise it doesn't actually matter and the more relaxed you are, the more relaxed the audience is. So now I just leave myself open and if people want to really engage with me, and if it is at the right moment, that is not in the middle of a routine, I'll talk with them.

MP: Has there ever been a heckle that's totally thrown you, you couldn't deal with?

OD: Yes and no. I got booed off once at Jongleurs and I don't know what happened and they were shouting, 'off, off, off' and they got very aggressive and I don't know what I did. But I've never had any racist heckling. A few people up North, yeah, 'get off ya Paki' and I've played around with it. I don't mind dealing with it, but I've had very little of it. I think it's because of the act I am, I come out very strong and when someone comes out really strong with a few big first jokes people are not inclined to heckle. I find people heckle if there's too much vulnerability. Vulnerability is a good thing, but it can leave your open to weakness. Then an audience will pounce. I think if you come out with material that says 'I'm here, I've got things to say, sit back people and listen', then by and large people do sit back and go 'fair enough – entertain me'.

MP: Can we return to stereotyping, which is obviously central to our concerns. It's characteristic of your act that you play with stereotypes in order to make people realise they *are* stereotypes, then you subvert the stereotype. Is that quite a conscious strategy?

OD: It's just the way it's happened because it's what makes me laugh. For example, I'd say, 'I'm so glad you're laughing because most people associate the Middle East with oil and phlegm and halitosis. I'm joking, we're running out of oil'. Having halitosis is so obviously not a specific feature of life in the Middle East, but for some reason it is to me. The tag line reinforces the fact that the halitosis bit is not even the joke. It means I hit on something that people on some level must have been thinking but would never dare say. I never analysed

it in any shape or form. I remember thinking, 'whether that's politically correct or not, that's funny'. I know so many people with bad
breath from the Middle East, myself included. My wife says you're
not out of this yourself, so I know it's about subverting those stereotypes. The whole point of subverting stereotypes is to create instead
some sense of the whole character, which begins with talking about
halitosis and then throwing in stuff that is unexpected, like 'I was
educated here. I spent two years here, I was sent to the Feltham
Young Offenders' Institute where I studied brutality and buggery ...
which got me a job at PC World Brentford.' Just throw in bizarre
comments so it becomes slightly surreal, and then it really becomes
PC or un-PC or whatever-PC. Iranians say that's an Arab accent and I
say, yeah, that's the whole point. It doesn't matter. It's trying to
create a world where PC just doesn't matter. The stereotype that is
not funny is the stuff like, 'hello, I am Arab and I'm a cab driver' or
'look at me, I have a kebab shop, yalla, walla!' I think that the whole
thing of subverting the stereotype is that you play with it and you
make it funny. And the playing with it is about connecting with
what people associate with the Middle East, so you connect with it
and them, and then you do a twist on the joke.

I'll give you two examples. One is the joke about 'you think we're
all so sexist in the Middle East and that's rubbish. People always
accuse me and even when I go shopping with my wife, people
always say, why does your wife walk 20 paces behind you? That's not
sexist, she's weighed down by the shopping.' You turn that around.
Another joke I did about Saddam Hussein, 'where is he now? He's in
jail somewhere ranting and raving and saying "I don't agree with the
war! And what kind of coalition is this?! Just Britain and America?
That's not a coalition. If that's a coalition, then famous singing duo
Renee and Renata, they are a coalition. Cockney knees-up Chas and
Dave, a coalition. However, Cannon and Ball remain a steaming pile
o' shit." ' So what you do is a bizarre comment that Saddam has
knowledge of populist British culture and indeed the British psyche,
in that he is also disarmingly accurate and able to make an ultimately winning comment. You play on the stereotype and what you
do is you try and dispel the stereotype, but then sometimes you
realise you've just confirmed it. That's when I've gone through and
analysed it afterwards, but I think that's the kind of structure to it,
playing with the stereotype and then undermining it.

MP: When that happens, do you think it breaks down barriers between
people?

OD: I think it does because it points out the stuff that is difficult. You are warming them to your culture by the simple fact that you're able to laugh at yourself. Stereotypes are only stereotypes, I feel, because they actually have a modicum of truth in them. It doesn't mean that everybody in the Middle East has halitosis, it doesn't mean that everybody's sexist, but women are more suppressed there and not as free as women in the West. It's an issue. And I think if you just play on that, the fact that we know it exists and we joke about it, people think okay, so they're aware of it too and they can joke about it and they can be ironic about it. Hey, they can laugh at themselves too! That's breaking the stereotype. I think that's where it works, that's how playing with the stereotype will actually alleviate it. That's what I believe, I don't know what you believe but that's the way I see it.

SL: Shall we move on to the material that you developed after 9/11? How did you feel about your act and comedy after the terrorist attacks?

OD: I felt I couldn't do comedy any more. I didn't leave the house for a couple of days, I was so nervous. Because I took my kids to school the next day and everybody was looking at me in a really weird way, as if I was personally responsible. So I thought, I'm staying at home, I'm just going to go home and not show my face for a couple of days. And then it became interesting. You must have read that I had a couple of shows on two weeks after 9/11 at the Bloomsbury Theatre, and I thought oh my God, and we'd already sent posters out with quotes from the reviews, Edinburgh reviews, like 'Burly but surprisingly athletic', but the last one was 'Middle-Eastern madman' and I said, 'that's it, recall the posters, forget it, just cancel the show'. But then my manager said, actually you can't cancel because of this, it will be the death of you. In fact, I had a corporate gig booked on the 13th and they withdrew me from that and all the work I'd had that week.

MP: Who withdrew you – the management?

OD: No, the actual corporate people said we don't want him any more; we're going to get Julian Clary or someone else. So I'm thinking this is it, this is going to be the death of me; it's the end of my career. There were certain jokes I was doing – not about suicide bombing, but I did a joke which ended with a bunch of Iranian football fans flying to Dublin and the Iranian fans were singing on the plane to Dublin, 'we are the Ayatollah's army, we're going to stuff the Irish twats, and we're really shake them up when we blow ourselves up' (with the punch-line) 'and that was the last message on the black box flight recorder' – and I remember thinking oh God, that's appalling. I have been doing appalling material, I am an appalling person, so I can't do comedy any more. Then I remember thinking, no, if I can just write some material about this, just write some jokes and deal with it, it could be the bravest thing I could do, and the shows were all packed anyway – they were all sold out. It was very interesting, perturbing and exciting all at once because there was a whole bunch of people that had rushed to give their tickets back on the night, there was talk in London of the Bloomsbury being a terrorist target, but at the same time there was a whole queue of 200 people waiting for returns. So about 100 people gave their tickets back in a frenzy and there was another 100 people who got those tickets, almost in an equal frenzy. I did nothing for two/three days and my wife said, come on, you've got to do these shows, so we sat down and we wrote some material. I realised I was actually very inspired by this and the first joke was, 'I'm here to make a stand because after 9/11 ethnic minorities are being attacked and in some cases even killed, and by continuing with the show, I'm going to make a stand about who I am.' There was a warm round of applause and I said, 'I'd like you to know that my real name is Sven, I'm from Gothenburg.' I did some other jokes, and in fact, the first ten minutes was just about 9/11, because it was what people wanted, needed in fact. So career saved, it was now down to the next business.

That is where my manager said 'you've gone up a level, and I think you should write a whole new show dedicated to 9/11. The chances are there'll be loads of other people doing this, but you're the first one so you're already ahead.' But by the time of the Edinburgh Festival I saw that actually nobody was doing a show like it. I think there was one show, a drag act called Tina C that had nothing to do with 9/11, but the poster was her two legs, these two stockinged legs and a plane going into the crotch area. I remember thinking that was a very risky marketing angle as the expectation was that he had some top-notch material on the terrorist attacks in New York. He, as a drag act, got a lot of flak because he was promoting himself as a 9/11 act, when in fact he barely touched upon the subject. People then came to my show as I really had dealt with the whole post-Taliban thing. It wasn't just 9/11, there was lots of stuff about the war in Afghanistan at the time and it dealt with all that, and it's been developed in the last couple of years and I don't do it any more. I've knocked it on the head now but at the time, when I think about it, it was brave. It was 11 months after 9/11 and I could see that audiences were packed and wanted to hear about it, and I could hear them bubbling and talking, saying 'I can't believe he's doing this', and I remember thinking deep down 'but why? I can't believe I'm the only act ...' and we looked on the Internet. Nobody. I was the only person in the whole world doing a proper one-hour show all about 9/11.

To his credit, Adam Hills did a show where he talked a little bit about some personal experiences post-9/11 and having problems, and even then I remember thinking he was still being very open talking about his experiences, but still he wasn't actually dealing with any of the political issues surrounding the subject, and indeed, why should he? Colin Murphy from Northern Ireland did some great routines too but no more than 5 minutes or 10 minutes. I'd just been to Montreal, the Montreal Comedy Festival is about three weeks before the Edinburgh Festival, and I saw the effect that I could have very clearly. They have these big gala nights, 2500 people, it's televised, eight acts come on and the last act is someone who, it's like his twentieth year in comedy, he's been to the Festival five times. They do a special, instead of doing seven minutes, he does 20 minutes and he's the star act of the night, and on my gala night it was an American comedian who's very well known in the United States. He is a big number-one star, a stand-up star, and the night before we did a warm-up gig at a place called Club Soda, and he went on before me and did this whole routine about, 'anyone been on a plane recently? I've got to tell you, any Middle-Eastern people here?' and someone put their hand up, and he'd take a picture and he said 'I've got the picture wiseguy.' He said 'listen you guys, can I ask one favour, when you get on a plane, could you take the turbans off because I don't want to sit there with my turban catalogue.' He went on 'I'm a Catholic, I don't walk down the aisle with a burning cross on my back so, take the turbans off.' He was getting big laughs because people were so excited about his 9/11 material. People said, 'wow, he's really dealing with the issue that we're really scared of Arabs and if you see an Arab on a plane, yeah, get them off.' I came on straight after him, very nervous but with high levels of energy that seemed to win the crowd over, and he didn't stay around to watch me. He left and then, at the gala night, he didn't know that I was on just before him and he didn't know who I was. I kept saying, 'hey, how you doing?' I said, 'I'm Omid, I'm on before you' and he must have assumed I was a fan.

I went on before him at the gala, and did enough to get a very warm reaction. He went on to do his routines and I watched it on the monitor and when he said, 'could you Arab guys take off the turban' – the audience were having none of it. I saw him thinking to himself, the panic in his eyes 'what's going on? I killed with this stuff last night.' And that's the power of comedy. That is the power because I got on first and won them over and he went on second and his stuff bombed (not all his set but significantly just this part of his set) simply because the people had experienced a shift in their minds. It made me think audiences can go either way. Simply with a force of personality, with technical ability, you can take an audience down a racist track, you could take someone down a route which is not particularly humanitarian but if you're good, and you're technically good, you can get laughs and you can go that way and the people will go with you. Fact is that night I got lucky. Due to the power of going on first, before this act on a big night with 2500 people, I was able to sway them, so that when they heard something unacceptable, they didn't accept it. They could have accepted it, if he went on before me. So in a nutshell, after Montreal and the Edinburgh festival, I inadvertently became a political commentator, but I still wanted to keep it entertaining, hence the absurdity, but I think I really grew up as a stand-up.

MP: Can you enlarge on the distinction you've made between inside and outside comedy? Obviously, in moving more to the inside, you're not abandoning the field of social, political comedy. How do they fit together?

OD: I'm far more interested, right now, in comedy set up more in terms of what I'm thinking about, something internally directed towards outside events. Whereas before it would be, here's an outside event, 9/11, and this, this and this happened, and I reacted like this and then these people thought this about me, and I thought that about them, and it was all very external. But internal stuff is more about your angst, about very detailed things that happened. 9/11 happened and I dealt with it but my main thing now, what I really want to do, is be less the kind of ethnic comedian banging on about 9/11 and ethnic issues, and be more a comedian who is totally accepted in the mainstream. He's just Omid Djalili, the comedian. Strange name, where's he from? Who cares! So if anyone says how do you feel being the only Iranian stand-up, it's not about that, I just want to be a comedian. Ethnic comedian is too much of a hook to hang yourself on and I realise I've outgrown that.

MP: You don't want to get kind of labelled and then be only that and nothing else.

OD: Yeah, because you're making a bigger point. A truly multicultural society will accept you just as a comedian and not as an ethnic comedian. But what we're talking about is the process of becoming that and I think 9/11 certainly helped speed that process up.

SL: If you hadn't commented on it, people would have raised questions about what your performance is all about, what your aim is through your comedy.

MP: Are there any topics that you would not make jokes about?

OD: I think it would be human suffering.

MP: You did say that earlier that you wouldn't make hostile jokes about Islam.

OD: Yes, I wouldn't do that, there's no point. Like I said, I wouldn't make jokes about Jesus Christ or Mohammed, Budda, Krishna or the central figures of my own faith. Billy Connolly has a fantastic routine about ... have you heard his Last Supper routine? It's brilliantly funny, where he plays out the last supper not in Galilee, but in Galashiels, the disciples are all a bunch of Scots drunks in a pub and they call Jesus the Big'n, 'you've got tee chip in mon, you've got to pay for this meal'. People thought it was very offensive at the time but I don't see that as making fun of Christ at all. Here's offensive in my mind. After 9/11, I heard a joke when someone's mobile phone went off in the audience and the comedian, I can't remember who it was, just said, 'oh no, that's not the 110th floor again'. I thought it was in very poor taste. We were discussing it on Radio Four and some comics were defending it saying 'that's a very good joke because it deals with people's fears'. I said, 'but people jumped out of windows and the comic was making fun, or making light of that'. If someone can find humour in that, I find it extraordinary. We all have a dark side, everyone has. I laughed out loud when I heard the joke that Elton John was rewriting Candle in the Wind for Mother Teresa, after she died – he's renaming it 'Sandals in the Bin'. Many people said, how can you laugh at that? It's just so silly – but the 110th floor – what is that? How people can think that's funny, I don't understand.

In conversation with Shazia Mirza

Friday 21 May 2004

SM : Shazia Mirza
SL : Sharon Lockyer
MP: Michael Pickering

SL: Your routine has been described as 'breaking new ground' by a number of people.

SM: Right, by who, *The Guardian*?

SL: Mark Thomas, *The New Statesman*. I wondered if you could just tell us a bit about your routine, if you could describe it.

SM: I'm sleeping my way to the top. No, well, my, routine, it's changed now.

SL: Has it?

SM: Yeah. I write every day you see and I am writing my new show at the moment. In my new show I don't talk about being Muslim or Asian at all, I talk a bit about being Asian, but I don't talk about being Muslim at all and I don't talk about my religion. I talk about my travels, I mean I've been to about 30 countries this year, doing stand-up and I talk about my travels and my experiences of being in those countries and it's also about temptation, how I'm tempted to do things, like I don't smoke and I don't drink and don't take drugs and I don't gamble and then I go to all these places, in all these different countries all over the world and every time I go somewhere I'm always tempted to do something. In this job and travelling on your own you do get tempted to do certain things and because I'm on my own I think I can do something like I'm in America or somewhere. I mean I was in Kosovo and I thought I can do something here and nobody would ever know and I'm always tempted, whereas I suppose people who are not of my religion or my culture maybe don't feel that temptation. I'm sure that people are tempted by different things. And like I went to Canada recently and they put me up in a casino and I kept going down to the floor every night to watch people gamble, because I found that fascinating. I've never been in a casino in my life and everyone would be gambling and it was full of old people with pots of change just gambling every night, every morning, every night, and I'd go there and I'd spend hours in the casino watching people gamble their lives, gamble everything away and I was tempted to do it, but I could see that it was an addiction for some people and I was so scared that if I did something once then I'd be an addict. But then I'd also go to my hotel room and there's like a fridge full of alcohol, or I'd go out for a drink with all the other comedians or the organisers and there's loads of free champagne and everything is free and I think, you know, I'm tempted to do these things and so my show really is about temptation and about my travels and about lots of other different things, but I never actually mention in the show that I'm Muslim. I never ever mention anything about my religion or my culture because I think that, sometimes, like I went to see an Irish comedian the other right, he's Irish, but he never once mentioned that he's Irish, but you knew from what he was saying that he didn't need to mention it. So I don't, and I feel enough people know me, and they know who I am, so if I say I don't drink they know why and I feel I don't need to mention that I'm Muslim, and actually it makes it more accessible if I just mention my vulnerabilities, that I'm tempted to smoke, I'm tempted to drink, I'm tempted to take drugs and gamble and shoplift and all these things. Actually I think that comedy is more about your experience and you don't need to tell people certain facts about yourself, you need to show them, so I'd rather share my experience than tell them a list of facts about being a Muslim, and what I should and shouldn't do and actually that I'm really human and that in my travels you know I am a human being and that everybody's fallible. It annoys me that people think that because I'm Muslim I must have morals, but it's not necessarily true that I'm not tempted and that because I'm Muslin I must be wonderful.

MP: You've said somewhere you only talk about your personal experience.

SM: I don't only, but I think every comic, the comedy comes from something they've seen or experienced, or they know about and I think that you have to, whatever you talk about you have to make it personal to yourself and that's what makes it funny and interesting really, it's to hear your point of view on it. Like if I went on stage and started doing stuff about being Irish and getting drunk I don't think people would believe me and also anybody can do that material, what makes it funny is that it has to be personal to you.

MP: Do you still wear the hijab when performing?

SM: No. When I first started I didn't, then I used to wear it, and now I don't and I don't think I will ever again.

SL: Why is that?

MP: Is that a conscious break from the past?

SM: Because I don't want to be seen as a Muslim comedian, I don't want to be seen as one-dimensional and that's all I can talk about and that's all that my life is about, because it's not at all. Also it's not very versatile and people are very narrow-minded and they see you dressed like that and they think oh, well she can't do this and she can't do that and they think of you in just one way. When I think about it, it is a one-dimensional image, but I'm not a one-dimensional person.

MP: Are there other things which are an inspiration to the material that you are doing now that is different to the past?

SM: I'd say I was more honest now. I think when you first start off in comedy you want to make people laugh and when you realise that you can do that, then you want to do something more challenging, like you want to tell more interesting stories. When you first go on stage you're desperate to get a laugh, now I'm not so bothered about that because I know I can get them. So I just go on and I just want to tell stories and be a bit more personal and a bit more interesting and you know in an hour's show there are so many different things, you can't just do gag gag gag. It's a show, you're taking them on a journey, you want to talk to them about it.

SL: So what type of people make up your audiences?

SM: Anybody and everybody really. I don't have a particular audience. I do have a big gay following actually, I do a lot of gay gigs, and gay people always come to watch me and then lesbians are very supportive to me – I wonder why ... I do loads of lesbian gigs. Even when I'm doing an ordinary show lesbians will come along.

MP: Have you become a gay icon?

SM: I don't know, I don't know why that is. I did a lesbian gig, I did three lesbian gigs last week, I went to Sweden recently and I did a gig for 15 female engineering students and when I turned up they were all lesbians and they said, oh well the reason why we invited you was because we thought you were. And I think that sometimes people make associations, that if you're a strong woman you must be a lesbian, if you're doing something brave you must be a lesbian. I don't think gay men think that I am, I think gay men just love it, they just think it's great. Women are supportive of me, well lesbian women are. But I would say I do straight gigs a lot.

SL: Are there age differences in your audience?

SM: No, last night they were really young and then I do, like I have loads of old guys come to watch me, middle-aged men come to watch me. Do you know I find that quite strange really. I look at them and I think, I don't think you'd normally go to comedy. I have a lot of middle-aged men, white men that come to watch. But I like doing young crowds. I don't know, but it really is mixed.

MP: Are there any particular kinds of response you are trying to generate according to who the audience is?

SM: No.

MP: If it is mainly lesbian are you trying to get a particular kind of response?

SM: No, I mean I do the same material, but in a lesbian crowd, last week I did some new material on how people think that I'm a lesbian and they liked that. I do that in a straight crowd and in a straight crowd they're a bit shocked and in a lesbian crowd they get very excited. I still do the same material though.

SL: But do you get different reactions from different audiences?

SM: Yeah. No actually, I did one last night in Primrose Hill which is very white middle-class Jewish, very rich and I was doing my lesbian material there and they were loving it and it was couples in there. So no, I don't think it is a different response, no.

MP: Do you ever have a kind of definite purpose behind the material, like to reduce the level of prejudice that may be there?

SM: No.

MP: Just mainly to make people laugh, that's your primary instinct?

SM: Yeah.

MP: Would you define yourself as a political comedian?

SM: No, I don't do any politics. Not like in Margaret Thatcher, Tony Blair politics. No I don't do that. I don't talk about the war, I don't do any of that, basically because I'm not interested in politics and I think that it is very boring and I don't think even established comedians are ever going to change the world.

MP: You very courageously made jokes about 9/11.

SM: So did a lot of white comedians.

MP: I mean that's political isn't it? The whole affair is political.

SM: But it doesn't make me a political comedian.

MP: Have you made any jokes about the Iraq war?

SM: No. I don't want to, I don't want people to think that that's all I make jokes about. I want to make jokes about anything.

SL: After 9/11 you made a joke about your name being on your pilot's licence. What sort of reaction did you get to that sort of joke?

SM: People all over the world loved it. They laughed, it was funny.

SL: Why do you think it was such a powerful, such a popular joke, if you like?

SM: Because it was funny, people really laughed, and it was brave and nobody had done anything like that and also maybe because I said it rather than another comedian saying it, it wouldn't have had the same impact obviously. And there was only a few people who could have done that.

MP: How would you differentiate your humour and comedy from other Asian comedy that has become very popular in recent years, such as *Goodness Gracious Me*?

SM: I think that was all sketches, I mean it's very general. I say that my comedy is quite personal and it's about my experience and it's about Shazia Mirza really and that I'm an individual person and I think that if you went and saw other Asian comedy, I mean there aren't that many Asian comics that do stand-up, but I'm sure that if you

did go and see one, there may be some common threads about being
Asian, but if it was good comedy it would be personal to them, that like
only they could have done that material because only they wrote it
from their point of view and I think that's what really characterises a
good comic, their material and their persona. So, like a particular comic
doing material that was specific to them, I could only imagine them
saying that material. I think that what makes somebody an individual
comic is that you want to go and hear what they have to say.

MP: Do you think that's particularly because it is stand-up, because it's
not something like sitcoms which tends to lend itself to stereotypes
more?

SM: Yeah, but I think like that even in sitcoms it still has to be a part
of what you think, or what you know or what you experienced to
write a sitcom, otherwise you would never have anything to write
about. I wouldn't write something which I don't know about.

SL: But how do you, if you're talking about your personal experience how
do you think your audiences relate to that, what do they make of it?

SM: It's personal, but it's also general. So, I could talk about not drinking,
but I can imagine what it must be like to drink. I mean everybody,
most people will have an experience of what it is like to drink, or would
have seen other people drunk. So, although I will like relate it back to
me in the end, I sometimes generally say I wonder what it would be
like to piss up a door in Leicester Square and everybody has sort of
watched that, or done that, or can imagine what that was like. I then
give my opinion on that, on why I wouldn't do it, or why I would do it
as it looks like so much fun, I wish I did drink and then I could do
things like that you know. So some comedians go on and will talk
about why they drink too much and or the different types of alcohol
and what they do to you and I can talk about how absurd that is to me,
why have different types of alcohol when at the end of the day all you
do is piss up a doorway in Leicester Square? They're all having the same
effect. Why have the different varieties, what's the point of that?

MP: You've become famous in quite a short period of time. Has that
been difficult?

SM: Anyone can be famous these days. I don't like to think of myself
as famous. I don't think about that, I don't think it's important.
I just like to do my work and it's really important to me that I write
new material all the time and become a better performer, because
without that, I'm nothing really. You see the people that do come
and see me, they don't want to hear me doing the same material
because they've heard it and when they come and see me again they

want to know what else I have to say and I think the more times you go and see a comic you feel maybe you know them a bit better. And that's what makes them interesting and it is always exciting for me to go and see a particular comic. I want to know what he's going to talk about that's going to be new. You don't want to go and see the same comic after like two or three years to see that they're still saying what they were saying three or four years ago. And so, whether they're famous or not, it's neither here nor there really.

MP: But you've become very popular in a short period of time, why do you think that is?

SM: I don't know about popular. I suppose I'll be popular when I'm selling out the Royal Albert Hall every night, then I'll think that oh maybe I'm popular, maybe people like me. But I don't think that popularity is as it stands now, I think that grows over many years and I don't want anybody and everybody to come and watch me, I mean I want certain people to come and watch me. You know I do like it that old people come and young people come and middle-aged people come, I like that, different variety, I like that and I'd always want to keep that and that happens over many years.

SL: I don't know whether this will apply to your more recent material, but with your earlier material, do you think any parts of your audience find what you do or what you say offensive?

SM: Maybe, but then I think, they have a problem, not me. I never set out to offend, I never make jokes about black people or disabled people or anything like that just for the sake of it, but my material is personal to me and often it's based on the truth so if they find it uncomfortable then often it's they who have the problem, not me, because I never make jokes about different groups of people.

MP: So have you ever come up with material and then thought, no I can't use this, it will be too offensive?

SM: No, sometimes I might change words around.

SL: Are you ever surprised by what people find offensive if they do find offence in your material, are you quite surprised?

SM: Yeah, and often I'm right, often they do have a problem themselves, and their problem is more to do with me than it is to do with my material, it's that they don't like me as a woman getting on stage being a comedian, regardless of what I say. Sometimes there are Muslim men who say, I don't think it's appropriate you doing comedy, to get on stage and do what you're doing, we don't find that appropriate. Muslim women aren't meant to do that. And I say that if they've been offended in the past, well they haven't seen anything yet. I'd expect them to be *more* offended now because I'm talking about much more controversial things or what Muslim men might think are more controversial.

SL: Also, I've read, or heard on some of the recordings on your web-site, that you have actually been attacked by Asian men in the earlier days because they didn't like the fact that you were standing up there talking, making jokes, and didn't see that as appropriate. Could you tell us about that?

SM: Yeah, they don't think it's appropriate, some of them think I shouldn't get on stage and also I think at the time they didn't like me talking about being Muslim either, making jokes about it. But it wasn't really my religion I made jokes about, it was more my culture. But I think it was more me really. A lot of times I used to get emails from people who criticise me but they'd never seen my show. I thought that indicated to me they didn't like me doing what I was doing, and it had nothing to do with what I was saying because they had never seen my show. They criticised the fact that I was doing what I was doing. I do think it that was more to do with that.

SL: How have your family and friends reacted to you performing stand-up?

SM: They just want me to get a proper job, and get married really.

SL: They still want that?

SM: Yeah. That's all they talk about. I don't think anybody takes com-edians seriously. They don't think of it as a proper job. They always go, do you make a living from that? I think they think it's a weird thing to do, but then you've got to be a bit strange to do it.

SL: Do you?

SM: There has to be summat not right, I don't know what.

SL: So the next question would be a natural follow-up, what's not right with you then if you're doing stand-up?

SM: I dunno, I'm still trying to find that out. I dunno. I was reading about another comedian the other day and the person who interviewed them said 'oh, you must have had a lot of demons to do stand-up', and the comedian said, 'well actually when I look back on it maybe I did'. But the comedian didn't know why 'til about ten years later.

SL: Right, so you might find out later.

SM: But I do love it. I love what I do so.

MP: Can we ask you a bit about stereotypes? Are there any stereotypes that you consciously avoid? I mean you mentioned a few already, such as those associated with black people or the disabled, are you conscious of those when you write your material?

SM: I avoid making stereotypes of Asian people, being Asian, and I never really talk about being a woman. A load of comedians go on and on about the differences between men and women. I've never done that in my life and I don't think I ever would.

MP: Well, the follow-up question to that is, are there any *topics* that you would deliberately avoid?

SM: I suppose I'm avoiding political material. I'm avoiding talking about things that I don't know about. Also things that other comedians do all the time, like differences between men and women. It's been done so much. I mean I can talk about things that everybody talks about, like smoking and drinking and getting drunk and it will also be from my point of view, which is the opposite, so I can do that, but not relationships, no.

SL: So do you think you're unique in that sense, that you provide a different perspective?

SM: I think certain comedians are unique in that they only talk about those things that people think are taboo. You know when all these men would go on and say they hated women, or complain about women, and certain female comedians would go on and complain about men and do the opposite and as a result people call them aggressive and lesbian because they break taboos.

SL: So the fact that you're talking about lesbianism and going into gay clubs, do you think that you're talking about taboo topics and mostly men have had problems with that?

SM: I think that anything a Muslim woman talks about is taboo, because you would never really hear her talk about anything. Especially in a comedy club. And I don't think, you know, if you go into a comedy club people have never really heard a Muslim woman's point of view on anything including on lesbianism. So it's all just a new thing, a new point of view.

SL: So what are you trying to do with that new point of view? Are you trying to challenge stereotypes?

SM: There's no denying white laddie blokes on the circuit and I suppose I'm putting a unique perspective being an Asian Muslim woman and I suppose I'm really trying to use that perspective to the best of my ability. There's a load of Irish comedians, but it must be hard for them because there's so many great Irish comedians that you think they all have to compete against each other to get their unique point of view across because they're all Irish. There will be some similarity of overlap because they're all Irish, but what makes them unique is that they talk, they make it all personal to themselves and I suppose I'm trying to sharpen my tools and use my point of view as best as I can and that will take many years. Now I can go on and not talk about being Muslim, but whatever I do talk about will be from my point of view and I'm trying to use that unique perspective really.

MP: When you're heckled, do you think that's because of who you are rather than your material?

SM: No I don't think it's either. Last night I was doing a gig and I was heckled by these white Irish guys. There had been loads and loads of men on and I was headlining and there'd been no Asian acts or anything, they'd all been white men. These white laddie blokes, Irish guys you know from Belfast, were drunk and were heckling me and whistling at me when I came on. They must have thought I would not be capable of dealing with them and then after, when I'd ripped them up and everything, they came up to me and they went, 'oh we feel really bad now, we feel really bad'. I said, 'Why? Because you thought I was a woman and I wouldn't be able to deal with you?' And they said 'we feel really bad, we shouldn't have done it'. All the audience were cheering and laughing because I'd really just torn the pair of them apart, and then they sat for the rest of the show with their heads down and I think they must have thought 'oh skinny little Asian woman coming on, she won't be able to deal with us because we're from Belfast and we're really really tough'. And maybe that is a perception that they have when I come on and I suppose that if I came on and was really girlie and really sweet and nice that would reinforce the stereotype that they have of the Asian woman, and they don't expect me to be the way that I am on stage. But that doesn't happen that much really. It happens sometimes. And I think it's more to do with being a woman than it is to do with being Asian, because a lot of people don't know that I'm Muslim and sometimes people don't think I'm Asian and so when I come on, it's more to do with being a woman, because a lot of times I'm the only woman on the bill.

MP: Did you have to learn how to deal with heckling?

SM: I think that people think that heckling is just such a minor thing, it's like eventually you won't have to deal with it because you have your own show in a big theatre and everybody's come to watch you. If you spend your whole 20 minutes dealing with a heckler I don't think that makes you a great comedian. I know that I can deal with them, but I don't want to hone the craft of dealing with hecklers. It's not as important as my material.

SL: So how did you deal with the two guys yesterday, you said you ripped them apart?

SM: Well I had material on Belfast you see and they didn't know that. So I said, where one of them was Irish and he started heckling me, he said something at the beginning, and I said oh where are you from in Ireland, whereabouts in Ireland are you from and he went Belfast, oh I said right Belfast, yeah right and I had loads of material about not being able to understand a bloody word he was saying to me and I had material about going to Belfast where I couldn't get a word in and couldn't understand a thing they were saying and I did a whole load of material on that. And he was really embarrassed.

[We would like to thank Tim O'Sullivan and the School of Media and Cultural Production at De Montfort University for financial help with the transcription of these interviews.]

6
Merry Hell: Humour Competence and Social Incompetence

Ken Willis

'The question is,' said Alice, 'whether you *can* make words mean different things.'
'The question is,' said Humpty Dumpty 'which is to be master – that's all.'

(Lewis Carroll, *Through The Looking-Glass*, 1992)

Most of us like to think we have a good sense of humour, so much so, in fact, that in personal advertisements it is the most common characteristic people use to advertise themselves and request others to have. Attempts to understand such a central aspect of our self-identity date from at least Plato[1] (*c.*350 BCE) and more recently humour has increasingly become the subject of academic research.[2] This has given rise to attempts to model humour along various lines, a development which has met with varying success. Here I would like to examine some of the more interesting models and make a contribution to the ongoing discussion. Let me make my own perspectives clear from the outset. Too often commentators and researchers feel that because having a sense of humour would seem to be a cultural universal, they are therefore obliged to make universal claims about their ideas and findings. While there may well be certain common denominators involved in the production and reception of humour (e.g., it does always seem to include an element of incongruity), I am wary of theories and models with sweeping claims of universality. As humour is such a fleeting and complex phenomenon, which can involve a combination of cognitive, affective, cultural, social, political and personal elements, much can be overlooked if it is depicted with brushstrokes too broad, and so I prefer an approach that tries to account for these factors closer to home, as a communicative interaction on a local level, and this is how this chapter will proceed. After a review of various models of

126

humour, I hope to make a variety of salient points concerning the following: differential humour competence and the place of power in differing interpretations; the interactive roles involved in humour; the tensions between public and private domains; and also to sketch in an outline of the nature of humour networks. I will then illustrate these ideas with two examples of humour made in public. Note that the notion of humour used here refers to verbal humour only and is inclusive, that is, it includes any verbal communications (from a one-liner to an extended piece of narrative) that intentionally (or unintentionally) provide amusement, though the actual examples used here are short. Also, given the aim of this collection, most of the focus will be on humour of a contentious nature. One further qualification, which may seem strange but is necessary, is that the discussion is of humour engaged in by adults with undamaged brains.[3]

Some models of humour

The concept of 'humour competence' was introduced in Raskin's (1985) Semantic Script Theory of Humour (SSTH), which claims to be able to assign the feature of funniness to texts. The SSTH draws on Chomsky's notion of 'linguistic competence' and its 'ideal speaker-hearer community' (1965) and consequently this idealised model of humour (and subsequent developments of it) is designed for a speaker-hearer community in which members' senses of humour are identical (Raskin, 1985: 58), for people who have no racial or gender biases and are not concerned by scatological, obscene or disgusting content (Attardo, 1994: 197), and where audience responses are 'essentially irrelevant' (Attardo, 2001: 30). As the discussion here *is* concerned with matters such as why, for example, an item of humour amuses A but not B, and who is in a position to determine dominant interpretations, we need to look at other ideas which *do* take account of the fact that, as people's social positions (and, hence, relations of power) are different, our senses of humour *cannot* be identical. Thus, the relevant aspects of the models of Raju, Hay, and Carrell will now be considered.

In her discussion of humour appreciation, Raju refers to people's 'reference groups' and 'identification groups', the former being the social groups in which *other* people place individuals, the latter being groups with which people identify *themselves*. She comments: 'A person's response to jokes which rely on racial or social stereotypes will therefore depend on how far his/her identification groups correspond with his/her reference groups' (1991: 80). Hay discusses humour support and in her

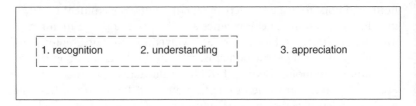

Figure 1 Hay's model of unqualified humour support (2001)

three-part model Element 2 (understanding) entails 1 (recognition), and Element 3 (appreciation) entails both 1 and 2, which can be illustrated as in Figure 1.

Here we can see that there is a gap between Elements 2 and 3 and that this gap is not bridged automatically, but will be bridged via negotiation with recipients' differing belief systems, so that people can, for example, show understanding of a joke but withhold appreciation should they so wish. (There is actually a fourth element in Hay's model and this will be discussed below.) Carrell, like Raju and Hay, recognises that the space between understanding and appreciation is vital and one that is not traversed without mediation. Factors which can influence humour appreciation are such things as religious beliefs, political convictions, and sexual orientation (1997a: 183). All these positionings involve power, a factor that is particularly important in contentious humour and one which will be returned to below.

In sum, then, these models recognise that because our positions in social life differ, so will our humour competences, and thus it isn't possible to carry out a blanket assignment of funniness to texts. Of course there *are* areas of overlap between our humour competences (a shared competence) and so many of us *will* find the same example of humour amusing. In relation to this Carrell speaks of 'humour communities' (1997b), an important point which will receive further treatment below. But first it is necessary to detail and exemplify some of the complexities of the idea of *differential* competence, looking in particular at the following topics: contentiousness, joke relations, and the relationship between appreciation and agreement.

Some aspects of differential competence

Let us start with a simple joke taken from the public domain.

A miser took all his money out of the bank for a holiday. When he thought it had had enough of a rest, he put it all back.

There are those who will find this amusing and those who will not, and one of the many reasons for the latter response could be that it is a rather weak joke. At this point it is worth noting Freud's distinction between 'innocent' jokes and 'contentious' jokes, where the latter involve, for example, something sexual, aggressive or cynical (1960, ch. 3). So for some, perhaps, the miser joke is childish, a little too 'innocent'. However, let us see what happens when some minor modifications are made to it:

> A Scot took all his money out of the bank for a holiday. When he thought it had had enough of a rest, he put it all back.

Simply changing the leftmost noun now makes this joke somewhat more contentious (the syntactic mechanics of the joke remain the same, please note). I would imagine that Scottish people and those who identify with them would not find this amusing. (If they also found the first version unamusing, they are likely to find the second doubly unamusing). Here is another version:

> A Jew took all his money out of the bank for a holiday. When he thought it had had enough of a rest, he put it all back.

Given the consequences of anti-Semitism within living memory, this joke is liable to cause even greater offence to many people. But even here some qualification is necessary. The second version may cause greater offence when told, for example, by an English stranger in a bar in Glasgow. Further, the third version may cause little or no offence when told by a Jew to another Jew (Freud's work is full of Jewish jokes in which Jews are not always seen in the best light.[4]) What we can see at work here is the reference groups and identification groups mentioned earlier by Raju, and, inextricably tied in with this, the power relations involved in such social groupings. As power is unevenly distributed throughout society, it becomes highly significant to the success of a joke who is telling what kind of joke to whom at what time and in what place. These relationships can be represented diagrammatically as in Figure 2.

This simple illustration actually represents very dynamic relationships, which are in constant flux. For instance, as we develop as social beings we not only move through time and space but also move in and out of different groupings and position ourselves accordingly, and in turn find ourselves positioned differently by others. A clear-cut example of this comes from British television. Angus Deayton was the host

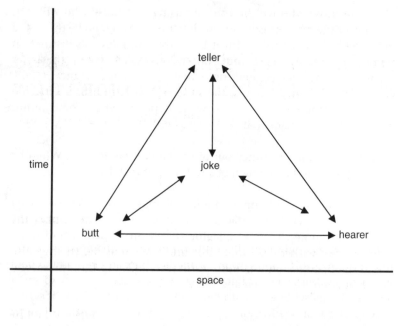

Figure 2   Humour relations

of the show *Have I Got News for You*, a topical news quiz in which two panels satirise the perceived misdeeds of politicians and celebrities, and as such, it occupies the moral high ground. In this context Deayton (and the panellists) could be said to occupy the role of teller, with the studio and broadcast audiences being the hearer, and the satirised being the butt. However, when Deayton himself became the subject of a running tabloid front-page news story concerning his sexual and drug activities, he found himself increasingly being positioned by the media and the panellists as butt. His position eventually became un-tenable and the BBC dismissed him. One of the show's team captains, the comedian Paul Merton, who had relentlessly ridiculed Deayton on air during this period, later explained that it was no longer possible for someone who was the subject of those stories to be the host of a show which satirised such people. That is, in that context, the butt could not be the teller. However, this does not mean that at any one time these three roles must always be occupied by three different people or groups. The relationships are much more fluid than that. For example, someone (a teller) can make a joke with a like-minded friend (a hearer) against a mutual enemy (a butt), giving a situation of two groups ('us and them'), or make a joke with a friend about their own group, so that all relations are in-group. An individual's self-deprecating humour elides teller and butt, and if we laugh at ourselves when alone, for example, all three roles are occupied by one person. And so on.

A further relevant factor here is that different people can appreciate the same text for different reasons. Powell's model of humour as 'normality vs. deviance' (1977) recognises that different people/groups recognise different norms and rules and consequently find different ideas and events funny, or find the same text funny for different reasons. For example, take an audience watching *Modern Times*, in which comic actor Charlie Chaplin plays an assembly worker having difficulties with the modern production process. Audience members of a left-wing persuasion might locate the problem in the conditions and relations of production and be amused by Chaplin's resistance to these. Those of the right might be amused by the incongruity of Chaplin's failure to conform to acceptable norms. 'We are not talking of abstract realities, but rather of a world of multiple realities and constructed meanings' (ibid: 54). (This situation will recur below in the discussion of *Till Death Us Do Part*.)

Another aspect to note is that the processes under discussion take place in an instant and are not always under our immediate control. We do not listen to a joke, ruminate on it and then, all things considered, decide whether to show or withhold amusement. Our amusement (or lack of it) is immediately present. In the discussion of Hay's model above we saw that the space between Element 2, understanding, and Element 3, appreciation, allowed room for the withholding of amusement. Hay adds yet another element – agreement. This means that, in *unqualified* humour support, appreciation of the humour also means support of the message, whatever it may be. However, she also notes that it is possible to support the humour through appreciation but cancel any agreement by such comments as 'That's cruel' and the like (2001: 76). But she further adds that some humour (she cites ethnic and sexist humour) depends on sharing a given attitude and so, in such cases, amusement always means agreement. Ronald de Sousa would agree. He calls such examples of humour *phthonic* ('malicious', 'evil') and claims that enjoyment of such jokes makes the amused person complicit in the breach of the moral code:

> In contrast to the element of wit, the phthonic element in a joke requires *endorsement*. It does not allow of hypothetical laughter. The phthonic makes us laugh only insofar as the assumptions on which

it is based are attitudes actually shared. Suspension of disbelief in the situation can and must be achieved for the purposes of the joke; suspension of attitude cannot be.

(1987: 240, emphasis in original)

Such points do take the discussion further but there are certain problems concerning cognitive/affective sequence (role of hearer), the nature of the role of the teller, and the strains between the public and the private which I feel are not as easily resolved as Hay and de Sousa might imply.

Concerning the first aspect (cognitive/affective sequence), Freud, perhaps the major proponent of the relief theory of humour (certainly the most detailed), argues that tendentious jokes use the joke-work (the cognitive) to evade the censor and give playful and acceptable expression to otherwise repressed or inhibited emotions (the affective). This raises the possibility of giving vent to feelings of which we are not always consciously aware. If this is indeed the case, does it mean that, for de Sousa and Hay, when someone expresses amusement at, for example, one of the modified miser jokes above, it is then too late to cancel the entailed agreement or that any such cancellation will be seen as insincere? Why is it possible to cancel the agreement of a cruel joke (which, of course, could also contain sexist and/or racist elements) but not of other types of jokes? There are those who anyway see no problem with such humour. Jacobson, for example, comments on attempts to defuse aggressive ethnic humour: 'Jettison the cargo of offence and you jettison the joke' (1997: 37). This purgative (as opposed to moral) view of humour would find no role for cancellation, any joke having served its purpose in appreciation alone. Indeed, is this not the folk view of the function of humour, 'to have a laugh', regardless?.[5] But the question for us here is: what is the nature of that amusement? There are no easy answers to these matters and they will no doubt remain the grounds of contestation. I would tend to agree with Powell that we are talking about multiple realities and constructed meanings, and I believe that what happens in practice is that the power relations present in any given context will decide what the dominant interpretation will be, and, further, that the nature of those relations will determine the consequences of such interpretations. Thus, in Germany in the 1930s, making jokes about leading Nazis led some people to be denounced and executed,[6] and in the USSR under Stalin, jokes criticising the regime could lead to the camps in Siberia.[7] In the United States in the early 1960s Lenny Bruce suffered various types of state harassment, and in

Burma in the 1990s two comedians, 'The Moustache Brothers', supporters of pro-democracy leader Aung San Suu Kyi, performed a satire
outside her home to the delight of 2000 supporters, but were imprisoned for seven years by the military for 'disrupting the stability of the
union'.[8] However, when in the 1990s Saddam Hussein sent assassins
into Kurdish-controlled northern Iraq to kill those that had taken part
in a film satirising him and his regime, local power won out, the assassins were caught, and the humorous not the murderous interpretation
prevailed in that region.[9]

The second point raised by the connection between appreciation and
agreement concerns the role of the teller. Klages (1992) focuses on
Helen Keller jokes in America, Helen Keller being the woman who
overcame the great adversity of being born deaf-blind and who is often
cited as a model for children to follow. Klages says it is possible for
women to analyse and reinterpret these jokes rather than to ignore or
censor them. To take one example.

Q: How did Helen Keller go crazy?
A: Trying to read a stucco wall.

Such jokes make us laugh and wince, says Klages; 'laugh' because they
criticise the saintly, sanitised and miraculous representation of Keller
in dominant cultural values, 'wince' because we should not laugh at
the disabled. She asserts that it can be a positive act to tell such jokes
because disabled women also 'have bodies that need to be, and have a
right to be, publicly visible, publicly represented, in their own terms,
and with their own differences' (ibid: 22).

This position raises some questions. Klages's main problem is that
she talks in the third person of the disabled being represented in 'their
own terms'. Can able-bodied comedians be sure that the terms of the
joke are the terms of the disabled? It seems unlikely the Helen Keller
jokes originated from deaf-blind people, but even if they did, is it then
the same performance with the same social significance for able-bodied
people to tell them to other able-bodied people? Once again joke
relations come into play. This is the 'team shirt' problem where, for
example, comedians feel justified in telling jokes about their own
group but can be suspicious of outsiders doing the same. There is also
the danger of an implicit elitism in the position of Klages, containing
as it does the suggestion that a certain self-selected group have a
licence to tell any kind of joke about any kind of butt as if they were
somehow above or outside of historical contingencies. It is likely that it

would only be possible to tell such jokes among close friends who would be explicitly aware of the ironic detachment involved, but this raises yet more questions about the teller's role and also points us towards the third point, the relations between the public and private, which will be addressed shortly.

The teller, rather than being simply a vehicle for the transmission of verbal signs, can actually have a number of roles. The strongest example in this regard is the professional comedian. Throughout history in a wide variety of cultures there has been a role for the comic figure, whether that be the court fools in ancient China or Egypt, the buffoons of classical Greece, medieval jesters, circus clowns, music-hall turns, movie comics, TV sitcom stars or club stand-up performers.[10] What they all have in common is a licence to play the fool, and a significant part of this licence is to transgress. No-one is more aware of this than the practising comedian, as just a small selection of comments from some of today's practitioners shows. 'The purpose of comedy ... is to take people where they are not sure they want to go. There is no unchartable territory' (Rich Hall in Lawson, 2000), and 'it's not my job to find anyone's comfort zones. I don't give a shit what people like, or think they like, or want to like' (Capurro, 2000: 138).

Another distinguishing feature of comic figures is that, unlike most other performers, it is difficult to separate out the comic persona from the 'real' person. As Welsford puts it when discussing Tarlton, Elizabeth I's jester: 'whereas Burbage ceased to be Hamlet when the play was over, Tarlton was Tarlton both on and off the stage' (1935: 312). Many comedians are unable (or choose not to) switch off their comic persona when giving interviews and making public appearances (audience expectations play a part here). For example, in the 1970s Peter Cook, then a leading comedy writer and performer and notorious for always being 'on', underwent therapy on the grounds that he no longer knew who he was (Cook, 2004), and two present-day UK comic figures, Ali G and Avid Merrion, will only give interviews when in character (see also Chapter 9). In such cases it is not always easy to attribute responsibility to comic utterances. However, this view can be qualified somewhat. Bob Monkhouse, a comic performer and writer for over 50 years, commented in an interview in 1984, 'I came into the business ... in order to get laughs but that meant inventing a persona, offering something that is not necessarily me, it's an invention, a construction' (Tolson, 1991: 186). For him, then, there was a clear distance between himself and his stage persona. The point that needs to be stressed here is that whatever the perspective taken on this matter, being a comic figure with a licence does not place people outside of social life or mean that comic talk has no social consequences, as we shall see below. This ambivalence of the comic figure is also paralleled of course in the material offered (humour), which is by design ambiguous. Thus, the comic figure can use any or all of these factors as an excuse should jokes cause offence, as, indeed, we all can when taking on the role of teller: 'It was only a joke.' But it is worth repeating that this does not mean such excuses will be accepted; in a world of multiple realities and constructed meanings the speaker of a comic utterance does not 'own' the meaning and cannot control hearer meaning.

The third point regarding appreciation and agreement is the tension between the public and the private. We all allow ourselves to behave in a more unbuttoned manner when in private, saying and doing things when alone or with close associates which we would not consider doing in public. Indeed, we might even condemn similar behaviour by others if carried out openly (unless, of course, some kind of licence has been negotiated or granted, as is the case with comic figures). This public/private duality parallels to some degree the friction between the conscious and the unconscious mentioned above, and, given the increased significance of personal politics in contemporary life, such conflicts can become difficult to manage. These strains are magnified by the degree to which anyone is a public figure, particularly at a time of increasingly intrusive news media. This is not to say that we are two wholly separate beings, one private, one public; for most of us most of the time there is a strong (if not complete) correspondence between our private and public morality. Though this means we may tell or appreciate jokes in private that we don't in public, I would suggest the distance between them, where it exists, is small. The psychic (private) censors discussed by Freud originate in social (public) disapprobation and it is this collective force of which we are all more wary and do our best to avoid by behaving, for the most part, appropriately. Most of us are able to distinguish clearly between public and private and display a tolerable level of social competence.

Humour communities/networks

In an attempt to understand differing humour competences, Carrell offers the concept of 'humour communities' (1997b), which she bases on Killingsworth's (1992) notion of local and global discourse communities. This asserts that global discourse communities, unlike local, are not restricted by physical site but rather, 'are defined by like-minded-ness, political and intellectual affiliation, and other such "special interests" and are maintained by widely dispersed discourse practices made possible by modern publishing and other communication technologies' (ibid: 111). For Carrell these relationships constitute 'abstract political systems' (1997b: 13). She says that those different audiences who, for example, watch a television situation comedy, whether as adults watching a repeat or as new fans not even born when it was first shown, 'constitute one humor community' (ibid: 14).

There is much of interest here but I have certain reservations, the chief one of which is that Carrell's is too much of a top–down approach. For example, she argues that people who watched the 1970s US sitcom *All In The Family* (*AITF*), with its main character of Archie Bunker, can be broken into two broad groups: those who agreed with Bunker's reactionary views and those who thought Bunker was the butt because of these views. That is, there were those who laughed with him and those that laughed at him. This show was the American adaptation of the 1960s/70s BBC sitcom *Till Death Us Do Part* (*TDUDP*) with its main character of Alf Garnett. The self-same observation about Bunker was at the core of the argument over *TDUDP* in Britain. Its writer, Johnny Speight, insisted that Garnett was the butt, but not all those who watched the show shared the irony. (There were also those, of course, who strongly condemned the show.[11]) What is noteworthy about Carrell's discussion is that for her both of the groups she identifies in the audience for *AITF* constitute *one* humour community. There are two main problems with this view. The first is that in this example the concept of community is stretched too far, so that, put simply, anti-racist viewers find themselves positioned with racist viewers without any say in the matter. Second, Carrell doesn't take into account different types of comedy performances and the different nature and compositions of their respective audiences. Sitting at home watching television programmes, one of which is this particular sitcom, is significantly different to actively spending time, energy and money to find and go out to see a comedy performance of your own choosing. Even if it were the case that all viewers of this sitcom actively created time to watch only this show, we are still not comparing like with like. It seems to me that it is in the latter case that people are more likely to associate with like-minded individuals who also share other 'special interests' and therefore are more likely to see themselves as part of the same humour community. But part of my quibble here is with the term 'community' itself and the problems of trying to define it, particularly in relation to such a polymorphic subject as humour.

With this and a concern for what is 'local' in mind, I would like to put forward the idea of 'humour network' as a more manageable concept.

Part of the problem with, for example, positioning racists and anti-racists together is that it ignores people's social relationships and their conceptions of self-identity. Drawing on models of social networks[12] allows us to sketch in such important factors and I hope gives us a more detailed and accurate picture of what is at work in communicat-ive interactions involving humour. Two concepts which are of great use in this regard are *density*, which refers to whether members of a person's network are in touch with one another independently of the person at the centre of a given network, and *plexity*, which is a measure of the range of the different activities people are involved in with dif-ferent individuals. In terms of density the relationships in the *TDUDP* situation could look something like this. (What is said below could equally apply to *AITF*.)

In this rather simple representation of A's humour network given in Figure 3, B, C, D and E also appreciate Garnett being the butt of the humour in *TDUDP*, and they share other ideologically similar humour connections with one another (for some of which see below), thus making up a (fairly) dense network. I would argue that those who agree

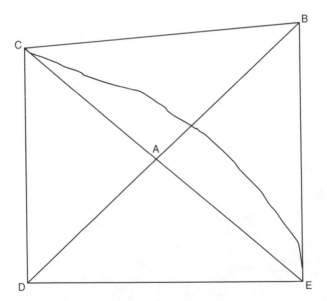

Figure 3   Part of the humour network of A

with Garnett's views are unlikely to be part of this network. Further, I suggest that the relationships A has with B, C, D and E will lean towards multiplexity, that is, there is likely to be a range of interactions and interests among them apart from humour, whereas the (passive) relationship A has with someone (F) that watches *TDUDP* in support of Garnett's views is less likely to be multiplex and may even consist of just viewing the same programme. In terms of *contentious* humour, A's and F's networks are unlikely to share connections except perhaps passively in infrequent cases like *TDUDP*, where there is an ambivalence concerning the butt. Such relationships can be illustrated thus (see Figure 4).

In Figure 4 representation of a very small part of A's and F's networks,[13] A is seen to have hearer connections with Jeremy Hardy and Shazia Mirza, stand-up comedians known to be, amongst other things, anti-racist. F is seen to have hearer connections with Jim Davidson and Bernard Manning, stand-up comedians known to have used racist material. A and F share a passive connection via *TDUDP*, but their perceptions of the show are different. Note that this representation

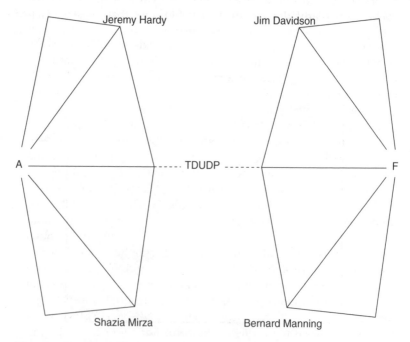

Figure 4 Fragments of A's and F's humour networks.

does not mean that, for example, A will not find any of Davidson's or Manning's material amusing, nor that F will not be amused by some of Hardy's or Mirza's material. But it does mean, I argue, that it is unlikely that A will identify with or make efforts to go and see either Davidson or Manning in a supportive manner, and similarly it is unlikely that F would identify with or make efforts to go and see Hardy or Mirza in a supportive manner. There would seem to be little or no overlap of their networks when considering these aspects of contentious humour. It is entirely possible, of course, that A may share a connection with F concerning other, *non-contentious* humour, but this would make up a different network. While this bottom–up approach does not allow an immediate view of the bigger picture, it does provide a starting point from which to build a more accurate, practical and manageable model which could be expanded when needed.

Two examples

Much of the foregoing discussion can now be drawn together in a look at two extended pieces of public humour. 'Public humour' merely refers to the fact that these examples are from sources which, through the media, had a widespread audience. Both involve female Conservative politicians, one as butt, one as teller. The former involves a comment made on a chat show, the latter a joke made during a speech at a private dinner, which was subsequently made public. I have chosen two different 'performances' of humour to see how well the above discussion can match different situations.

The first example comes from the television show *Politically Incorrect* (*PI*), which is a hybrid between a chat show with celebrity guests and a discussion programme, with the host, the comedian Bill Maher, nominating the various topics (Maher, 1999). *PI* is a regular chat show in America and on its short run in the UK it ran for five consecutive evenings on Channel 4 from 10.00–10.30 p.m. As its name implies, it sets out to discuss topical issues in a way which may not always consider the sensitivities of a complex pluralistic society. One-half of the audience was American and one-half British. Similarly, the panel of guests usually consisted of two Americans and two Britons. The topic of this particular extract is 'sex in this country' and the participants are: Bill Maher (BM), the male American host; Richard Belzer (RB), a male American actor/comedian; Julie Kirkbride (JK), a female British Conservative Member of Parliament; Lynda La Plante (LL), a female British writer; and Elle Macpherson (EM), a female Australian model.

BM's concern was to discuss why the British had elected a female prime minister, Margaret Thatcher, but also had pictures of naked women as a regular feature of tabloid national newspapers ('Page Three Girls'). His nomination of the topic as 'sex in this country' initiated a stretch of banter about all manner of things sexual: enjoying sex, changing sex, homosexuality, pornography, and also Margaret Thatcher. This was a cooperative interaction with much humour and humour support. Of note is that during these exchanges BM and RB, who knew one another before the show, worked together to establish that RB was a strong supporter of feminism, whereas BM was not. However, the *bonhomie* was punctured by the following exchange. JK, presumably because she is a Conservative female, was expected to answer this question of why the British elected a female leader yet at the same time have 'Page Three Girls'.

50.   JK: We appreciate all women's talents. [*Panel laugh*] As great polit-
          ical leaders

51. | and as other | things. I mean what's wrong | with that?
52.   EM: | There you go |
53.   RB: | But Margaret
                                                       | Thatcher
                                                       | really

54.   in the end turned out to be (1.0) a man, didn't she? [*Smiles wryly,
      shrugs*

55.   *shoulders and lifts hands at sides, palms upwards. General laughter
      and some*

56.   *applause. RB continues in sing-song voice*] I don't know if she
      qualifies [*General

57.   *laughter continues*]

58.   JK: [*Laughing*] The great conspiracy theory!

59.   BM: [*Straight-faced*] Now see that to me is a sexist comment
          because you're=

60.   RB: =Now that to | me was a joke|
61.   JK: [*To BM*] | You tell him! |

62.   BM: Yeah| | Yeah but you're saying because
                                          | she was strong>

63.   RB: | Now wait a minute |
64.   BM: >she had to be a man
65.   RB: No I think (.)
66.   BM: [*Knowingly*] Aaah!
67.   RB: Not because she was strong (1.0) because she was <u>mean</u>
68.   EM: | [*unclear*]_ |
69:   JK: | [*unclear*] <u>the same!</u> | [*smiling*] Shame!

We see that the humour relations, having started out as very similar for the discussants, suddenly change with RB's comment in 53.[14] He may feel, from the progressive position that he had earlier established, that he is joking at a right-wing butt; however, in choosing to focus contentiously on the very topic – gender relations – on which he had established that identity, he positions himself separately from the others. At first JK and EM show an amused response (this may be out of politeness) but once BM objects they immediately and forcefully cancel any idea of agreement (61, 68, 69). RB tries to use his role as comedian (he *is* a practising comedian, the comment *was* delivered with a theatrical pause and gestures) and the nature of the utterance (a joke is by design ambiguous) to extricate himself (60), but when someone has to *explain* a joke, that is strong evidence of failure, and it is the interpretation of the comment as sexist which prevails.

We should also note that this type of chat-show talk is deliberately designed to be overheard as opposed to, say, everyday talk between friends in private, but at the same time the turn-taking system is largely extemporised as in everyday informal talk, and so what occurs is, as Alaoui notes, the private putting its imprint on the public, 'thus generating talk which is halfway between talk that is produced as private and that whose design exhibits its production for overhearing' (1991: 388–9). RB's 53 is not, then, a private joke between close friends shot through with irony, in which he is deliberately mimicking the role of bigot. He makes a public blunder and the medium serves to magnify it for many to see and judge. He himself must have thought that this line would be appreciated and this is partly understandable, for he has seen a whole variety of humorous comments from various panellists on the topics of sex, gender, nudity, Thatcher, and so on, not only go unremarked but meet with an appreciative reception by both panel and studio audience. Yet suddenly this topically relevant line about Thatcher and gender is assigned a different value by other discussants. We can guess that up to this point in this context, the panellists are part of the same (or a very similar) network and that this sudden rupture serves to underline the point that such networks are not a given, but are dynamic phenomena which emerge from and are transformed by interactions.

It is also important to emphasise the power that is at work in these exchanges. The viewer is left feeling that RB has made a sexist remark and has been socially censored for this. The chief determinant is the fact that it is the host and the majority on the panel who band together to assign this meaning, and that in this specific context – five people on stage in front of a studio audience, with a television audience at home –

it is the discussants at the centre who have speaking rights. It is there that most power resides, and within this echelon it is, of course, the host who holds most power. When BM condemns the remark and then is supported by JK and EM, it does not matter that the majority response of the studio audience was amused laughter (i.e., they saw it as a joke). The majority view of the panel with the host at the head holds sway. This, of course, does not mean that this is the only interpretation, because we are discussing 'multiple realities', and no doubt there are those who will see it as amusing not sexist or will see it as amusing *and* sexist (and some who will see it as amusing *because* it is sexist[15]). But it is the panel's interpretation which dominates the show.

The second example comes from a speech made by female Conservative MP Ann Winterton in February 2004 at a dinner in Whitehall to discuss Anglo–Danish relations, which was hosted by the Danish shipping company Maersk. Before coming to the joke, a little background information is necessary. In May 2002 Winterton was dismissed as the shadow agriculture minister by the then Conservative leader Iain Duncan Smith when she made a joke at a rugby-club dinner in her constituency about a Pakistani being thrown out of the window of a moving train because Pakistanis are 'ten-a-penny in my country'. In early February 2004, 20 immigrant Chinese cockle-pickers working without permits for extremely low wages were drowned in Morecambe Bay.[16] This occurred at a time of widespread media coverage, much of it sensationalist, about 'illegal immigrants'. At almost the same time the new Conservative leader Michael Howard, in an effort to distance his party from the far right on such an important issue, made a hard-hitting speech against the British National Party, condemning their racist policies. It was in this charged atmosphere that a week after Howard's speech, Winterton told a joke in which a shark, bored with eating tuna, suggested to another that they should go 'to Morecambe for a Chinese'. When this was reported in a national newspaper Howard dismissed her from the parliamentary party.[17]

The relations in the joke are quite marked. Winterton, as we have seen, has a history of racist joking, and just as she had previously told a joke in which Pakistanis were 'ten-a-penny', here her relations to the butt are also those of superior/inferior. In relation to her, the Chinese generally are ethnically, culturally and linguistically distant, something 'other'; these particular Chinese, moreover, had no legal status in the UK, their labour was reprehensibly exploited by gang masters, they had no representation, and in the scripts at work in the joke they are equated with food. In terms of the distribution of power, there is a great inequality between the teller and the butts, in the teller's favour.[18] Even though she is an elected public figure with all the attendant responsibilities that such a position entails, and had even been warned by a fellow-Conservative MP not to make a joke that might cause offence, she chose to tell this joke to an audience gathered together to discuss international cooperation, containing, amongst others, MPs from opposing parties.

It is also necessary to note that the nature of the talk was not the give-and-take banter of a small group where meanings are collaboratively and extemporaneously constructed, as in the previous example, but was someone making a speech (a prepared monologue) to a captive audience. Responsibility is therefore easier to attribute. Further, although this was a 'private' dinner, it was not private in the sense of, say, having a dinner at home with family and friends, although it was private in that the general public and news media were excluded. Many of the people there were strangers to one another, and many were public figures. She must have been aware of these crucial factors and that an MP speaking at such an event could not be an entirely 'private' matter (though she did try to use the 'private' nature of the function as a defence). While the after-dinner speaking rights she enjoyed conferred upon her a certain licence, she once again overstepped the mark. Her joke was met with silence, and one Labour MP in the audience was so incensed that he reported it to the news media. In this case, then, there could be no question of hearer agreement as there was simply no appreciation. Nor, given her history and the speaking context, was there any possibility of her falling back on the 'it was only a joke' excuse.

The public/private issue is significant here. Tragedies often give rise to jokes and this Morecambe Bay joke was already circulating in the public domain before Winterton told it. Although it is the racial element that is uppermost in this joke, it can also be seen as being in the tradition of disaster jokes. Sick-joke cycles usually occur within local networks where such jokes are ideologically acceptable and tellers feel themselves to be on safe grounds. In the letters column of *The Guardian* newspaper (28.02.04) a number of correspondents commented that they had already heard the joke before this incident. One correspondent noted that her colleagues at work had told it but she expected politicians to show higher standards, while another thought that it was equally wrong for anyone to tell such jokes. Yet another thought such jokes exist in a separate 'humour space' where there is no such thing as a racist or sexist joke, a point strongly at odds with this discussion. While agreeing with the second correspondent that it is just as immoral (or at least amoral) for individuals to tell this joke in private networks, the significant difference of a politician telling the joke is that in the existing scheme of things her office endows her (rightly or wrongly) with a certain moral authority and, further, her words are empowered by the mass media, all of this giving greater weight to her utterances, which have a national audience. That is, the immediate social and political consequences are far greater than these jokes being told within private networks, though, of course, the existence of the latter is not without social significance. Telling a joke to what was, in effect, a public audience meant that Winterton stepped outside of an imagined safe network into, as it were, the worldwide web of humour networks, and such a contentious joke was guaranteed to come up against opposition. Although in this country Winterton is far more powerful than the butts, at present in the UK there is a general acceptance of multiculturalism backed, if necessary, by laws against racial discrimination. These prevailing conditions were manifested in the warning she received before her speech, the silent reception of the joke, the leaking of it to the press, her dismissal by the party leader and the widespread condemnation of the utterance. These are the chief determinants in the assignment of this particular meaning to her joke. Other interpretations are available, but they are not the ones which dominate.

Conclusion

This discussion has shown that the seemingly simple pleasure of cracking jokes can be a precarious undertaking in a contemporary pluralistic society in which human rights are promoted, pressure groups proliferate, and personal politics are commonplace. This is especially the case for public figures (actors, comedians, politicians and so on) whose utterances are represented through mass media that court controversy, and even more so for those whose previous talk has caused heated debate. Such complex situations can in part be understood through the use of models of humour which recognise the interactive nature of such exchanges and thus show that a number of interpretations are possible (differential competence). The disputes about the social meanings of contested utterances are usually resolved by the power relations involved, and can range from verbal disagreements between a few individuals through to the exercise of various degrees of state control. On a local level it may be possible to shed some light on such matters by considering people's humour networks and a tentative attempt at this was made, though the explanatory power of such a preliminary sketch remains to be seen. What is clear is that when such conflicts arise, a dominant interpretation will emerge in most cases. As Humpty Dumpty observed, the question of what the words may or may not mean becomes, rather, a matter of who is in a position to enforce a particular meaning.

Notes

1 See Lauter (1964).
2 The multidisciplinary *HUMOR: International Journal Of Humor Research* has been published since 1988.
3 See McGhee (1980), for the development of humour in children, and Brownell and Gardner (1988), for some neuropsychological aspects of humour.
4 Woody Allen and Jackie Mason also come to mind here.
5 That old folk saying 'Laughter is the best medicine' has now become a form of alternative therapy. See, for example, Holden (1993). Also note the recent increase of laughter clubs, a phenomenon originating in India.
6 See Hillenbrand (1995).
7 See Dolgopolova (1983) for a collection of jokes from the USSR.
8 See (Pilger), 1996, and Hilbreth (2002).
9 See Harding (2003).
10 See Christen (1998), and Janik (1998).
11 See Husband (1988).
12 I draw on Milroy (1980) here.
13 This model is two-dimensional and static. To more accurately represent the connection it needs to be three-dimensional and mobile.
14 See Willis (2003) for full transcript and discussion.
15 See Schutz (1995) for a blunt discussion of 'political correctness' and humour.
16 The death toll subsequently rose to 21.
17 She was reinstated in the parliamentary Party in March 2004. In July 2004 she was reselected by her constituency party in Congleton, Cheshire, to stand again at the next general election.
18 This is not to draw a picture of the Chinese as innocents. Chinese humour also, unsurprisingly, deals in stereotypes (see Kowallis, 1986). Further, after the attacks on the USA in September 2001, the following joke about the event was in circulation in Shanghai: Bush asked the attackers why they destroyed the World Trade Centre, to which they replied, 'Sorry, there's no World Trade Centre on these maps of ours. They must be out of date.' This was a reference to the US excuse for bombing the Chinese embassy in Belgrade during the Balkans conflict, which killed a number of Chinese (Groffman, 2001).

7
Privacy, Embarrassment and Social Power: British Sitcom

Frances Gray

Bland beginning

A middle-aged man strolls down the high street. He reaches a department store with plate glass windows. He takes a furtive look around. There is nobody in sight. He positions himself at the corner of the building and raises one arm and one leg. His reflection in the glass looks out at us – a mild-looking chap in spectacles apparently floating like a starfish in mid-air. He titters, and walks on.

This image – from the credits of Harry Worth's sitcom *Here's Harry* – will be recognisable to anyone who watched television in the early 1960s. It is as inoffensive an image as comedy ever produced, which is why I have chosen to begin with it. For I am concerned with a feeling that might seem like small potatoes in the arena of ethical discourse, that of embarrassment.

There are powerful emotions fuelling the delivery of humour – anger, aggression, scorn – and the response of its target – rage, humiliation, misery – which seem automatically to demand ethical judgements: from the perpetrator, from the victim, from the audience. Debates about what it is permissible to mock tend to be predicated upon assumptions about the target: whether an individual or a group is vulnerable or too powerful, whether a joke serves to change or aggravate a situation. Narrative comedy complicates the mix further: its targets are fictional and in theory, one cannot hurt a fiction; but we are aware that things are not quite so simple. All arguments, however, that explore laughter's relationship to powerful emotions assume clear boundaries between joker, audience and target; the joker acts, the target suffers, the audience laughs (or not).

146

The reason I focus on embarrassment is that, although a much milder emotion, it is, whether we are dealing with fiction or reality, equally real for all parties. Audiences do not necessarily share the sexual or violent feelings fictional characters appear to experience, certainly never to an equivalent degree; a production of Shakespeare's *Macbeth* seeks their complex judgement of the hero, not a mass desire to rule Scotland. But it requires no effort to make them experience a fictional character's embarrassment: it just happens. Embarrassment does not mean sympathy with a character's actions – often the reverse – but it does involve the sense of privacy violated, of being an unwilling observer of his *re*actions to what is happening to him, a sense of guilt for speculating about feelings the victim would prefer to conceal. There may also be a sense of observing (im)moral attitudes – racism, sexism or sheer nastiness – which are not reproved, imparting discomfort at our powerlessness to change the situation. Embarrassment is a real physical sensation on the skin and in the stomach: it leaves us with a sense of our own, real, damage. Situation comedy has to negotiate with this phenomenon – even Harry Worth at his most harmlessly silly; and it is with the kind of assumptions on which he did so that I wish to begin.

Television, transparency and ethical norms

Television became a social force to be reckoned with in Britain in 1953, when many households bought their first set to watch the Coronation. The timing of this mass purchase suggests unanimity between the BBC and the public about television's function. The current affairs programme *Panorama* announced itself as 'your window on the world'; many broadcasts could have said likewise, as if television showed 'reality' untouched by bias or self-consciousness. There were documentary 'windows' on everything from public institutions to the seabed, offering 'objective' commentaries in markedly similar tones of voice. Drama also partook of this transparency; naturalistic playwrights like John Hopkins and Alun Owen provided a 'window' into private worlds, using the intimacy of a small screen in the living room to offer delicate dissections of family life.

'Transparency' also suited situation comedy, which offered a permanent group of characters who resembled, and shared the values of, its middle-class audience. Asked to define its ethical stance, sitcom might have quoted Northrop Frye's definition of comedy as gentle corrective 'designed not to condemn evil but to ridicule a lack of self-knowledge' (1949: 63). A distinctive pleasure of the form was the gradual deepening of dramatic intimacy, allowing it to become, as Neale and Krutnik observe, a microcosm of broadcasting, 'concerned with reaffirming cultural identity, with demarcating an "inside", a community of interests and values, and localizing contrary or oppositional values as an "outside"' (1990: 242). In a typical sitcom, domestic or community harmony would be threatened by the desires of an individual, who eventually returned to the fold with differences resolved: laughter was directed less at the individual who (mildly) violated social norms than at the comedic mechanisms triggered in consequence: lies, disguises, hiding and confusion – all were resolved as the half-hour ran its course.

While sitcom was, and is, socially conservative in its dependence on shared ethical norms, it could never be ethically static. Over the decades it engaged in slow but definite negotiation with cultural change. British comedy of the 1950s contained no black or gay characters and barely mentioned divorce or single parenthood, while Jimmy Edwards's public school comedy *Whack-o!* (BBC TV) treated corporal punishment for children as a joke. The next 50 years saw a series of almost imperceptible shifts in the way sitcom constructed the position of women, the family, the rights of minorities and children. It could challenge viewers by showing the comic triumph of characters they might perceive as exotic or dissident (implicitly validating their moral stature) or by presenting the correction of a racist or sexist attitude as a necessary precondition of resolution. But it did so on the assumption viewers shared an ethical consensus with the figures on the screen. Some might have a more conservative or radical point of view than the protagonist – but they would find their stance represented and respected within the protagonist's community. While occasionally sitcom threw up a popular monster such as racist Alf Garnett in Johnny Speight's BBC TV sitcom *Till Death Us Do Part,* he was a clearly designated butt for scornful mockery; the main function of laughter was as lubricant for social relations. Sitcom did not just show a community in action, it created one.

The eccentric in the frame

One kind of sitcom positioned the viewer differently: the comedy of eccentricity. This centred not on a social group but on an individual at odds with the world; the world invariably won; the laughter elicited might therefore be seen not as moral correction but as something more ethically dubious: cruelty, an assertion of superiority, an act of social exclusion, or a sign of shared embarrassment. However the relationship between viewer and comic actor transformed the cruelty, though in different ways on each side of the Atlantic.

American sitcom of eccentricity was a British television staple in the 1950s – notably *I Love Lucy* and *The Phil Silvers Show* – shown on ITV and BBC respectively. The titles hint at their attraction: they showcase a loved performer in a persona, which shares his/her characteristics but is clearly a dramatic construct. Lucille Ball co-starred with her real husband, Desi Arnaz, and incorporated her pregnancy into *I Love Lucy;* her character, showbusiness wannabe Lucy Ricardo, got into scrapes which gave Ball the opportunity to display her matchless talent for slapstick. Lucy's domestic experiments ended with exploding loaves, her attempts to ogle film stars in disguise ended in disaster. However, the nature of the laughter was defined by the way the structure manipulated the boundaries of naturalism so that the performer was not observed through a 'window on the world' but through a clearly drawn frame of artifice. When Lucy donned an elaborate disguise to convince film star William Holden that they had never met, she set fire to her false nose while lighting a cigarette and with magnificent nonchalance dunked the Pinocchio conk in her coffee; she showed no sign of humiliation; the camera, centred firmly upon her, made it clear that this was a bravura piece of physical acting which left the guest star on the sidelines, reduced to audience admiring superior talent. Phil Silver's character, Sergeant Bilko, was discomfited when trying to con money out of the dimmer members of his platoon – but the cartoon sequence at the beginning of the show made clear that these unsuccessful scams existed to showcase Silvers's rapid-fire patter, swivelling manic eyes and grace of movement.

Thus, though the comic plot might mark a character as butt, a figure potentially to be excluded or despised, the laughter was shot through with admiration for the performer. It also drew on another assumption. Lucy Ricardo and Sergeant Bilko were struggling to succeed in a tough world. Lucy – like Ball – was married to a Cuban immigrant seeking to prove himself, and her efforts mimicked his; Bilko was a working-class man finding an unorthodox path through an institution. They might be unsuccessful – and Bilko morally dubious – but their aspiration guaranteed the sympathy of the audience, reinforced by awareness that the performer was living out the American dream. There was no dissection of the psychological basis for this aspiration, but there did not need to be; it served to bind performer and viewer into a community.

The eccentric in the window

British comedy of eccentricity took a different path. Its conventions are embodied in a line from the first of the genre, *Hancock*. Tony Hancock, transforming a routine stint of jury duty into *Twelve Angry Men*, turns emotively to his fellow jurors and cries, 'What of Magna Carta? Did she die in vain?' British sitcom centred upon characters as doomed to obscurity as Hancock's imaginary martyr. The arena in which their aspirations rose and fell was that of class. While Lucy and Bilko had career goals, British eccentrics had fuzzier ambitions: to claw their way into a particular social group or force a little respect from those higher in the pecking order.

Such a summary, however, implies endorsement of hierarchy and pleasure in the humiliation of an outsider. This is a position which might have caused Hancock's audience considerable embarrassment; in the era of the Welfare State many would have considered it ethically dubious. In practice the interplay between audience and eccentric was as complex as in the USA.

British TV audiences were as aware of Hancock the performer as US audiences were of Ball. His highly publicised private life, his rows with scriptwriters Ray Galton and Alan Simpson and his interview in John Freeman's probing series *Face to Face* left them in no doubt of the gap between the tormented actor and the character he played. But unlike *Bilko* or *Lucy*, the series studiously avoided the acknowledgement of this gap. Its originality lay in its use of naturalism.

Hancock, Galton and Simpson had considerable success with the radio sitcom *Hancock's Half Hour* for two years before it debuted on television in 1956. The persona at its heart, Anthony Aloysius St John Hancock, was already a solid creation – pretentious, snobbish, ignorant, shifty and pompous, but also curiously vulnerable. On radio he got into funny situations with funny characters played by comic actors like Sid James and Kenneth Williams. The move to television marked a new departure. Although the self-dramatising Anthony Aloysius made the most of them, the situations created for him over the next five years were humdrum: he was a juror, a blood donor, he decided to get married and vainly chatted up a succession of women over a frozen TV dinner for two as if he were playwright and actor Noel Coward. If he clashed with officialdom in the person of a policeman or a doctor, this did not involve a well-known comic 'name' bringing his own style to the role, but an actor performing a policeman or a doctor as he would in a play. Hancock made the technical aspect of the show support the style. He refused to exploit for laughs the inevitable mishaps that arose during recording, such as a wobbling set. Increasingly, schedules were organised to permit more close-ups, a device common in naturalistic television drama but new to sitcom. Hancock's talent lay in the flexibility and variety of his facial reactions; rather than comic ' mugging' *á la* Ball they offered access to the interior life of his character.

This was a risky strategy in a comedy grounded on a persona invariably punished for his social pretensions. It presented viewers with a dilemma: they could treat Anthony Aloysius as an object of scorn, endorsing the moral status of the class code which punished him; or they could respond to the humanity revealed by the sensitivity of the actor, replacing laughter with embarrassment.

Embarrassment, because it erodes the boundary between audience and butt, is a risky option in comedy and is generally kept in check by precise narrative boundaries. If viewers thought Lucy experienced humiliation during a slapstick set piece, it would undermine their comic pleasure. American eccentric comedy rarely permits a character to be alone or in an intimate situation where feelings need to be articulated. Galton and Simpson, however, confronted this problem head-on and made the risk part of the pleasure: they opened up the psyche of the character to the audience. In an episode called *The Bedsitter* they abandoned 'situation' altogether.

The Bedsitter is a half-hour soliloquy in which nothing happens. It begins with Anthony Aloysius trying to blow smoke rings. He hurts his lip. He pouts. He roots through the medicine cabinet. He puts some butter on the burn. Struck by the way the protruding lip makes him look like French star, Maurice Chevalier, he does a quick impression. He ponders the word 'bicuspid'. He tries to read philosopher Bertrand Russell, shifts to a thriller but finds he can't manage without a dictionary, scratches, fancies a chocolate but there's only one left in the box, 'Marzipan. Oh dear, oh dear.' He tries combing his hair in different styles and wonders if he's getting old. No, he tells himself, 'You're like old cheese ... old wine' (Hancock and Brent, 1986: 104).

The precisely observed detail of Hancock's social interactions offered the audience mixed pleasures. Everyone knew what it was like to confront a tight-lipped authority figure; they also knew that it could be managed with less self-absorption and greater adroitness. Hancock's inept attempts to show off placed him in the midst of a struggle for social dominance, and rendered him fair game as an object of mockery. But alone, at the point when he should be at his most vulnerable, he ceased to be a comic object and became a subject. He was not involved in a power struggle, and so could not lose. He was not needy, and so could not be hurt. He might exhibit desires that were silly, or pretentious, but the focus was on his childlike and unselfconscious absorption in fantasy. Hence his inner life, made visible to the camera, was not an expression of hurt snobbery or frustrated aspiration, but pure play, experimentation with different identities for its own sake. The unselfconscious soliloquising tapped into a dimension the audience shared; while they might never behave like Anthony Aloysius in public they could certainly imagine themselves in a world less restricted. The visibility of his fantasy life thus offered a kind of comic excess. He transcended embarrassment, so the viewer could do so too.

The vitality with which this endowed him encouraged a laughter that did not spring from the aggression of a social group excluding an outsider, but was grounded in a moral position more positive and generous. When he tried to pass as an Old Etonian or a Coldstream Guard, or boasted that the blood he was about to donate was 'one hundred per cent Anglo-Saxon with perhaps just a dash of Viking', (ibid: 106) viewers might laugh at his snobbishness, but their access to his playful subjectivity made the hierarchies to which he aspired pale in comparison. Week by week, he failed to make the social grade, and week by week he bounced back, fuelled by a vigorous inner child infinitely more attractive than the rigidly codified world that rejected him.

The eccentric as class warrior

If Anthony Aloysius was a snob he was thus also a hero of the class struggle. There was certainly no suggestion anyone should be content in a situation he described as 'frustration, misery, boredom, worry and insomnia.' (ibid.) His character was inextricably associated with his address, 23 Railway Cuttings, East Cheam – clearly a house in the downmarket end of a smart upper-middle-class district, one in which, Hancock pointed out, 'I've done everything except be indecent ... O I can tell you where every knot is in the wood. Where I burped. It's like a bloody death cell ...' (ibid: 94) *Hancock* made it clear that the comedy of eccentricity in a classbound world was inevitably a comedy of entrapment; generations of comic heroes went on to test the boundaries of their social traps, and by implication our own.

They did so with varying degrees of intensity but the avoidance of embarrassment through the revelation of subjectivity was always a vital component of the comedy. Harry Worth's little joke in the window was a private moment in the life of a character whose assaults on the *status quo* were those of an innocent bumbler. But it was also poss-ible to delineate the trap with greater intensity. Galton and Simpson followed their work on *Hancock* with a BBC sitcom about two rag and bone men, *Steptoe and Son,* one of the most merciless dissections of family life to appear on television. It centred on the ambitions of 40-something Harold Steptoe – like Hancock's, social, intellectual and erotic – and his longing to escape his anarchic father Albert who invariably brought him down to earth.

The reason for *Steptoe's* appeal is located by Neale and Krutnik in 'the way it represents a *spectacle* of inverted bourgeois decorum for a bour-geois audience: one has to know the "rules" in order to recognise and to find funny the ways in which they are broken' (1990: 251). This cer-tainly applies to the old man's violation of middle-class manners – he eats pickled onions in the bath and tackles the ones he has dropped in the filthy water with extra relish; or to the moments when Harold's wincing pretentiousness proves inadequate to his current social target – he ruins his chances at the local dramatic society, pronouncing 'polo pony' as 'polopony', while Albert wins a major role by speaking purest RP [received pronunciation]. But the smug bourgeois exclusivity sug-gested here is prevented by the intimacy with which Harold is exposed. We see him alone in the street taking imaginary applause after the dis-astrous theatricals. One episode, *Loathe Story,* invaded his dreams: he is shown muttering in his sleep about the petty defeats inflicted by his father; eerily, he begins to speak in the old man's voice: 'Snap. Down the snake you go. Hotel on Mayfair. Two thousand pounds. Beat you. Checkmate. Beat you ...' (Galton and Simpson, 1988: 83). He sleep-walks into Albert's room, picking up a meat cleaver on the way.

The intensity of this insight into Harold's subjectivity puts the comic response at risk: it could be a source of, rather than a relief from, embarrassment. But the very acknowledgement of the reality of his feelings is our guarantee that he will not act on them; awake, Harold is a moral man. The establishment of his humanity, however, is a judge-ment on the class to which he aspires. In the same episode he visits a psychiatrist – who, throughout the consultation, doodles women with enormous breasts. Although constructed as 'superior' by his thera-peutic role as well as his class, his indifference underlines Harold's decency.

The comedy of eccentricity and entrapment mutated to fit tech-niques as varied as those of Hywel Bennett in the ITV sitcom *Shelley,* a workshy misanthropist with a good deal of sexual charm, and the gawkily acrobatic John Cleese as the snobbish hotelier in the BBC sitcom *Fawlty Towers,* a character whose private moments suggested an inarticulate despair, conveyed in frenzied bodily movement; alone, he crouched and leapt like a contorted frog or gave his car 'a damn good thrashing' for breaking down. But however varied its format and however extravagant the action, sitcom still depended on the idea of television as a one-way 'window'. The interiority of the characters was exposed without acknowledgement of an audience by performer or camera and no frame-breaking to give the viewer tacit permission to admire the comic skill involved.

This included a doubled-edged relationship with language. Since Richard Sheridan's first play *The Rivals* brought Mrs Malaprop to the stage, a character's struggle with the discourse of a higher social class has been a comic staple. The British eccentric was rarely self-consciously witty; he might have funny lines, but always in a context that disallowed his capacity for *le mot juste.* Harold froze to inarticulacy trying to impress in the wider world. However, his tirades to his father have an impressively marshalled lexis:

> How romantic. The junkyard by moonlight. A setting worthy of Antony and Cleopatra. They had the Nile, you had the Grand Union Canal. They had a barge. You had a junk cart with the horse taken out. They had their pyramids. You had your ten-foot pile of old ballcocks and gas stoves. The inscrutable face of the Sphinx watching over you, or next door's tom-cat with its ear torn off – what's to choose?
>
> (ibid: 160)

This bravura performance is, however, as distant from the arena of power as Harold's dream. Harold is not trying to gain anything, except temporary triumph over his indestructible father, nor is the actor, Harry H. Corbett, wooing applause in his own persona like Ball. Rather, it is a gift to the audience, a moment of comic excess. It is a joke about comedy itself, an acknowledgement that too close an adherence to a simplistic idea of exclusive laughter, a refusal to acknowledge the value of the person laughed at, can constrict comic pleasure. A similar moment occurs in *Fawlty Towers* when Basil briefly transcends his oily snobspeak to a pair of unattractive diners and makes what may or may not be a Freudian slip:

SYBIL: A sherry, perhaps, would you like a sherry?
MRS HALL: That would be very nice.

COLONEL HALL: Two small and dry.
BASIL: Oh, I don't know ...

(Cleese and Booth, 1977: 179)

Such lines remind the audience that eccentrics are, morally, on the same side as ourselves; their desires may be petty but they stand head and shoulders above the 'small and dry' world to which they aspire. This can only be the case as long as there is no element of self-consciousness; an eccentric aware that his privacy was not absolute would lose the childlike dimension that prevented his own sense of embarrassment and thus our own; his moral integrity could no longer be taken for granted. A later era of comedy was to explore exactly that loss.

The ethics of reality: the comedic and the commodified

The sitcom audience from *Hancock* to *Fawlty Towers* might criticise individual programmes, argue about language or behaviour or be selective in their viewing. On the whole, however, if they discussed programmes, it was in terms of what they showed rather than of the medium showing them. Inevitably, though, the generation which grew up with the box in the corner as a given object began to investigate it as a cultural phenomenon. With the rise of new disciplines – feminism, media studies and cultural studies – the study of gender, power relations and language fed back into the making of programmes. The form and the ideology of earlier programming were challenged from within and without.

New technologies abetted this process. Early equipment was cumbersome and documentaries involved teams of editors and lighting technicians. But with the rise of new technology like digital video, it was possible to plant a camera as a 'fly on the wall' in any setting; the evolution of the webcam allowed subjects to film themselves, empowering them to shape the filming. At the same time, Thatcherism introduced swingeing cuts in broadcasting budgets and a market-led approach. A popular new format, the 'docusoap', cost a fraction of the budget of a serious documentary – or indeed of a sitcom. Docusoaps such as *Driving School* and *Airport* (both BBC TV) created 'characters' out of participants who could act 'naturally' in front of the camera. Acting 'naturally' involved a high degree of conscious performance; participants became part of a team building a persona and engineering situations where it could display itself to full eccentric advantage. The process was not unlike the way that Hancock, Galton and Simpson evolved Anthony Aloysius. Hancock, however, had a clearly defined, if stormy, relationship with his comic alter ego; his work was always predicated on the assumption that he controlled his persona. The persona displayed – often for our laughter – in docusoap was not the result of a creative process within the individual but of simplification – and exploitation – of that individual by others. Once ratings dropped, the programme makers would start again with a new location and dump their 'stars' with no regard for their feelings.

The genre took a leap forward at the end of the 1990s with Channel 4's *Big Brother,* which placed a group of people in a closed environment under permanent cameras. To surveillance it added competition: viewers were invited to vote weekly to evict participants and award a cash prize to the survivor. This made it controversial. Some, pointing out that more people voted than in the 2001 elections, saw it as democracy in action; others perceived it as voyeurism. The controversy underlined questions about its ethical limits. Bernard Clark defended *BB* as 'rentertainment,' (2002: 13) pointing out that lives were only 'borrowed.' Bought or borrowed, however, participants became objects. Frequently one was foregrounded by the editors as comic butt – for example the fluffy Welsh hairdresser Helen in *BBII*, given to questions like 'Is there chicken in chickpeas?'

For the participants *Big Brother* might have felt like documentary, in that their actions had no structure and the camera never stopped watching; for the editors, however, with the power to select what was shown in prime-time, it was sitcom: a sitcom without closure, so that the correction of an individual in a half-hour episode became sustained mockery; a sitcom which removed everything that shaped participants' uniqueness – family, work, relationships – so that the sense of an eccentric stepping into the private space of play was lost; and a sitcom too in that it used real people as if they were fictions to be laughed at without consequences in the outside world. As Ben Thompson remarks, 'the commodification of the self which reality TV entails is also a comedification' (2004: 397).

Meanwhile the media explored their power to embarrass the participants *after* they had exhibited themselves. The *Sun* ranted, 'Please leave our lives immediately ... You are not celebrities, you just happened to be part of a TV freak show which is now over ... go back to your jobs. We don't care about you anymore' (7 July 2001). The erosion of the private space for play eroded the idea of laughter as sympathetic enjoyment of the eccentric, the *Sun* evidently preferring Bergson's definition: 'a sort of social gesture. By the fear which it inspires, it restrains eccentricity, keeps constantly awake and in mutual contact certain activities of a secondary order which might retire into their shell and go to sleep' (Palmer, 1984: 63). The denizens of the *Big Brother* house, cameras in their bedrooms to catch their eccentricities all night long, might have liked Bergson's caveat that *real* laughter, as opposed to cases that are elementary, theoretical and perfect, reflected more complex responses to social relations. As I write in early January 2005 the academic Germaine Greer has just walked out of a 'celebrity' version of *Big Brother* – which had gone out of its way to ensure both quarrels and physical discomfort among the participants – denouncing its endorsement of a 'school bully' culture that would be widely imitated in the outside world. If she is right, the 'democracy' created by the programme is extending beyond the choice of winner; the audience is implicitly invited to engage in the process of comedification in their own back yard.

Reality – the new comedy?

As market-led channels tiptoed towards the new millennium, increasingly disinclined to experiment, reality TV seemed set to replace sitcom. However, sitcom took some of the lessons of *Big Brother* on board. Once the self-revelation of eccentric characters in a power struggle over money, status and audience became a regular television event, sitcom's use of interiority was ripe for re-examination. The old sense of watching private play without embarrassment on either side could be recreated by the viewer watching repeats of *Fawlty* or *Hancock* or *Steptoe*, but it was, perhaps, no longer possible to invent such a character. A new possibility had emerged, however – to allow the eccentric televisual self-awareness. This went beyond parody (like Rob Reiner's *This Is Spinal Tap*), implicitly questioning the ethical basis of reality TV by exploring its relationship with both embarrassment and power. The eccentric's desire for social status was replaced by the desire for celebrity; his moments of playfulness for personal enjoyment became conscious self-exposure to a camera with the power of the medium behind it. In an early example of the emerging genre, Chris Langham's *People Like Us* (BBC TV), about an inept broadcast journalist, the viewer was laughing not simply at the character but at the deft satire on media intrusiveness. With Rob Brydon's *Marion and Geoff* (BBC TV), in which a cuckolded chauffeur confides his deluded optimism about his marriage and children, the exposure of private thoughts was performed in apparent innocence about its possible impact; the audience were aware of the potential for their own embarrassment if they did not allow their laughter to mellow into compassion. Implicitly, they were positioned on the side of Keith the chauffeur; this meant not only that they were ranged against the selfish wife who exploits him, but that they were also questioning the ethics of the medium and the comedification process.

The Office, by Ricky Gervais and Stephen Merchant, first aired on BBC2 in the summer of 2001, advanced this questioning with a more varied relationship to the fly-on-the-wall. Characters were not only aware of their status as comedified selves; they were also aware of humour as discourse. This distinguished the central character David Brent from his predecessors: Harold Steptoe and Basil Fawlty were too busy trying to copy the language of a higher class to attempt wit. Consequently they never needed to define humour. David Brent wanted celebrity, and he knew that here 'humour' mattered more than class; consequently he did need to define it, at a point when humour had become an ethical minefield. Legislation about race relations, sexual discrimination and disability – and the rise of alternative comedy – made it difficult for anyone to be unaware that a joke standard in the 1950s would now have a very different reception. 'Political correctness' was itself a subject of jokes. Not all the public were sympathetic to the notion, but those who continued to make sexist or racist jokes knew that they were engaging in a discourse which might result in a judgement against them, whether ethical or legal.

This awareness was further complicated by a myth beloved of Western society, and the English in particular: that humour is not simply a quality one might possess, like righthandedness, but an indication of personal value. Hence the plethora of lonely hearts ads pleading for a GSOH [good sense of humour] and the widespread teaching of humour as a coping skill in contexts as varied as the boardroom, the care home and the jail service. An individual lacking 'humour' is seen as morally deficient – even if laughter may involve colluding with the victimisation of oneself or another. Hence to be a master of humour, to be one of the class that decides *what is funny* is to assume power over the rules of social interaction.

Mark Thompson, Director-General of the BBC, announced at the Edinburgh Festival in 2004 that 'Investment in and promotion of comedy is probably more important today than it has ever been.' David Brent would have phrased this less elegantly, but he would undoubtedly endorse the idea of the comedian as both investor and product; relentlessly, he tried to establish himself as a 'boss ... who's basically a chilled-out entertainer', marketing himself as a comedian to the fly-on-the-wall, while trying to use humour to dominate the workplace.

The joke was that he could never acknowledge this lust for power, even to himself, and so was endlessly flummoxed by the consequences of his actions. Brent welcomes new workers with a carefully rehearsed (racist) joke which results in a triple-barrelled put-down: once as a black man enters just in time to deflate the punch-line, remarking a little wearily, 'It's not the black man's cock one, is it?' (Gervais and Merchant, 2003: 36); again when trapped by his female boss in a linguistic minefield; she is sophisticated enough to deconstruct the joke's 'ethnic stereotype', a phrase that mystifies Brent, who stumblingly translates her rebuke into his own language as 'Some of them can be a little bit sensitive' (ibid: 39); and finally, when he tries to regain power as boss and humourist, assuring complainants: 'You'll never have another boss like me' (ibid: 47). Brent is ridiculous because he recognises his mania to be the one who decides *what is funny* only as a guarantee of his GSOH, rather than a subconscious wish for power at any moral cost. 'If you get a coloured gent in the audience', said the purveyor of racist jokes Bernard Manning, 'he throws back his head and laughs.' He added, chillingly, 'If he's got any sense' (Gray, 1994: 26). Brent, benignly trying to make his courteous subordinate Oliver at home by announcing his admiration for Sidney Poitier, grasps that intentionally racist jokes are offensive; what he cannot understand is that his own humour, never private or playful, can only operate in the arena of power and thus will always offend. It is, however, all too clear to the fly-on-the-wall. Rather than the pleasurable excess of the playful and often more articulate private self revealed by the selective 'window on the world', the camera in *The Office* reveals a persona constructed for the consumer and spiralling out of control because the viewer, forced to play that consumer, is helpless to stop it:

> There are limits to my comedy. There are things that I will never laugh at, like the handicapped, because there's nothing funny about them, or any deformity. It's like when you see someone look at a little handicapped, and they go, 'Oh, look at him, he's not ablebodied, I am. I'm prejudiced.' Well, at least the little handicapped fella is *ableminded*. Unless he's not, it's difficult to tell with the wheelchair ones. So, just give generously to all of them.
>
> (Gervais and Merchant, 2002: 115)

If viewers are *not* embarrassed by this speech it is because it jams so many failures of discourse control into a small space that the very excess is pleasurable. The second series, however, seemed to insist on embarrassment. Among the new staff is a young woman in a wheelchair; Brent, in charge of fire drill, starts to haul her down the emergency stairs, gets tired and pontificates 'Obviously in a real situation we'd take her all the way down, but this is just a drill, so I think we can leave her here' (Gervais and Merchant 2003: 65). As she is abandoned on the stairs, the camera pulls away as if *it* is embarrassed, stressing that Brent is showing more than linguistic ineptitude in a phrase like 'the wheelchair ones' and that our own laughter must involve some kind of ethical judgement.

In the end that judgement is sought not on Brent but on the medium that has spawned him. The characters in the series who do not court the camera are free to have a more complex relationship with humour; for Tim and Dawn, a bright young couple who yearn for each other and never muster the courage to admit it, it is pleasure for its own sake (Tim plays a series of creative practical jokes on Brent's rigid sidekick Gareth, including setting his stapler in jelly) and a subtextual way of energising their agonisingly slow courtship. Laughter and play are thus reclaimed for the interior, private world as opposed to the fly-on-the-wall.

Brent does, across the run of *The Office,* become humanised, but at considerable psychic cost. The series alerts the viewer to a savage aspect of reality television ignored by those making it a sitcom substitute. The comedy of eccentricity occupied an eternal present; reality shows move in time. They involve change, and that is painful. From the outset, redundancy is a real possibility in *The Office;* the first series ended with actual job losses, announced by Brent with characteristic egocentricity – 'That's the bad news: the good news is, I've been promoted' (Gervais and Merchant 2002: 250). A wider world is also present, although it is mediated through one of Brent's on-camera attempts to grab the moral high ground through our culture's fetishisation of laughter:

> Yeah, sure, she'd say she's the boss, yeah, but there should be no ego when you're pulling together to create something good, yeah? It's like, Comic Relief, yeah? I'm out here in Africa and I'm seeing the flies and the starvation ... and she – if she is the boss – she's in the studio with, you know, Jonathan Ross and Lenny Henry – and they've got their suits on. They're doing their bit, they're counting the money. Good luck to them. But, their hands are clean, while I'm down here in the office with the little starving kids ...
>
> (ibid: 29)

At the end of the second series, in which he has persistently tried to undermine the authority of his bosses with humour at the expense of doing any work, he is made redundant. He receives this news on Red

Nose Day, dressed in an ostrich outfit. Briefly, the camera reveals his utter panic and terror.

This is a comedy of entrapment in which the trap wins – not on the cyclic basis that allows Anthony Aloysius to bounce back and fight another day but as a single event on a time line that continues to move forward. Brent's world has a rigid hierarchy of which *visible* aspects are comic – Gareth's title of 'Assistant *to* the Regional Manager' is a source of continual struggle over the preposition of power – but the real control is offscreen; only the *effects* of the real power source are visible, and hence there can be no comic struggle with it. Rather than an unacknowledged source of privileged insight, the camera reveals itself to be confined to the trap too, unable to show who really controls Brent's world.

More polemical ending

By making us aware of those external power relations *The Office* implicitly demands that viewers should undertake the work of the old, humanising 'window on the world' which showed us Anthony Aloysius or Harry Worth as subjects rather than comic objects. When Brent's shock indicates he is aware of his own inner emptiness the moment is deeply embarrassing: for Brent, for his bosses who have to get through the unpleasant business of sacking him, and for us. This is partly because it is so very public: while other characters occasionally cheat the camera by refusing to play up to it (Tim switches off his lapel microphone when he wants a moment with Dawn) Brent does not seem to know how: he has been playing to camera even more than usual on his Red Nose Day high. His fate is not a comic comeuppance in the eternal cycle of sitcom, but has real economic and social implications. The viewer is no longer certain what to do with the laughter sparked by the sight of Brent in his ostrich outfit: it is undeniably there, but it is laced with guilt and discomfort. The camera has made us an unwitting part of Greer's 'school bully' culture, and we have to decide what to do about it.

In the new millennium we will be increasingly less likely to meet Harry Worth enjoying his moment of silliness with the window. Reality TV has redefined the boundaries of fantasy and play; it may be that it will make them impossible. The comic eccentric, safe in his window on the world, could recruit us as warriors against the sillier side of the class struggle or just to join him in an untouchably private space where he could protect us from embarrassment. Brent and his like cannot: but that sense of discomfort in the stomach and that heat on the face demand that we think hard about the ethical use of television.

8

Comedies of Sexual Morality and Female Singlehood

Deborah Chambers

Introduction

A group of popular television situation comedies circulating among Anglophone nations since the 1990s show how situation comedy has been reshaped to feature the lives of single women. White, professional women are being identified as the source of shifting lifestyles and morals in comedies such as *Sex and the City* (HBO and Channel 4), *Absolutely Fabulous* (BBC TV), *The Vicar of Dibley (BBC)*, and *Ally McBeal* (Fox and Channel 4). These are echoed in films such as *Bridget Jones's Diary* and its sequel which explores anxieties associated with finding a partner, sustaining intimate relationships and breaking down traditional forms of gender identity. Key themes of dating, being 'unattached', working in a masculine profession, non-marital sex, lone parenthood and cohabitation are delved into from the perspective of heterosexual urban women in their thirties and forties. Focusing on the independence and sexuality of the single woman, these comedies are morality plays structured by a comedic engagement with gendered identity.

A striking feature of these narratives is the characterisation of women's single status as a problem which, through humour, becomes a source of profound pleasure for audiences. We are invited to pore over the incongruities of female singlehood. The pleasure of the female singleton sitcom text involves a nervousness about the predicaments of the single woman in her attempt to carve out an identity that transcends the conventional married, domestic role. Making singlehood into an *issue* is a process focused mainly on women since heterosexual white men's single status remains largely uncontested (unless situated in the context of post-divorce or 'mid-life crisis'[1]).

A long history of labelling unmarried women as deviant confirms the deep unease with which female autonomy has been traditionally regarded in Western societies. Spinsterhood began as a legal term in the seventeenth century but, in stark contrast to the positive image of the bachelor, it carried negatively charged meanings. A fear and hatred of single women, epitomised by their association with witches in folk tales and religious customs, ensured that they were often left unemployed and poor. The nineteenth-century denunciation of the spinster as a female deviant was articulated through the image of a plain or ugly middle-class governess figure who received little respect (Jeffries, 1986). However, singlehood offered choice for women with wealth and education, with examples from the nineteenth century of single women pursuing careers in journalism and novel writing. Public anxieties about the sexual energy of the spinster in the 1920s and 1930s were fuelled by sexologists who advocated sex only as part of marriage. The fact that Marie Stopes's *Married Love* (1918) declared sex to be just as important for women as for men prompted even more concern about the spinster (Jeffries, 1986; Oram, 1992).

Despite recent research evidence that many women who live alone enjoy their single lifestyle,[2] the historical unease with the unmarried woman remains with us today, borne out by sociological studies of attitudes towards them (Stock and Brotherton, 1981). The status is deviant in narratives ranging from Victorian novels, to inter-war Hollywood Melodrama, to 1950s and 1960s British films (see Fink and Holden, 1999). Today, spinsterhood remains a deviant spectacle. And this is despite the fact that the single person household is now one of the most rapidly rising household types in Western nations including the USA, Britain and Europe (see, for example, Heath and Cleaver, 2003; Chandler et al., 2004).[3]

With a focus on sitcoms, this chapter examines the role humour plays in popular fiction in articulating changing attitudes towards sexual morality and female singlehood in a post-feminist age. The humour serves to interpret shifting anxieties about the moral principles associated with romance, sex, marriage, work and friendship in singles comedy. Here comedy acts as a powerful device for investigating the moral uncertainties concerning women's increasing sexual and economic independence, as 'bearers of a new world'.[4] I argue that through the use of irony, humour functions to perpetuate the prejudices against the single woman. It portrays her as both aggressor and victim. It gives licence to audiences to simultaneously scorn the singleton as an assertive subject representative of rampant individualisation and, conversely, to treat her as victim of social fragmentation: a lonely, isolated and marginal subject incapable of commitment. I argue that the female body, narcissism, unrequited love, insecurity and confession are sites of ironic humour and moral ambiguity in female singleton sitcoms, preserving powerful ideas about the disorderliness of being 'without a man'.

From family sitcom to women's sitcom: the unruly woman

Whereas the television sitcom began in the 1950s by focusing largely on the antics of 'the family' (Spigel, 1992), today's sitcoms reflect the upsurge in single person households resulting from delayed marriage and rising divorce rates from the late twentieth century. Examples of the ways that situation comedy has traditionally used the family as the site for staging humour are shown by early American comedies. In an episode of *Father Knows Best* (1954–63, CBS and NBS), called 'Margaret's Vacation', wife Margaret is bored with doing housework and wanders off from the family home to a downtown club where she entertains the idea of becoming a beatnik before being hauled back to her claustrophobic suburban dwelling (cited in Spigel, 1997). Through comedy, the conventions and constraints of family morality were affectionately mocked but, paradoxically, with the effect of confirming and reinforcing the nuclear family form as inevitable.

By the late 1980s, a 'golden age' of female comedy was identified by the American news media,[5] exemplified by *Rosanne* (ABC), *Murphy Brown* (CBS), and *Designing Women* (CBS). This cluster of sitcoms addressed the experiences not only of unruly married women but also *single women*, with the 'normal' family and marriage hovering in the background as a moral aide memoire. Significantly, the protagonists in these new women's sitcoms were represented as 'unruly woman': disorderly, unstable, strident women. *Rosanne*[6] epitomised this disruptive female creature, which has a long history both in high art and television sitcom (Rowe, 1990, 1995). Her working-class status, obesity, sexual awareness, tattoos and breach of conventional standards represented the disruptive qualities of feminine excess and laxity (ibid: 410). Rosanne literally *embodied* unruliness, allowing her to transcend her role as an object of sexual and domestic desire to serve her own interests. As such, the character of Rosanne invited reprisal from patriarchy and the ideology of middle-class decorum (Butler, 1993; Chambers, 2001). While a key strand of contemporary comedy is the objectification of the fat female body as a *problem* in a society that demands thinness, female obesity also embodies gender ambiguity and instability (Hole, 2003). Rosanne refuses to perform a consistently subordinate role: she is both powerful and subordinate. Rather than simply being the butt of the comedy, the fat female body represents a threat to patriarchy.

In the American sitcom, *Designing Women*,[7] Delta Burke as Suzanne Sugarbaker was also portrayed as badly behaved on and off screen, and was fired after five seasons. She was single but, like Rosanne, was obese and was depicted in the press as brazenly outspoken, contemptuous of motherhood and she dressed in a sexually provocative manner. Suzanne's disdain for motherhood and childbirth was based on the statement: 'Why do they think you must be married and a mother? I don't mind being alone; I'm very self-sufficient'.[8] As Butler says, her main crime was a lack of interest in men, and a failure to get her weight down to make herself attractive to them.

Rosanne's and Delta/Suzanne's obesity and unruliness rendered these characters *excessive*. Both characters constituted icons of unruly femininity. Obesity signified both a loss of *personal control* as sexy, to-be-looked-at femininity (Mulvey, 1975), and a retrieval of *public control* as someone less feminine and to be reckoned with. The fact that Burke attracted so much media attention prompted the producers to dedicate a whole show to the issue of women's obesity, titled 'They Shoot Fat Women, Don't They?'.[9] This was echoed a decade later in *Sex and the City*'s 'They Shoot Single Women, Don't They?'. The fat woman and the female singleton are linked in their potential to connote unruliness and subversion (Hole, 2003: 321). Size, disorderliness and single status were key attributes, linked together, then, to signify excess in women's sitcoms.

Female unruliness plays a crucial role in later female singles comedies such as *The Vicar of Dibley*, *Absolutely Fabulous* and *Sex and the City* which rely on rendering women both absurd and liberated through the accent on feminine excess. Importantly, these comedies pushed beyond the barrier of the traditional family setting, to be located in sites such as the public sphere of paid work and the city. Yet they persistently refer back to a traditional familial sexual morality which they transcend, yet by which they are judged as deficient. Singleton sitcoms are, accordingly, inherently polysemic. By incorporating quite oppositional values, humour functions to explore the moral tensions of female independence through multiple meanings. Jeremy Butler (1993) draws on Paul Attallah's (1984) concept of 'discursive hierarchy' for an understanding of unruly women's sitcoms. 'Discursive hierarchy' contributes to an understanding of the way various systems of meaning in situation comedy are either validated or discredited. 'Discourse' is deployed as a system of representation or language that works ideologically to fix the meaning of a particular topic (Fiske, 1989: 14). It works in such a way as to make those meanings appear commonsensical in serving the interests of the particular section of society from which the discourse originates.

Following Fiske, Attallah (1984) uses discursive hierarchy to uncover the ways in which aspects of situation comedies can be identified by the importance given to each of the discourses operating in specific circumstances. Extending Attallah's concept, Butler argues that a meta-discourse is generated in a TV programme, structured by specific discursive hierarchies within it. A hierarchy of conflicting discourses is measured according to 'ideological priorities that obtain within the host culture'. The point is that a number of conflicting moral discourses are set in motion in sitcoms, in order to provoke the tension needed for humour. In many women-centred sitcoms of the 1980s certain disruptions, such as those associated with unconventional modes of femininity, were repressed through the validation and restoration of a patriarchal framework of values by allusion to conventional romance discourse as a legitimate and authentic goal. The collision of feminist and patriarchal discourses then came to the fore with the unruly, outspoken woman exposing some of the absurdities of family life for women.

Singlehood as feminine excess

The single woman who enters a male-dominated profession, as in *The Vicar of Dibley* or *Ally McBeal*, allows the exploration of this collision of feminist and patriarchal discourses in contemporary comedy. Irony, satire, caricature and masquerade are central. Bodily presence remains crucial, often expressed in bodily extremes. The female singleton is highly sexualised or coy, obese or extremely slim, tarty or frumpy, bohemian or fashion fixated. The funny female body provides, then, some clues about how humour represents and produces new feminine identities. Transmitted between 1994 and 2000, the BBC's *Vicar of Dibley* is an example of a female singleton comedy in which female obesity, singleness and women's advancement into male-dominated vocations are themes used to explore ideas about the independent woman. Feminine excess, displayed by the weight and assertiveness of Dawn French, is exploited as a site of humour rooted in moral rupture, both as power and punishment.

A new female vicar surprises the parishioners of the quiet rural village of Dibley in the form of Geraldine Grainger, played by Dawn French. She is, however, not only the wrong sex but also both single and excessively overweight. At one discursive level, this single, fat woman takes up too much public space; her fatness signifies the embodiment of power (Hole, 2003). Geraldine is opposed at every opportunity by David Horton, hostile, pompous, self-opinionated chair of the parish council, who feels threatened by her. He is determined to remove her from the parish in Episode 1. Yet she overcomes village antagonism by charming parishioners with her fun-loving optimism. How can this contradiction be played out?

The hierarchy of conflicting discourses operates by subordinating the threat of a woman entering a man's profession. It works by superimposing on the monstrous-feminine subject, who occupies both a man's job and a grotesque fat female body, an intriguing depiction of the vicar of Dibley as cuddly, attractive and therefore harmless. She is both a public figure with authority as vicar, yet her duties can be interpreted as maternal. Her obesity, signifying the (feminist) threat of entering a man's space, is transformed into both maternal femininity and a personal weakness for chocolate. Sex and food are, as Hole (2003) points out, mutually exclusive desires within the context of normative femininity. Geraldine's potential power is rendered trivial by a (patriarchal) foregrounding of her obesity as comic and maternal.

A necessary theme in female singleton sitcoms is failed romance. Not only is this vicar's power discredited by her gender and her weight, but also by unrequited love. Her sexual desire is tamed by her quest for old fashioned romance. Wishing to marry, she takes a fancy to David Horton's brother, Simon with whom she has a brief but passionate affair before finding out he has a girlfriend.[10] This is further punishment for taking on a male role. She is, then, fated for several reasons: for being single, for being overweight, for occupying a man's profession, for being sexually demanding *and* for searching for traditional love and romance. Her penalty makes her likeable and manageable. The need for the character to be accepted in the community as 'normal' means she must be unthreatening: so humour also functions to mock Geraldine's excess, causing her to be hilariously self-deprecating.

Absolutely Fabulous takes feminine excess a stage further by exploring it through the personal anxieties of two middle-aged, debauched women. The humour in the sitcom is focused on the characters of Edina and Patsy as female caricatures, as monstrous feminine: chaotic, hysterical, single, 'mature' women. *Ab Fab*, launched in 1992, was so successful it ran, with a break in between, until January 2004. Edina Monsoon, a 40-something PR [public relations] person played by Jennifer Saunders, is a member of the idle rich: a spoilt brat more childish, volatile and impulsive than her mature 20-something daughter Saffron (Julia Sawalha). Edina lives off the alimony provided by two ex-husbands. Unable to grow up, she is trapped in 1960s youth culture: but her take on life lacks the political consciousness of the period, and is fastened on its self-indulgent features. Her whole personality reeks of excess: she overindulges in shopping, all kinds of stimulants and alcohol. She staggers from one fad to another (Buddhism, colonic irrigation, extreme diets) and from one crisis to another. When things go wrong, she makes a complete spectacle of herself, being loud and offensive.

Edina runs her own PR business but works infrequently and ineffectually. She spends most of her time with her best friend Patsy Stone (played by Joanna Lumley), fashion director of a glossy magazine. Patsy also rarely works and her excessiveness is further conveyed by her trashy appearance and a number of bad habits: substance abuse and sexual rapaciousness. Her amorality is indicated by the fact that she slept with her boss to obtain her glamorous job. Patsy sports a ludicrously tall blonde beehive hairstyle, too much lipstick and is dependent on Edina economically and for companionship. As such she is deeply jealous of Edina's prim and moral daughter. The very virtuous Saffron is central to the humour by acting as a moral counterbalance to the wicked Patsy and as comic foil to these two irresponsible middle-aged women.

Reminiscent of *Rosanne* and *The Vicar of Dibley's* use of humour, Terrie Waddell (1999) refers to the display of feminine excess in *Ab Fab* as female grotesque, associating it with medieval carnival culture wherein large women were signified as abundance. Celebrated and honoured during the two weeks before Lent, women were allowed to break free from feminine conventions. Similarly, taboo female behaviour, such as being drunk in public, is explored in *Ab Fab* with images of feminine decorum being ruptured as a key feature of the independent woman.

The feminist style of the humour in *Ab Fab* dominates in a number of ways that emphasise the *disorderliness* of being without a male partner as menacing. First, the absence and irrelevance of men is significant. The four main characters are women, with men such as Saffron's father putting in rare appearances. Second, the clownish characters of

Edina and Patsy, and their playing out of mid-life crisis allow a blazing critique of conventional representations of motherhood and family life by ridiculing the maternal instinct and notions of women's liberation (Waddell, 1999).[11] This challenge to patriarchal discourses is lost in later singleton comedies such as *Sex and the City*.

The amoral urban spinster: *Sex and the City*

Public preoccupations with the lives of professional, single women pro-liferated from the late 1990s, as part of the fashion for 'personal narrat-ives', characterised by the rise of a whole new genre of Chick narratives: Chick news columns, Chick Lit, Chick Flicks and Chick sitcom. Here, subversive images of the female grotesque are overlaid and arguably eclipsed by a return to representations of the stylish inde-pendent woman, wracked by narcissism, who failed to get married by her late thirties. Within explorations of deviant behaviour among single women, feminine excess and transgressive aspects of feminine decorum continue to be sources of humour, shifting from excessive weight, swearing, drinking and smoking, to excessive slimness and self-disclosure about sexual hang-ups and exploits. The grotesque female subject is no longer obese, though a large bottom was a significant aspect of Bridget Jones's imperfect character. The singleton was self-absorbed, needy and self-deprecating. And the disorderliness of being without a man was articulated as a deficiency.

The emphasis on self-disclosure and self-discovery in female single-ton narratives forms part of a new theme of humour across the popular media. Tales such as *Bridget Jones's Diary* and *Sex and the City* typify a trend in autobiographical and confessional narratives characterised by a public personalisation and sexualisation of relationships. Exemplify-ing the cross-mediated, hybridised nature of the genre, Helen Fielding's 'Bridget Jones's Diary' column began life in the British newspaper, the *Independent* in 1995 and moved to the *Daily Telegraph* in 1997. It was then published as a book in 1996,[12] launched as a film in 1999, and a sequel in 2004. Framed within the traditional heterosexual romance fantasy of Jane Austen's *Pride and Prejudice*, *Bridget Jones's Diary* was set within the parameters of self-conscious, post-modern reflexivity. This approach and attitude was also reflected in Candace Bushnell's column in the *New York Observer* which acted as the basis of the TV sitcom *Sex and the City*, launched in 1998. Coated with lashings of irony, this eruption of female singleton fiction embodies the rise of a new, parodic 'girlishness' (Heller, 1999: 12).

These 'chick' narratives were riddled with paradoxes in the representation of the single woman, sanctioning women's revelations of personal insecurities, vulgar habits, sexual conquests and sexual defeats
(Heller 1999). This, then, is the font of the humour. The confessional
characterises the reflexive references to previous popular narratives,
setting up an apparently critical distance from romance myths through
the use of post-modern irony (Whelehan, 2000). Negative attitudes to
single women are conveyed in the British press, for example, in the
context of single mothers, 'selfish' career women, 'ladettes' and young,
female 'binge drinkers'. Through self-conscious references to feminism
and the media's ambivalent attitudes to single women, irony serves to
hide the ethics of humour.

Today's singleton sitcom humour forms part of wider popular cultural articulations of the single professional woman as a symbol of negative social change. The humour works by conspiring with traditional
prejudices, fuelling the notion of female singlehood as a form of
deviance. It exposes the single woman's narcissism and insecurity, con-
trasting her with the patriarchal notion of the virgin and mother-figure
of femininity of a mythical bygone era: pure, altruistic, self-sacrificing
and nurturing. Fated as female deviant, today's single woman figures
both as aggressor and victim. On the one hand, she is presented as
someone free to break social rules and transgress cultural boundaries.
This is exemplified by the promiscuous Samantha in *Sex and the City*,
whose freedom and independence we are invited to envy. On the other
hand, the female singleton is portrayed as a sad, lonely and socially
subordinated individual. The tomb stone with 'spinster' carved on it in
a dream sequence of *Bridget Jones: Edge of Reason* (2004) provides this,
albeit ironic, sense of dejection. We are provoked into laughing both *at*
and *with* this disorderly subject by fuelling former gender prejudices.

In the television serial *Sex and the City*,[13] the contradiction of envy
and scorn works by the humour feeding on public anxieties about a
post-traditional, individualised urban society. This show centres on the
candid and sexual gossip of a group of smart, urban, professional,
30-something female singletons. Importantly, the series ditches the
traditional settings of family or neighbourhood community, typical of
earlier women-centred sitcoms, in favour of downtown metropolitan
chic. First released in 1998, *Sex and the City* was one of the first TV
sitcoms to provide a forum that venerates heterosexual women's *group*
friendships as a context for exploring female sexual desires. The hot
gossip about sex is the glue that binds the characters of Carrie,
Samantha, Miranda and Charlotte together. As Arthurs (2003: 93) states:

Aesthetic boundaries replace moral boundaries so that men who can't kiss very well, who smell, who are too short, or whose semen tastes peculiar are rejected on those grounds.

This seems to promise, then, a subversive discourse of humour.

At one level, the power of metropolitan, affluent, professional and single-status femininity is being flaunted in *Sex and the City*. The 'to-be-looked-at-ness' of female characters jettisoned by Rosanne, Burke, French and the *Ab Fab* duo, is celebrated with a vengeance by *Sex and the City's* insolent and feisty protagonists. However, feminine excess is signified not by obesity but by excessive thinness and insecurity. Cloaked in the glamour of New York chic, these women have bodies carefully sculptured to mirror the sexy young female models presented in women's glossy magazines, with the latest hairstyles, make-up, clothes and accessories worn and flaunted in a number of settings: fashionable art galleries, restaurants, clubs and bars. Paradoxically, while the gossip between these women is typically set in trendy Manhattan eating places, the protagonists are so slim that food barely passes their lips. Excess and self-denial go hand in hand.

Following Mary Ann Doane (1982), the emphasis on the theatricality of femininity is so excessive in *Sex and the City* that it too becomes a masquerade. Although masquerade offers a radical potential to the narrative, this is disavowed by a slippage in which the women's bodies, actions and anxieties are represented as commodified self-gratification and fetish (Akass and McCabe, 2004: 179). At another level, then, *consumer culture* replaces the *ethical self* as an ideal (Arthurs, 2003: 93). The pleasure-seeking, post-modern, singleton female subject is rendered profoundly *amoral*. The humour works on a particular, materialistic version of femininity, a market-led post-feminism focused on consumption and 'style' (Whelehan, 2000). The protagonists' agency is fated by their lack of self-confidence and their faith in consumerism (Arthurs, 2003). The consumption of fashion and men signifies overindulgence and hedonism which, in turn, signifies feminine excess.

The selfish singleton

Christopher Lasch's (1979) pessimistic interpretation of individual agency in modern urban society highlights the problems people have in adapting to the processes of social fragmentation characterising late modernity. He observed the acceleration of narcissism: a rising tide of self-love and an increasing reluctance by rootless individuals to care for and share with one another. In an urban landscape of atomised, self-centred subjects, the modern individual becomes intensely self-absorbed, restless and fragmented, with no moral universe in which to anchor his or her identity. In contrast to individuals in the past who drew on society as a means of personal progression, the narcissist is isolated and obsessed with survival of the inner self and the desire to stay young.

The fear of encroaching narcissism and individualisation raises important ethical questions about how the 'personal' is being constituted, as a *gendered* subject position during late modernity. Significantly, female singleton humour provides a channel through which these issues can be pored over. For example, in *Sex and the City*, our four Manhattan women are labelled self-absorbed, fickle and reckless. At the same time, they are cast adrift: necessarily *orphaned* through the narrative absence of their parents and wider kin, in a metropolitan quagmire of shifting values. The focus on the expanding single phase of women's life course as comedy allows the popular media to proclaim selfish singlehood as an essentially feminine trait. The moral codes of humour in female singleton comedies work by mocking and contesting growing *female* autonomy as selfish femininity. Since male autonomy has been at the centre of the Enlightenment project of the rational self it remains unchallenged (see Lloyd, 1984; Pateman, 1988). By rendering the female singleton amoral and irresponsible, women's apparent freedom and choice come to stand for the sense of social decline.

A crucial theme of *Sex and the City*, like all Chick fiction, is unrequited love as the punishment for female independence. This is played out through the use of familiar constructs that define the ideal woman in order to highlight the grotesqueness of feminine singlehood. As Kim Akass and Janet McCabe (2004: 178) point out:

> The comedy works by juxtaposing the two classic patriarchal fantasies of virgin and whore – fantasies that are projected onto women, and in so doing, introduces us to the raw material which will be used time and again throughout the series to create humour.

Playing with this deceit of a patriarchal signifying system that defines the female self, the conventional romance fairy-tale narrative is scrutinised and pored over in *Sex and the City*. Irony is the humorous device used by the characters to negotiate these patriarchal tales (Akass and McCabe, 2004). While exploring the dilemmas of being unmarried, the protagonists frequently draw the conclusion that being single is preferable to faking happiness with a man, as exemplified in the episode, 'They Shoot Single People Don't They?'[14] (Arthurs, 2003). The fantasies of heterosexual romance, the search for Prince Charming, and perfect motherhood are explored in the show, but friendship and consumption are either chosen or offered as the favoured refuge. Or are they?

While a feminist discourse is drawn on as a system of representation that challenges the sexual objectification and subordination of women, it is repeatedly destabilised by the presence of oppositional discourses through the use of irony. Like narratives such as *Bridget Jones's Diary* (1999), its sequel, and *Ally McBeal* (1998), the emphasis in *Sex and the City* is on the *neediness* of single women (Whelehan, 2000): these women are always defined by their relationship to men. Despite the intermittent celebration of single status, and despite their smartness and apparent confidence, the moral outrageousness of the brazenly expressed sexual desire of these women is disarmed by the ironic treatment of singlehood as an unremitting dilemma: as a marginal status. The irony hides this prejudice.

The championing of feminist ideals is undermined by the single woman's preoccupations: her desire for Mr Right and 'happily ever after', her celebration of sexual independence, yet her fear of being perceived as a slut. The radical potential of mocking patriarchal myths, emphasised by Carrie Bradshaw's narrative agency, is further disavowed by anchoring the characters within both *consumer* and *confessional* discourses that work to expose this neediness. Thus, as Akass and McCabe (2004) argue, we find that these daring, smart, single women find it difficult, if not impossible, to shake off the myth of seeking true love. For example, the four women are invited to the stylish, fairy tale wedding of an unlikely celebrity couple in the episode, 'I Love a Charade'. The wedding prompts them to believe that the single woman's pursuit of Mr Right is legitimate. As Akass and McCabe (ibid: 198) put it:

> It reminds Samantha that she is still hurting over her recent split with Richard Wright, Charlotte that she may be falling in love with her 'just sex' Harry Goldenblatt, Miranda that she feels more for Steve than she is willing to admit, and Carrie that she should take another chance on romance with Jack Berger. But it also reveals how the series never seriously questions the pursuit of Mr Right as a worthwhile goal, summed up by Carrie: 'Some people are settling down, some people are settling in, and some people refuse to settle for anything less than butterflies.'

The breakdown of extended kinship networks and traditional community ties in late modernity forces individuals to become self-reliant,
both materially and emotionally. The erosion of traditional authority
means that individuals must *actively choose* their sexual partners rather
than rely on marriage alliances once formed by the parents. Forsaken
by family and traditional community, urban subjects rely on their own
resources, forced to create their own forms of togetherness in order to
create a coherent life course and identity (Beck and Beck-Gernsheim,
1995 and 1996). Love has become a central part of the rise of individualism and the most important way of finding meaning in life (Beck
and Beck-Gernsheim, 1995). Anthony Giddens (1992) states that men
and women are now developing relationships characterised by 'conflu-
ent love', an emotional and sexual equality based on a 'pure relationship' no longer bound by the needs of sexual reproduction or tradition.
Since today's singleton is no longer controlled by the rules of tradition,
she forms a self-identity in the context of the 'pure relationship': a
relationship entered into voluntarily and contingent on delivering
satisfaction to both parties (Giddens, 1992: 58). Freedom to choose and
end intimate relationships is critical to the way the humour works in
Sex and the City to convey the unmarried woman as both aggressor and
victim. This pure relationship is more democratic than relationships in
the past: it is a contract between two equal individuals which can be
ended when one or both partners wish to leave. The conditions of the
relationship are subject to continuous renegotiation: we stay together
'until further notice'.

Giddens's (1992) views about individualisation as a democratisation
of relationships in late modernity may appear more optimistic than
Lasch's narcissistic loner, but the voluntary nature of personal relationships raises important issues about the vulnerability of commitment
and emotional security which get played out in female singleton
narratives. Through ironic humour, audiences are alerted to the pitfalls
of modern day spinsterhood in *Sex and the City*. By exposing the *vulnerability* associated with the freedom of being able to choose ones own
relationships, these women become victims. This unruly subject is
dogged by superficial relationships characterised by short-lived
romances, one-night stands and the fear of emotional rejection. *Sex
and the City's* satirical humour invites audiences to laugh at the retribu-
tion delivered to smug, self-satisfied single women who seem to 'have
it all', who appear to be succeeding in a man's world at a man's game.

Within attempts to explore the anxieties of today's ephemeral
relationships in popular media narratives, urban societies' fears get pro-

jected on to those new social groups who emerge, apparently confid-ently, from the late modern system of fragmented social ties. The humour implicates single women in citing individualism and rampant narcissism as the cause of social decay. Her demand for equality in inti-mate relationships allows the humour to confirm an assertive dimen-sion to the character of the female singleton: she is pushy, needy and dissatisfied with the men she dates. The narrative ensures that she gets her comeuppance later. She must then disclose her disappointments to her friends within a confessional discourse. This over-confident woman is rendered hilarious in symbolising the wider moral panic about fem-inine individualism. Treated as a threat to the moral fabric of society, sardonic humour allows an exploration and then sets up a denuncia-tion of women's independence.

Sex and the City's Samantha represents the most strident and excess-ive aspect of femininity but, importantly, she is also rendered victim: she regularly crumples under her own vulnerabilities. Despite being morally outrageous, Samantha's fear of being judged badly by men and predatory women is a persistent trigger of humour. In one episode, she faces public humiliation when attempting to banish her facial wrinkles with something more extreme than Botox injections. Unveiling her new look at Carrie's book launch, she reveals the gruesome, red-raw effects of a too-recent chemical face peal. But she tries to 'save face' by pointing out that women should not be pressured into covering up their efforts to combat ageing: 'Women shouldn't have to conceal in the shadows because they've had cosmetic surgery which society nearly demands of them' ('Plus One is the Loneliest Number'[15]). And in the episode called 'The Big Time',[16] the onset of the menopause is signified as humiliation rather than a triumph, such that it prompts Samantha to make love to an unexciting older man. But on discovering her menstrual flow while love-making, Samantha celebrates rather than suffering embarrassment at being caught in a predicament, declaring that there are 'plenty more hot studs in this hot, pre-menopausal woman's future'. As Akass and McCabe (2004: 192) state, 'one taboo replaces another'. The independence and boldness of female singlehood can be celebrated as long as it is, at the same time, humorously denunciated.

The confessing singleton

Confession underpins female singleton humour as a spectacle. It acts as the framework for the hilarity and absurdity of the singletons' predica-ment and, in *Sex and the City*, serves to seal group friendship. Self-disclosure allows hilariously outrageous thoughts and actions to be broadcast. And this reflects contemporary trends, since intimacy must be continuously monitored as part of the reflexive project of the self and is regularly subjected to scrutiny and reflexively organised as part of our lifestyle and self-identity. Under conditions of ontological insecurity, the management of anxiety becomes a highly valuable personal skill.

In the past, the sense of self and regulation of personal behaviour traditionally stemmed from the family, religion and education. Today's independent, isolated individual has medical counselling, forms of personality management, self-help books and manuals that advise on self-improvement. Lasch (1979: 140) asserts that this emphasis on the individual and self-help exemplifies the narcissistic personality. Life becomes an endless search for psychic self-help, of 'getting in touch with one's feelings', of 'learning to relate'. However, for Giddens, the rise in expert systems is a positive feature of late modernity. It allows individuals to act reflexively by evaluating and using the knowledge from therapists, sexologists and psychologists to help assess their intimate relationships. The self-help literature is aimed at affirming individuals' right and obligation to make a strong commitment to themselves, helping individuals face the ontological insecurities of modern life. Confiding is therefore an important personal tool: you must 'love yourself' and 'be in touch with yourself' before you can commit to others (Knorr Cetina, 2001). Sardonic humour exploits the central role self-disclosure plays in the management of the modern feminine self: a person's 'feelings' are exposed and pored over to portray a disorderly female subject.

Ironic humour appears to render the confessional discourse of Chick comedy both subversive *and* conformist. These singletons apparently undermine dominant discourse by talking about topics deemed taboo by a patriarchal discourse. Menstruation, menopause, single parenting, blow jobs, premature ejaculation, male impotence and homosexuality are all commented on with relish. The confessional discourse allows these women to *confront* their neediness according to Akass and McCabe (2004: 183) who state that 'talking about sex may yet provide an emancipatory strategy to help women change the stories and reconfigure the fairy tales in their favour.' The female confessional, here the butt of humour, is not only a 'space of women's hystericalisation, but is also the space of feminist politics: it takes a second woman to help confer meaning on the first woman's experience' (Modleski, 1999: 22, cited in Akass and McCabe, 2004). The humour works to expose taboos, confer solidarity between the women, and through the use of *double entendres*, it also apparently debunks traditional romance narratives.

At first blush, then, it would seem that the critique of patriarchy's romance discourse is rescued by generating subversive humour through a confessional discourse. The friendships and dates with men get played out by exposing and thrashing out personally embarrassing situations and scandals. As Arthurs (2003) asserts, the show offers a site for the self-reflexive satirical investigation of sexual taboos and respectability. Is the confessional therefore a source of strength, signifying subversiveness by addressing taboo subjects? While this emotional discourse is highly pleasurable and ruptures taboos, the comedy reminds us that it is also profoundly risky, involving humiliation. The radical bid for autonomy is derailed by the protagonists' excessive emotional vulnerability and the reminder that singlehood is *spinsterhood*. The assumption among Carrie and her friends is that the singleton is a profoundly marginalised category. The confessional mode drives feminism down the hierarchy of discourses by allowing the neediness of the women to eclipse the pleasure and wisdom of their status. It undermines the protagonists' power by confirming the status of unmarried woman as lack, as UN-something. The single woman thereby experiences spectacular humiliation in searching for alternative self-fulfilment. Accordingly, the humour forms part of the management and regulation of single women by exposing them as victims, emphasising that independence is a highly risky business.

As one critic, Stacey D'Erasmo states:

> The new single girl, tottering on her Manolo Blahniks from misadventure to misadventure, embodies in her very slender form the argument that not only is feminism over. It also failed: look how unhappy the 'liberated' woman is! Men don't want to marry her![17]

The image of victim works, then, through the confessional, centred on the independent woman's failure to find romance and form a family of her own. It works by disregarding or trivialising the wider set of social conflicts affecting the roles of women in late modernity: the conflict between women's employment and economic independence, and women's assigned nurturing role, making them responsible for the caring of society's young and elderly. The confessional constitutes a site of struggle in exploring women's identities, but satirical humour evokes the isolation conveyed by *lack of family ties* to render a fun-loving, independent singleton a vulnerable, self-absorbed, amoral subject. To underline this desolation, Sarah Jessica Parker, who plays Carrie, is depicted in the media as 'a wanton, desperate woman roaming the streets of New York' (Rudolph, 1998: 13). Accordingly, the female singleton is denied the status of heroine, of champion for a new feminism or even a new, woman-centred ontology. The patriarchal fantasies confirming traditional family values remain intact. Personal vulnerability guarantees the intensity of the women's friendships. Ultimately, though, these stray singletons' dependence on one another is treated as a substitute for marriage.

Conclusion

Today's woman's sitcom is part of a new genre in which singlehood apparently stages a challenge to patriarchal discourses. The humour does not, however, expose the moral dilemmas of singlehood in a neutral fashion. Through a series of comedic devices involving irony, the female singleton is characterised as unruly and vulnerable. The self-reflexive irony masks yet at the same time reinforces social prejudice against single women. Against a background of rising single-person households and professional single women who occupy public space and delay marriage, the comedy confirms the disruptiveness and failure of being without a male partner. It exposes the dilemmas of decorum and decency associated with the anxieties of being single, of bonding with friends rather than family, and struggling to deal with the myths of traditional romance narratives. The female singleton is both an object of desire and scapegoat who embodies the aspirations and social problems of late modernity: the desire for self-determination leading to the collapse of family values, a breakdown of community, encroaching selfishness and urban fragmentation.

Forming part of a rising moral panic about selfish individualism, the humour surveys women as problematic subjects who are increasingly demanding equality in the workplace *and* in their private lives. Women's agency is castigated for disrupting traditional patriarchal structures and discourses, for jeopardising traditional family values. Women's quest for self-fulfilment and equality in intimacy is apparently being sought 'even if it clashes with the needs of spouses and children and even if it leads to the break-up of a marriage', as sociologists such as Andrew Cherlin (1992: 38) suggest. Women are being blamed for withdrawing from their responsibilities as nurturers and carers in favour of the search for personal autonomy, prompting governments to express concern that women's increased participation in the workforce and independence may result in a declining supply of carers.[18] Meanwhile, men's freedom and choice in forming social and personal relationships remains largely uncontested. Although an enormous amount of caring is celebrated in *Sex in the City* in the form of friendship, such compassion is invalidated as a social bond that exists outside the traditional nuclear family. Ironic humour works to regulate and discipline the female singleton who is reined back under patriarchal control within sitcom narrative resolutions. As a morality tale, female singleton humour warns us that despite being a growing category, the female singleton remains a subordinated subject: a spinster.

Notes

1 See, for example, *Manchild* (BBC, 2002). The series starred Nigel Havers as Terry, Anthony Head as James, Ray Burdis as Gary, and Don Warrington as Patrick. It was, however, quickly designated a flop, indicating that the exploration of men's personal weaknesses within a confessional discourse remains taboo.

2 See, for example, Forsyth and Johnson (1995); 'Going Solo' BBC Single Life Survey (2002).

3 Longitudinal data from UK Censuses between 1971 and 2001, for example, corroborates other research indicating that increasing numbers of non-retired people are living alone, with single occupancy households rising by 31 per cent (Office for National Statistics, 2003). This trend of living alone is a characteristic across Europe (Kaufmann, 1994).

4 See Oram (1992).

5 For example, Jane O'Reilly (1989) wrote an article in the *TV Guide* titled 'At last! Women worth watching' (quoted in Butler, 1993).

6 *Rosanne* premiered on ABC in 1988.

7 *Designing Women* was produced between 1986 and 1993.

8 Quoted in Kiester (1986: 56).

9 The title refers to the film, *They Shoot Horses Don't They*, from a novel by Horace McCoy.

10 'Autumn', Series 3, Episode 1.

11 Gary Burn, '*Absolutely Fabulous*': British Situation Comedy, available at: www.museum.tv/archives/etv/A/absolutelyfa/absolutelyfa.htm

12 Published by Picador.

13 *Sex and the City* (HBO) was aired from June 1998 to February 2004 on US and British television networks.

14 Episode 16.

15 Session 5, number 5.

16 Season 3, number 8.

17 Quoted in Akass and McCabe (2004: 8–9).

18 See, for example, the document produced by the British government, 'Caring about Carers: A National Strategy for Carers' (Department of Health, 1999).

9

The Ambiguities of Comic Impersonation

Michael Pickering and Sharon Lockyer

Introduction

Impersonation is an ambiguous term. It can be viewed positively, as for instance when we say of a certain act that it is a good impersonation or when we regard a certain comedian as an effective impersonator. It can also be viewed negatively, so drawing on other meanings of the word. This happens when we use it in its associations with imposture, duplicity, fabrication and fraudulent practice. The word impersonator is then more or less equivalent to the old-fashioned, but still effective description of someone as a mountebank or quack. The description makes us think of falseness, trickery and manipulation. By implication it carries the accusation of cheating or being a cheat. The accused stands indicted of having usurped someone else's role or identity for an underhand purpose. The negative connotations attached to the term do not usually apply to the profession of acting or comedy, for then impersonation generally has a positive sense, with the label of impersonator as comic entertainer being regarded as wholly legitimate, but it would certainly carry at least some of these connotations if we regard a particular comic impersonator as trading on a demeaning or derogatory stereotype, whether of gender, ethnicity or some other social category. The term would then be one of ethical criticism, involving a negative evaluation of the impersonation.

In this chapter we argue against the polarisation of the term's positive and negative semantic dimensions. We need to keep the term's intrinsic ambiguity of reference and meaning constantly in view, not least because it strikes to the heart of our ideas about theatre and acting. Both of these nouns are similarly ambiguous. They may denote dramatic performances that are greatly valued, but also be used for purposes of critical exposure, as for instance when someone is impugned for being theatrical or when someone's attempted demonstration of sincerity is dismissed as 'merely acting'. The ambiguity of both positive and negative meanings is central to the directions which critical evaluation can take in response to particular acts and performances, both on stage and screen, and in everyday action and interaction. We draw on the semantic ambiguity when we make a judgement about good or bad acting or, in the case of impersonation, about false and genuine identity, with both positive and negative judgements implying a contrast with their opposite. Critical judgement relies on this contrast, for without it both aesthetic and ethical values would be seriously diminished.

This is too simple because it assumes that we always know how to make such judgements. It assumes that we understand that such judgements will be appropriate to the case and context to which they are applied. This is not necessarily so. We are confounded not so much by the ambiguities involved in the notion of impersonation, but rather by particular acts of impersonation and how we should respond to them. This is especially the case with comic impersonation, for then we may respond to the ambiguity of persona and person with hesitancy, uncertainty or caution, knowing we could move in alternative ways but not feeling surefooted enough to take steps decisively in either direction. We need also to recognise that the reliance of judgement on a contrast with an opposing evaluation can become ossified into a fixed set of binarisms, such as masculine/feminine, white/black, rational/irrational, which then provide a fertile breeding ground for stereotyping and ideological constructions of the Other. This constitutes a refusal of ambiguity. Remaining open to ambiguities means moving interactively between the different options of interpretation they point towards and refusing their polarisation. The strategy in this is of trying to avoid ill-considered jumps into peremptory judgement.

Impersonation and offence

Working with an initial sense of hesitancy and uncertainty of response, and attending closely to ambiguities as part of the process of interpretation and evaluation, seems to us especially important in relation to comic impersonation. One of the most pressing reasons for this is that comic impersonation permits offence, or at least a considerable extension of the ethical limits within which this is allowed. The limits are never fixed or even clearly defined, for if they were the possibilities open to humour and comedy would be seriously constrained. When a comedian dresses as another, and acts in character, this extends the potential scope of humour, allowing it to encroach on what would be taken as ethically dubious territory if the performer was 'playing it straight'. It becomes considerably more difficult for the butt of a witticism or joke made by a comic impersonator to react with hostility when they feel they have been deliberately offended, and not only because the rhetoric of justification for humour slips so readily into position. The difficulty is due primarily to the fact that a negative reaction would not be directed at a 'real' person. Reacting in this way to a comic persona or assumed media personality would suggest a gross lack of sophistication, or an overweening propensity to take oneself too seriously and of not being able to 'take a joke' or laugh at oneself. That would only compound the comic damage and perhaps give it a degree of permanency it wouldn't otherwise attain. It would make the targets of the humour appear doubly foolish. Being the butt of a comic impersonator puts more pressure on people to laugh at themselves, along with the audience, than would be the case with a 'straight' interviewer who is making jokes at their expense. The most appropriate positive response, apart from joining in with the laughter, is to parry the wit with further wit, even to the extent of upstaging the comedian.

What is specifically peculiar to comic impersonation is not only that it permits offence but also that it makes light of the offence at the same time. This is possible precisely because the offence is placed within a comic frame. The comic frame prepares, intends and sets the ground for a non-serious response. A 'perception of incongruity, absurdity, perversity – insideoutness or upsidedownness' – generates amusement or hilarity so long as this is simultaneously accompanied by an assurance, especially in a disharmonious situation, that in spite of the comic disorder, things are nevertheless somehow *in order* (Guthrie, 1903: 258–9). It is the comic frame that provides this assurance. At the same time as the assurance is given there arises the difficulty of knowing how comic is the comic offence. We all know that what is said in jest can sometimes be meant in earnest. The comic offence may leak back into serious discourse, or be taken as having a serious point above and beyond the immediately comic frame in which it is uttered, either through frame-jumping or code-switching by the comedian or through divergent responses and interpretations on the part of any individual audience member. Again, the difficulty is greatest for the butt of the humour. It involves a switchback ride of negotiation. How are the impersonator's utterances and accompanying facial or bodily gestures encoded, within what frame or register are they being made, how are responses to be made to the ambiguities of meaning involved in the talk, and within what modalities of social and cultural interchange are issues of identity and difference to be conducted? Negotiating these questions require various moves and shifts in which it is potentially easy to take a fatal false step. The ritual test in the synthetic impersonator/guest relation involves ensuring that this never happens.

We want to explore issues concerning intention and understanding, utterance and response, and identity and difference as these are raised by the ambiguities of comic impersonation and offence. In doing this we focus on two contemporary examples of comic impersonation: Mrs Merton and Ali G. These particular examples are chosen because they illustrate two types of impersonation within the same gender category, but involving women of one generation disguised as women of another generation, and men of one ethnic category disguised as men of another ethnic category. In embodying these types, Mrs Merton is relatively straightforward so far as our understanding of the impersonation is concerned, though what is achieved within the impersonation is at times quite subtle. With Ali G the lines of switchover in the impersonation are considerably blurred, leading to interpretative difficulties which are nevertheless integral to the humour. These differences seem to us intriguing and worth trying to unravel. The ambiguities that are central to our discussion lead us to move alternately in two ways. We're concerned with the aesthetics of comic impersonation and how it is able to achieve certain modes of joking relationship. At the same time, we want to consider the ethical questions raised by such aesthetics and how the discourse of comic impersonation may be critically negotiated. As should be clear by now, these alternative ways of considering humour and comedy are thematically central to the book as a whole.

Mrs Merton and Ali G

Mrs Merton (Caroline Aherne) was pioneered in local radio in the North West of England as a spoof agony aunt before transferring to a BBC TV chat show that ran for five series between 1995 and 1998. The persona was of an ostensibly prim, demure, middle-aged, lower middle-class woman from Stockport. Aherne wore clothes that were decidedly out-of-date – floral print dresses, sensible sandals, thick spectacles with old-fashioned frames, greying hair in a perm. Her whole sartorial ensemble was a deliciously studied antithesis of glamour and chic. The studio setting complemented this in its mimicry of ordinary homeliness: a coffee table with lamp alongside Mrs Merton's armchair, a live audience of mainly elderly folk, and a comfy sofa for the guests – billed on the cover of the video for the second series as 'the sofa of dreams', a sly play on the well-known alternative name of 'Theatre of Dreams' for Manchester United's Old Trafford stadium. In the focal centre of this setting, Mrs Merton was posed as somewhat parochial, sweet and naïve.

Aherne used this demeanour, along with her costume and make-up, as a screen from behind which she could ask rude, provocative or challenging questions of her celebrity guests, make sudden descents into sexual matters, or sally forth with some outrageous double entendres. The impersonation allowed her to turn on their head such conventions of the chat show as acquiescence to the celebrity status of her guests, affirmation of their achievements, fame and prestige, and confinement of the host or hostess to instigating or prompting the talk rather than being in discursive command of its direction and flow. Such subversions of form were generated, licensed and protected by the comic impersonation. The theatrical persona was effective in inhibiting a hostile response from the guests to whom she had said something untoward, rude or insulting. The ambiguity baffled some guests – was this insolence a joke, or for real? – as for example when she asked athlete Kris Akabusi: 'Do you have to plan your tactics before the race or do you just try and run faster than the other blokes?'; or when she said to the soap opera and *Carry On* actress, Barbara Windsor: 'That's what I love about you Barbara, you're one of us ... You're like a big film star, but you're still as common as muck!' Perhaps most notoriously, having first disarmed her with praise for being 'very pleasing on the eye', she asked Debbie McGee the seemingly innocent question: 'but what first attracted you to the millionaire Paul Daniels?'

Like Mrs Merton, Ali G (Sacha Baron Cohen) did not cross-dress, but whereas her manifestation of provincial middle-age seemed to be quite 'true to life', to use the age-old expression, Ali G embodied a deliberately exaggerated copy of cosmopolitan hip-hop youth. He dressed and spoke as, to quote TV producer Harry Thompson, 'a disaffected wannabe homeboy of the suburbs, the kid stuck in Staines who dreamed of Compton or Watts' (Collins, 2000: 2). The dream was lived out in the clothes and lingo: Tommy Hilfiger skull cap, wraparound yellow shades, bright yellow sportswear, Lion of Judah pendant, heavy gold rings and exorbitantly priced trainers, accompanied by gangsta-style argot and streetwise hand and arm gestures. The choice of Staines in Middlesex was apposite as the backdrop to the dream. It is a typically bland English town whose only claim to fame is that it was the place where linoleum was first commercially manufactured. In the words of the local journalist, Shannon Kyle: 'Staines hasn't got much of an image' (Stuart, 2000: 7). Existing socially in Staines while living imaginatively in places like the Bronx was central to the Ali G act. The absurdity of the contrast was the source of the comedy.

Ali G's comic persona succeeded precisely because it represented cultural failure. It was appreciated as a comic impersonation because we know we cannot slip out of our social selves at will, that it is nonsense to assume, as does Glenn Ward, that 'we can more or less freely fabricate our identities for ourselves' (1997: 124). With the singular exception of confidence tricksters, such fabrication is the preserve of actors and actresses, who of course only maintain the illusion of being someone else for a limited (and licensed) duration. While Ali G's wigger persona was considerably more ambiguous than this, its source in youthful white fantasies of crossing the ethnic tracks is clear enough. Michael Eboda has written of how the Radio 1 rap DJ Tim Westwood, the white, middle-class son of a bishop, stopped the music at the 1997 Notting Hill carnival and addressed the crowd: 'Right, I want all the white people to move to the back and let my big-dick niggers come to the front.' This risky play on an entrenched black stereotype met with a roar of approval from both white and black people in the crowd. Apparently, Cohen considered Westwood's whiteboy appropriation of hip-hop culture to be hilarious, 'and so the character of Ali G was born' (Eboda, 2000: 12; see also Leigh (2000) on Westwood, and Bennett (1999 and 2000, ch. 6) on wigger appropriations of hip hop).

His first manifestation on television was on Channel 4's *The 11 O'Clock Show*, a five-series, late-night satirical sketch show that ran between 1998 and 2000. In his mock-media billing as the 'Voice of Youth', he conducted a series of interviews with such figures as politicians, judges, retired soldiers and media celebrities who were at first unaware that the interviews were spoofs and they were being stitched up. (Later on, such guests as the Beckhams and ex-Tory MP Neil Hamilton were aware of this but proved more or less willing lambs to the slaughter.) We confine our attention to these spoof interviews because of the ways they compare and contrast with those conducted on *The Mrs Merton Show* (in 2000, Ali G went on to have his own programme, *Da Ali G Show*, on Channel 4). When the show was first aired, some of the television audience thought Mrs Merton was an actual person and wrote to compliment her. Her guests of course were keenly aware of Mrs Merton's comic impersonation and the subversive play on chat show conventions that were integral to the programme. She usually asked questions or made remarks specific to the lives and identities of her guests, whereas Ali G was interested in tackling certain 'big questions' or topical issues facing contemporary Britain, such as education, religion, war and the environment. Ali G's interviews were usually one-to-one, with no one else involved, while Mrs Merton used a studio audience to provide laughter, occasional applause, and questions or comments when invited to participate. For both, comic impersonation served as a means of guying their guests, ridiculing them, stringing them along or sending up their pretensions, pomposity or pride. Through their impersonation they were able to deflate powerful or prestigious figures. By feigning innocence or stupidity they inveigled people into talking about delicate or even taboo topics of conversation. The humour hinged on the ambiguities of meaning, role-play and identity and the perturbations of their interpretation, ranging from the interviewee apparently not realising that the discourse involved was comic, to the delicacies of negotiating the best or most appropriate response.

Ambiguities of interpretation

In his celebrated monograph on jokes, Freud noted that 'the great, the dignified and the mighty ... are protected by internal inhibitions and external circumstances from direct disparagement' (1905/1960: 149). The degree of protection they enjoy is dependent on the hierarchical structure of the society in which their status is inherited or acquired. Even though this is less so than in Freud's time, the comic ridicule in the interviews of Ali G and Mrs Merton continued to require the removal of this protection for the tables to be turned and the disparagement to be effective. The humour associated with the disparagement then seemed to exonerate Ali G's offensive language and sometimes brash treatment of certain difficult or sensitive topics. A characteristic technique of Mrs Merton was to ask an innocuous question or offer a flattering statement so as to lull her interviewee into a state of false security before dropping a bombshell question or remark. For instance, when talking to glamour model Melinda Messenger, she suddenly delivered a double whammy question: 'Of course, there's more to you than just your breasts isn't there, because you won Rear of the Year Award as well didn't you?' After talking to ex-footballer and football pundit Jimmy Hill, she announced that 'we have another old man coming on now'. The demure smile so often accompanying these pronouncements belied the intention to comically insult her guest. The humour was achieved by switching abruptly from guileless sweetness to barbed sarcasm, so taking her guests off guard and making their deflation part of the amusement.

Humour in everyday life generally relies on an assumed contract between those party to it. This was clearly not the case with some of Ali G's and Mrs Merton's guests, even though they had willingly contracted in to the talk. The tacit contract then applied more specifically to the interviewers and 'us', their media audience, who are indirectly elevated by the comedian in gaining a sense of superiority over those in positions of authority or prestige. Such figures were excluded from the discursive relationship active within the contract, whereas audience and host or hostess shared 'a delicious intimacy, which is pleasurable and powerful in itself' (Purdie, 1993: 5). This was achieved through witnessing a sudden (if temporary) descent from seeming superiority, power or prestige. It is there that the amusement lay. The audience recognised the joking situation, along with the host or hostess, so were party to any comic incongruity that went on. With our two examples, the extent to which the guest became the butt of the joke depended on whether or not they were cognisant of what the changed humour contract facilitated, and the manner in which they responded. What seemed to happen then was that – in Ali G's case for instance – his crudeness or crass stupidity were, within the temporal span of the exchange, exonerated by the humour generated by the farcical out-of-contrast responses of those enjoying elite or celebrity status. This created the enjoyment of a temporary superiority gained from being 'in the know' so far as the impersonation and its motives were concerned; we went along with and tacitly endorsed the impersonation when in other contexts it would have been met with a wholly or partially negative evaluation.

This was somewhat more complicated in *The Mrs Merton Show* because she had a studio audience as well as a television audience. An interview may have been interrupted by an invitation to the studio audience to participate, to comment or ask their own questions, whereupon, in her usual unassuming manner, Mrs Merton could toy with them as she did with her guests. The collusion between hostess and audience remained intact despite these sallies, for what remained paramount was the comic strategy of backing her guests into an awkward corner and belittling them for the amusement of her mock-studio and media audiences. The temporary suspension of their celebrity status or self-arrogated aggrandisement was what counted, both for the humour and for the pleasure of temporary superiority enjoyed in seeing people of power, wealth and fame brought down to size and treated 'just like another household product, like bleach or cheese' (Parker, 1998: 8). Mrs Merton's questions were deliberately meant to embarrass or deflate – to remind her guests that they were not as powerful or significant as they may have assumed, as their celebrity status may have suggested, or their hostess's charm and ironically performed politeness may have initially confirmed. The ambiguities of meaning in her conversation were generally open to those who had ears to hear them, while in Ali G's *11 O'Clock Show* interviews they were closed off to his interviewees. With the former the humour derived from the degree to which guests were willingly duped; with the latter it derived from audience awareness that the interviewees had been unwillingly duped. For example, this happened to Tony Benn, the socialist politician and writer, who was asked to take part in a television programme designed to introduce young people to politics. He wasn't particularly surprised at Ali G's questions since he tends to lament, and do what he can to overcome, the de-politicisation of contemporary youth. He found these questions absurd, crude and offensive, as for instance when Ali G seemed to regard Margaret Thatcher as a communist, or when he claimed that all 'bitches' became pregnant simply in order to get on benefit. Benn was completely hoaxed by Ali G's apparent ignorance and naivety, but stood his corner and engaged in a serious debate with the issues that were raised (Benn, 2000; cf. North, 2000)

Regardless of these differences, Ali G and Mrs Merton both exploited their personae in order to beguile their interviewees into responding to their questions. For example, Ali G used deviations from standard English as these are standard in his adopted patois – 'Is it because I is black?' became a catchphrase – while Mrs Merton spoke a more standard English in a somewhat diluted East Lancastrian accent. She used the guise of her persona to be both coy and frank at the same time, as for instance when she referred to sex or intimate parts of the body. Her advancing age, apparent parochialism and outward respectability added to the comic value of her rude or insulting statements and questions. In both cases the impersonation enabled the two comedians to make offensive comments that would not otherwise be sanctioned, in what was again an instance of comic licence where characters are constructed 'so that an audience can engage with the action and yet be barred from implication with it' (Purdie, 1993: 75). In an ordinary social setting they *would* inevitably be drawn into implication with it, and that is the crucial difference associated with the comic impersonation, not to mention the mediated relation to it. The issue of comic licence in these cases was legitimised by the ways in which the characters were stereotypically identifiable as an ultra-trendy youth and nosy old lady, but because audiences were simultaneously aware of both persona and person concealed behind the persona, what was said retained its quality of ambiguity, enabling it to operate in both comic and serious discourses at one and the same time. Was that a joke or meant to be taken straight? Was the utterance sincere or insincere? Such questions couldn't be answered straightforwardly, as they can in everyday social interaction where the limits between serious and comic discourses are more strictly maintained (though of course ambiguity and pretence occur there as well). Ambiguities were at the helm of the comic discourse in both cases.

Questions and comments from Ali G and Mrs Merton involved a studied mix of astute intelligence and feigned naïvety or obtuseness – and again this was used to beguile their interviewees. The naïvety and obtuseness drew them in under a false assurance even when they knew they would be gulled, with the humour being primarily if not exclusively at their expense. The qualities they feigned protected them when they said things that in other contexts would have been deemed offensive, as overstepping the mark. Their sharp-witted intelligence showed at the same time in their ability to gauge when they had reached the limits of comic risk beyond which the humour would fail. In different ways both audiences and interviewees had to accept that they were being taken to such limits for the sake of fun. The emphasis was on the fun rather than the offence; even Mrs Merton would occasionally (though perhaps disingenuously) say 'only joking'. The risk was nevertheless crucial to the humour, for interviewees didn't expect some of the questions directed at them by characters who appeared to lack sophistication or intelligence, or in Ali G's case with his first set of interviews, who appeared unlikely to constitute a threat to their image and reputation. In both cases, guests at times responded to questions within the framework of serious discourse, patiently explaining their position or point of view and attempting, at least initially, to maintain the framework they were unaware was being subverted by the comedian, for comedians in general are constantly on the lookout for 'the discursive display of opposing interpretative possibilities' (Mulkay, 1988: 26). At any time the ground could disappear comically from beneath their feet.

In such contexts, any question or statement, even any word or single reference, can be taken in two ways, its ambiguity regarded as an open opportunity to confound the divisions between seriousness and comicality. The humour lies in the awareness of this on the part of the comedian and either initial or total lack of awareness of it on the part of the interviewee: do they get the joke or not? And how will they respond? As we indicated at the outset, the trick is in being alert to ambiguity and willing to run with it, while the test is failed if the intent is to nail down utterances to a fixed and unitary meaning. When this happens, interviewer and audience move between alternative scripts while the interviewee sticks to only one of these in a way the audience regards as in itself naïve, obtuse or incompetent. If the audience doesn't recognise or accept these shifts, the humour will fail and the ethical question of offensiveness would then be on the cards. Aesthetic enjoyment of humour in these cases depends on participants embracing the ambiguities at play, being willing to be taken back and forth from one regime of discourse to another, or to accede to the shift between one semantic association and another, as in the pun's 'bisociation of a single phonetic form with two meanings', its 'two strings of thought tied together by an acoustic knot' (Koestler, 1964: 64–5).

An example of dual meaning occasioning this split between impersonator/audience and comic butt occurred in Ali G's interview with the Tory MP, Sir Rhodes Boyson. Ali asked 'Sir Rhode' about one of his pet subjects, discipline in schools, so baiting the trap for the next question, when the pun was sprung: 'Do you believe kids should get caned?' 'Sir Rhode' was snared by the single literal meaning of the word caned; being ignorant of its synonymous use for getting stoned on marijuana, he agreed in earnest. Ali G's comic triumph – 'Wicked man, you believe kids should be caned, even in school' – was assured when 'Sir Rhode' emphatically repeated the end-phrase – 'Even in school'. Popular culture rose in splendid ascendancy over official culture as Ali G lured his 'victim' further on by asking: 'Don't you think if you get caned in school you can't concentrate as well?' Still not realising he was holding only one semantic string, 'Sir Rhode' replied: 'Well, I was caned and I've concentrated all my life'. This enabled Ali G to pull the acoustic knot even tighter – 'YOU were caned! Respect, man!' – as if this upright pillar of the Establishment was a lifelong participant in the drug culture he so opposes. The comic absurdity was complete.

Gary Younge summarised the source of this absurdity when he wrote of Ali G: 'the less his interviewee gets the joke, the funnier the joke' (2000: 3). By contrast, Mrs Merton didn't usually seek to play on anyone's ignorance in this way, for part of the appeal of her show was in waiting to see if her guests appreciated the barbs cast in their direction and could respond in good part to remarks designed to deflate them. To take a similar example involving different meanings dancing on the head of the same word, Mrs Merton made deft play on the word 'column' when interviewing the portly *Daily Mirror* astrologer, Russell Grant. The primary meaning of the word referred to his daily newspaper article, but through this another sense of the term reared its head in metaphorical reference to a cylindrical shaft or pillar. The pun made the primary meaning secondary in favour of direct sexual allusion combined with indirect mockery of her guest's rotund appearance. The bisociation of phonetic form involved in this was accepted by all parties, including the butt of the joke. There was no confusion between mainstream and subcultural meanings of a word on which the punning operates. It was the confinement of the pun to a word known and accepted in both of its operational senses by all participants that allowed the butt to respond harmoniously within the joking frame initiated by Mrs Merton. We can best illustrate this by clearly distinguishing the main component parts of the chat in the table below.

Camera shot and scene	Speaker	Facial Expression	Vocal Track
CU of Mrs Merton sat in her armchair	Mrs Merton	Straight faced	And you know your column really sticks out I've always thought, I bet you can't see it yourself
	Audience		HA HA HA HA HA HA HA
CU of Russell Grant throwing his head back laughing	Russell Grant	Smiling, aware of the play on words	Darling I am going on a diet and hopefully I'll be able to see it in the future
	Audience		HA HA HA HA HA HA HA
CU of Mrs Merton with cutaway to RG	Mrs Merton		Do you ever look at your own column in the [M]mirror and compare it to all the others?
CU of RG	Grant	Straight faced, but then starts to smile	That's the only way possible these days
Same frame for RG	Mrs Merton	Not in shot	I bet it is yes

The humour here is old and new. It is in continuity with the humour of the old music hall and the old male republic of the pub, and it descends directly from the English humour associated with comic seaside postcards, especially those of Donald McGill. For instance, one of these depicted a middle-aged man with a huge paunch, under which sat a small child; the caption read: 'Can't See My Little Willy'. Another showing a man holding a monster stick of seaside rock, the bottom of which rests in his crutch, reads: 'A Stick of Rock, Cock?' (Buckland, 1984: 63 and 97; see also Orwell, 1942/1977; Alderson, 1970; Green, 1976). Against the long lineage of such sexual puns, the excerpt displays various innovative features in transgressing the generic rules and norms of the chat show. Such transgressions were initiated in earlier shows by Dame Edna Everidge and Clive Anderson, particularly in tending to dominate the discursive space available, broach sensitive or taboo issues, refuse rites of deference to guests and attack their amour propre. Mrs Merton adopted these features while also specialising in comic insults. These were rarely as humiliating as some of those administered by Edna Everidge (Tolson, 1991), but they directly undervalued, challenged or contradicted a guest's positive face and did not permit mitigation, repair or redress. In his discussion of these insults, Martin Montgomery (1999) has shown how they combined compliment and insult in such a way as to accentuate the negative evaluation, or manipulated ambiguities of meaning in order to facilitate the face-threatening remark. Guests usually ignored or evaded the implied secondary meaning, especially when it related to what is usually regarded as private or personal, but occasionally, as with Russell Grant, the threat to face would be openly accepted and playfully entered into, so in a way saving face gracefully, or at least more effectively than through evasion or tacit acceptance of the temporary loss of face. In all cases the open ambiguity of the person/persona distinction allowed a continual oscillation between actual insult and mock insult, and serious and comic registers, in such a way as to keep guests or members of the studio audience on their toes but never able to react legitimately as the offended party. The physical appearance of the persona guaranteed the acceptability of the verbal utterances and so transformed insults into humour. This was quite different to the humour of Ali G where confinement of the interviewee to serious discourse meant condemnation as an abject failure to appreciate the joke. It was the interviewees who then became the joke, whether deservedly or not depending on the butts in question and how they stood in your estimation of them.

Ethics of identity

We have noted that the comic impersonations of Ali G and Mrs Merton played upon two existing stereotypes, the wannabe gangsta rapper from the South East of England, and the prim, but saucy nosey-parker from the North West. The aesthetics of their comedy were dependent on the way the stereotypes were developed within their personae. But there were notable differences in the extent to which the personae were identifiable, reliant on the initiating stereotype and dis-sociable from the person behind the ethnic or generational mask. Although to begin with some members of the television audience regarded Mrs Merton as a 'real person', people were generally aware of the impersonation, and of some difficult aspects of Aherne's off-screen life that were pried into by a prurient tabloid press. Aherne remained clearly distinguishable from any comic personae she adopted.

In previous sections, we have pointed up the ways in which the two comedians used their personae in different ways even though the impersonations in themselves opened up similar comic possibilities. The stereotypical features of Mrs Merton's persona were playfully, almost affectionately referred to and played with by Aherne, while their reference to regressive provinciality was almost celebrated in their demonstrative visual and aural echoes among members of her region-ally homogenous studio audience. It was almost as if Aherne was dress-ing up as a putative older version of her erstwhile provincial self, as if this was the future and she had remained 'up north', never having become a television comedian, actress and scriptwriter. Impersonation in her case provided the ground for her comic manipulation of seman-tic and discursive ambiguities in her talk show, but the two sides of these were generally kept open, just as the distinction between person and persona remained clear. This was not the case with Ali G.

Ali G was an extreme version of the ambiguity inherent in imperson-ation. This created various difficulties. Little is known of Cohen beyond the fact that he is a Jewish Cambridge graduate. Even these small morsels led to the question of why an educated white man would want to play an uneducated, misogynistic, homophobic black man? Cohen's refusal to participate in interviews out of character, or to offer any personal information beyond coming from a north London Jewish family and being a university graduate, only helped to fuel debate about either his persona or his relation to it. Such debate revolved around the question of who was impersonating whom in the persona he presented. This was an updated wigger, that much was clear, and the few biographical details known made the contrast between a white public school boy and a black streetwise kid obvious from the start. But was he a white, Jewish or Asian wannabe? Or was he a white man pretending to be a white man pretending to be black, a white man pretending to be an Asian pretending to be black, or a Jewish man pretending to be an Asian pretending to be a white man pretending to be black? The permutations seemed endless. Were these multiple ambiguities some kind of satire on post-modernist suppositions about the fluidity of identities? Had the persona been deliberately constructed as multilayered in order to critique Romantic conceptions of authentic, unitary, internally coherent individualities? Was this to over-intellectualise the issue? Maybe it was, but who was being mocked in the impersonation? It was this question which cut to the heart of the controversy.

The pretensions and obsessions of 'yoof TV' were clearly in the frame, but why not then create an ageing character seduced by the glamour and fashion of the 'mee-ja' and fawning over every latest youthful trend? The answer to this question lies in the whole point of the impersonation presented in the original interviews conducted by Ali G, for there it was set up in order to dupe interviewees into thinking he was 'for real' and responding accordingly. These have been celebrated as media comedy because they deflated figures of fame, authority and power by making them give 'straight' answers to comically intended questions or outraged responses to outrageous observations. A conventional interview with a representative of the legal system would involve serious questions concerned with justice or the procedures of jurisprudence. Ali G suggested to Judge Pickles that women should not be chosen as jury members because when 'they have the painters in', everyone – as he finds with his girlfriend, 'me Julie' – is guilty. In these uses of it, Ali G's impersonation was intended both to blend in with and become indistinguishable from the stereotype, and to annul the person behind it so far as his 'victims' were concerned. Without this, the comedy would have fallen flat. If they, as well as the television audience, had been aware of the impersonation qua impersonation, as audiences were with Mrs Merton, the spoof 'yoof' interviews would have failed to be funny. Without the protection of comedy, they would have been plainly offensive. It was only when people began to ask about who was being represented in the impersonation that the question of black stereotyping came to the fore.

Extending from the early nineteenth to the late twentieth century, there has in Britain been a popular entertainment tradition of blacking up by white people, as there has in North America and elsewhere, with Jewish men prominent in various acts and shows on both sides of a blackface Atlantic (see Rogin, 1996). While the British tradition needs to be understood in its own historical and cultural contexts, we have inevitably to ask if or to what extent Ali G represents a latter-day version of the practice of blacking up, whether in Britain or the United States. There are clear differences – but can Ali G be dissociated from the tradition that comes before him, particularly as this was associated with racist stereotypes of black people? Some black people evidently felt that he couldn't, precisely because of this negative cultural legacy. The comedian Curtis Walker objected strongly to Ali G: 'I don't like the concept of a white guy playing a black guy and when he is playing to a stupid stereotype it is even worse ... If we were to flip the script, would a black comedian be allowed to dress up as a Hasidic Jew, make jokes about being a tight-fisted, highly ambitious mummy's boy and do a similar sketch?' (Eboda, 2000: 12). This is a legitimate question because of the similar legacy of derogatory stereotypes associated with Jews and Jewish culture. Walker explicitly compared Ali G to Al Jolson, one of the most famous Jewish exponents of blackface minstrelsy, while comedian and TV presenter, Richard Blackwood, regarded the humour as being directed primarily at black men and the kinds of stereotypes 'we are fighting every day' (Malik, 2002: 104). Comedians Felix Dexter and Gina Yashere compared the media frenzy over Ali G with the relative disinterest shown to black comedians themselves, and the ghettoised slots in which they do appear as, specifically, black entertainers (Lenny Henry being the token exception). Other black people take a significantly different view, offering praise instead of criticism.

Paul Gilroy, for example, has been effusive in his admiration for 'shape-shifting' Ali G, seeing him as a protean representative of an emergent multicultural Britain, a critical response to post-imperial melancholia and a celebration of a vertiginous post-colonial cosmopolitanism. He thinks left-wing and anti-racist critics are misguided in situating Ali G in the long blackface tradition of imitation and exploitation, dismissing them as 'the positive-image school of cultural critique' (Gilroy, 2004: 146). For Gilroy, criticising Ali G on the grounds of cultural appropriation, dilution or mongrelisation is anachronistic; it fails to see how the humour plays on 'contemporary anxieties over the integrity of marginal identity and the fluctuating value of minority

culture' (ibid.). Along with this, 'the central unifying joke underpinning all Ali G's work is supplied by an antipathy toward the stultifying
US styles and habits that have all but crushed local forms of the black
vernacular and replaced them with the standardised and uniform
global products of hip-hop consumer culture' (ibid: 147). We can see
this satirical take easily enough in the comic incongruity of the Staines
Massive or the adolescent sexual fantasy filtered through US ghetto
slang with which Ali regaled the *Staines & Ashford News* when he spoke
of dreaming about 'bonin Mariah Carey while havin Jennifer Lopez
trombone me from behind' (Stuart, 2000: 1). There was clearly this
satirical element in the persona and act, but at what price? As Gilroy
acknowledges, there were also 'hordes of illiterate juveniles' for whom
Ali became a hero (2004: 147). Anti-youth aspersions aside, we're back
with the Alf Garnett syndrome of anti-racist critique being misinter-
preted as racist celebration. Is the Alf Garnett syndrome an inescapable
problem in a pluralist culture, and can we separate the stupid from the
sly Ali G? Along what line can we distinguish subtle and pliable audience decodings from crassly literal acceptances of his comic impersonation? Where does studied multicultural undecidability end and
unstudied racial prejudice begin?

This is where Curtis Walker's question about Jewishness is pertinent.
The impersonation is neither susceptible to being used in a two-way
manner, nor amenable to being used by blacks themselves (a point of
contrast with such British Asian comedy as *Goodness Gracious Me*). Since
it is not it tends to block subversion of the stereotype from within, and
encourage its reinforcement from without. This is especially the case
when such ambivalence surrounds the issue of whether the racial
stereotype is being identified with or lampooned, and whether
entrenched prejudices of class, religion and race are being ridiculed or
upheld. Of course, the ambivalence was central to Ali G's popular
appeal, for in creating a melange of subcultural styles and symbolic references he signified in a number of different ways at once and pulled
punters and critics into a perilous guessing game. He invited them to
misinterpret his own misinterpretation. But again, where does this leave
the stereotype? Does the laughter undermine or underwrite the stereotype? When Ali G asked James Ferman, Director of the British Board of
Film Classification, 'why did they ban Chocolate Orange?', does this
appear to stem from the wannabe or from the stereotype on which the
wannabe parasitically draws? Who is the mocker and who the mocked?
When Nicholas Lezard wrote of Ali G that 'one of satire's purposes is to
afflict the comfortable and comfort the afflicted, but *whom* does he

afflict?', this again was a fair question and not a species of misplaced liberalism (Lezard, 2000: 6, our emphasis).

It could be said that Mrs Merton's comic persona invited a nostalgic celebration of a past Northerness in English regional culture – all cobbled streets, flying ducks and homemade jam. This would not only confine nostalgia to clichéd associations and a one-dimensional regret for changing times. It would also ignore the way everyday down-to-earth provinciality became valued over and above metropolitan glamour and sophistication, and the way the relative openness of the persona/person relation was used comedically in continuity with a sub-versive matriarchal tradition in English culture. This is where the nosey-parker stereotype was turned into something much more incis-ive and honest. Mrs Merton's ambiguities were in the end more those of discourse in relation to experience, rather than discourse with refer-ence to identity, whereas Ali G's teetered equivocally between both. For this reason, as Gary Younge pointed out, Ali G's act was finely bal-anced on the thin edge between social satire and racist buffoonery, leading inevitably to contradictory responses and contradictory sources of laughter. This means that there cannot be a central unifying joke underpinning all Ali G's work, but it does mean that the joke itself is possible precisely because our lives are ethnically entwined in contem-porary multicultural Britain. Although this allows the polysemous codings of Ali G's comedy, the problem nevertheless remains that while anyone can play at being black, you still have to be white to be white.

Bibliography

Adorno, T. W., Frenkel-Brunswik, E., Levinson, D. J., and Sanford, R. N. (1950) *The Authoritarian Personality*. New York: Harper & Row.

Akass, K., and McCabe, J. (2004) 'Ms Parker and the Vicious Circle: Female Narrative and Humour in *Sex and the City'*. In Akass, K., and McCabe, J., *Reading Sex and the City*. London: I. B. Tauris, pp. 177–98.

Alaoui, Sakina Mrani (1991) *Aspects Of Discourse Structure Of Humorous Anecdotes In Ordinary Conversation And Chat Shows*. PhD Dissertation: Strathclyde University.

Alderson, F. (1970) *The Comic Postcard in English Life*. Newton Abbot: David & Charles.

Altemeyer, B. (1988) *Enemies of Freedom*. San Francisco: Jossey Bass.

Apte, M. L. (1985) *Humour and Laughter: An Anthropological Approach*. New York: Cornell University Press.

Arthurs, J. (2003) '*Sex and the City* and Consumer Culture: Remediating Postfeminist Drama', *Feminist Media Studies*, 3(1), pp. 83–98.

Attallah, P. (1984) 'The Unworthy Discourse: Situation Comedy in Television'. In Rowland, W. D. Jr., and Watkins, B. (eds) *Interpreting Television: Current Research Perspectives*. Beverley Hills, CA: Sage, pp. 222–49.

Attardo, S. (1994) *Linguistic Theories Of Humor*. Berlin: Mouton de Gruyter.

Attardo, S. (2001) *Humorous Texts: A Semantic And Pragmatic Analysis*. Berlin: Mouton de Gruyter.

Bakhtin, M. (1970) *L'Oeuvre de François Rabelais*. Trans. A. Robel. Paris: Gallimard.

Bakhtin, M. (1981) *The Dialogical Imagination*. Ed. M. Holquist, trans. C. Emerson and M. Holquist. Austin, TX: University of Texas Press.

Bakhtin, M. (1984) *Rabelais and his World*. Trans. H. Iswolsky. Bloomington, IN: Indiana University Press.

Beaver, A. (2003) 'Rushdie to Speak at Philo Talk', *The Daily Pennsylvanian*, 14 January, 2003. Available at www.dailypennsylvanian.com/vnews/display.v/ART/2003/01/14/3e23bb8cf272f?in_archive=1 [accessed December 2004].

Beck, U., and Beck-Gernsheim, E. (1995) *The Normal Chaos of Love*. Cambridge: Polity.

Beck, U., and Beck-Gernsheim, E. (1996) 'Individualisation and "Precarious Freedoms": Perspectives and Controversies of a Subject-Oriented Sociology'. In Heelas, P., Lash, S., and Morris, P. (eds) *Detraditionalisation: Critical Reflections on Authority and Identity*. Oxford: Blackwell, pp. 23–48.

Benn, T. (2000) 'How I Tamed Ali G', *The Guardian*, 30 March, p. 5.

Bennett, A. (1999) 'Rappin' on the Tyne: White Hip Hop Culture in Northeast England', *Sociological Review*, 47(1), pp. 1–23.

Bennett, A. (2000) *Popular Music and Youth Culture*. Basingstoke, London and New York: Macmillan – now Palgrave Macmillan.

Bergson, H. (1911) *Laughter: An Essay on the Meaning of the Comic*. London: Macmillan.

Billig, M. (2001a). 'Humour and Hatred: The Racist Jokes of the Ku Klux Klan', *Discourse and Society*, 12, pp. 267–89.

Billig, M. (2001b) 'Humour and Embarrassment: Limits of "Nice-Guy" Theories of Social Life', *Theory, Culture and Society*, 18(5), pp. 23–43.

Billig, M. (2002a) 'Freud and the Language of Humour', *The Psychologist*, September, 156(9), pp. 452–5.

Billig, M. (2002b) 'Henri Tajfel's "Cognitive Aspects of Prejudice" and the Psychology of Bigotry', *British Journal of Social Psychology*, 41, pp. 171–88.

Billig, M. (2005) *Laughter and Ridicule: Toward a Social Critique of Humour*. London: Sage.

Blee, K. M. (2003) *Inside Organized Racism*. Berkeley: University of California Press.

Boskin, J. (1987) 'The Complicity of Humor: The Life and Death of Sambo'. In Morreall, J. (ed.) *The Philosophy of Laughter and Humor*. Albany, NY: State University of New York Press, pp. 250–63.

Brand, P. Z. (1998) 'Parody'. In Kelly, M. (ed.), *Encyclopaedia of Aesthetics*, Vol. 3. Oxford: Oxford University Press, pp. 441–4.

Brandist, C. (2001) 'The Bakhtin Circle', *Internet Encyclopaedia of Philosophy*. Available at http://www.utm.edu/research/iep/b/bakhtin.htm [accessed December 2004].

Brian, J., and Martin, M. D. (1983/1987) *Child Care and Health for Nursery Nurses*. Amersham: Hulton.

BBC Single Life Survey (2002) Available at http://www.bbc.co.uk/goingsolo/ results [accessed 20 February 2005].

Brownell, H., and Gardner, H. (1988) 'Neuropsychological Insights Into Humour'. In Durant, J., and Miller, J. (eds) *Laughing Matters*. London: Longman, pp . 27–43.

Buckland, E. (1984) *The World of Donald McGill*. Poole, Dorset: Blandford Press.

Burn, G. (n.d.) 'Absolutely Fabulous: British Situation Comedy', available at: http://www.museum.tv/archives/etv/A/htm1A/absolutelyfa/absolutelyfa.htm [accessed 12 October 2004].

Butler, J. (1993) 'Redesigning Discourse: Feminism, the Sitcom and Designing Women', *Journal of Film and Video*, 45, pp. 13–26.

Byrnes, S. (2005) 'Man Behaving Adly', *The Independent*, 31 January, pp. 4–7.

Calico Soul. (2004) 'Meeting Salman Rushdie'. Available at http://www.calicosoul. com/archive/000203.html [accessed 17 February 2005].

Capurro, S. (2000) 'Comfort Zones'. In Vidal-Hall, J. (ed.), 'The Last Laugh'. *Index On Censorship*, 29(6), Issue 197, Nov/Dec 2001, pp. 134–8

Carrell, A. (1997a) 'Joke Competence And Humor Competence', *Humor*, 10(2), pp. 173–85.

Carrell, A. (1997b) 'Humor Communities', *Humor,* 10(1), pp. 11–24.

Carroll, L. (1992) [1865, 1872] *Alice in Wonderland & Alice Through The Looking Glass*. Ware: Wordsworth Classics.

Cashmore, E. E. (1987) *The Logic of Racism*. London: Allen & Unwin.

Cashmore, E. E. (1982) *Black Sportsmen*. London: Routledge.

Chambers, D. (2001) *Representing the Family*. London, Thousand Oaks and New Delhi: Sage.

Chandler, J., Williams, M., Maconachie, M., Collett, T., and Dodgeon, B. (2004) 'Living Alone: Its Place in Household Formation and Change', *Sociological Research Online*, 9(3). Available at http://www.socresonline,.org.uk/9/3/ chandler.html [accessed 6 January 2005].

Cherlin, A. (1992) *Marriage, Divorce, Remarriage*. Cambridge, MA: Harvard University Press.

Chomsky, N. (1965) *Aspects Of The Theory Of Syntax*. Cambridge, MA: The MIT Press.

Christen, K. A. (1998) *Clowns And Tricksters. An Encyclopedia Of Tradition And Culture*. Santa Barbara, CA: ABC-CLIO.

Clark, B. (2002) 'The Box of Tricks'. In Cummings, D. (ed.) *Reality TV: How Real is Real?* London: Hodder & Stoughton, pp. 1–16.

Clark, T. (1980) 'Manet's *Olympia* in 1865', *Screen*, 2, pp. 18–42.

Cleese, J., and Booth, C. (1977) *Fawlty Towers*. London: Contact.

Coard, B. (1971) *How the West Indian Child is Made Educationally Sub-Normal in British School System*. London: New Beacon Books.

Coleman, J. (1994) 'Black Children in Care: Crisis of Identity', *Runnymede Bulletin*, October, pp. 4–5.

Collins, M. (2000) 'Hold On To Your Hats', *The Guardian*, 27 March, pp. 2–3.

Cook, P. (2004) 'Peter Cook – At A Slight Angle To the Universe', *BBC2 TV Broadcast*, 18 September.

Critchley, S. (2002) *On Humour*. London: Routledge.

Davies, C. (1988) 'Stupidity and Rationality: Jokes from the Iron Cage'. In Powell, C., and Paton, G. E. C. (eds) *Humour in Society: Resistance and Control*. Basingstoke: Macmillan, pp. 1–32.

Davies, C. (1990) *Ethnic Humour Around the World*. Bloomington: Indiana University Press.

De Sousa, R. (1987) 'When is it wrong to Laugh?'. In Morreall, J (ed.) *The Philosophy of Laughter and Humor*. Albany, NY: State University of New York Press, pp. 226–49.

Deckers, L. (1993) 'On the Validity of a Weight-Judging Paradigm for the Study of Humour', *Humor*, 6(1), pp. 43–56.

Dentith, S. (2000) *Parody*. London: Routledge, New Critical Idiom Series.

Department of Health (1999) 'Caring about Carers: A National Strategy for Carers'. London: Department of Health. Available at http://www.dh.gov.uk/ PublicationsAndStatistics/ [accessed 20 February 2005].

Devine, P. G. (1989) 'Stereotypes and Prejudice: Their Automatic and Controlled Components', *Journal of Personality and Social Psychology*, 56, pp. 5–18.

Doane, M. A. (1982) 'Film and the Masquerade: Theorising the Female Spectator', *Screen*, 23, 3–4 Sept/Oct, pp. 74–87.

Dolgopolova, Z. (1983) *Russia Dies Laughing: Jokes From Soviet Russia*. London: Unwin Paperbacks.

Douglas, M. (1968) 'The Social Control of Cognition: Some Factors in Joke Perception', *Man* (new series), 3, pp. 361–76.

Dummett, A. (1984) *A Portrait of English Racism*. London: CARAF.

Dundes A. (1987) *Cracking Jokes: Studies of Sick Humor Cycles and Stereotypes*. Berkeley, CA.: Ten Speed Press.

Dwivedi, K. N., and Varma, V. P. (eds) (1996) *Meeting the Needs of Ethnic Minority Children: A Handbook for Professionals*. London: Jessica Kingsley.

Easthope, A. (1988) *British Post-Structuralism*. London and New York: Routledge

Eboda, M. (2000) 'We Can All Take Ali G's Humour in Our Stride', *The Independent*, 12 January, p. 12.

Edwards, D. (1997) *Discourse and Cognition*. London: Sage.

Edwards, D., and Potter, J. (1993) *Discursive Psychology*. London: Sage.

Eysenck, H. J. (1971) *Race, Intelligence and Education*. London: Temple Smith.

Fine, G. A. (1983) 'Sociological Approaches to the Study of Humor'. In McGee, P. E., and Goldstein, J. H. (eds) *Handbook of Humor Research*, vol. 1. New York: Springer, pp. 159–81.

Fink, J., and Holden, K. (1999) 'Pictures from the Margins of Marriage: Representations of Spinsters and Single Mothers in the Mid-Victorian Novel, Interwar Hollywood Melodrama and British Film of the 1950s and 1960s', *Gender and History*, 11(2), July, pp. 233–55.

Fiske, J. (1989) *Television Culture*. New York: Methuen.

Forsyth, C. J., and Johnson, E. J. (1995) 'A Sociological View of the Never Married', *International Journal of Sociology of the Family*, 25(2), Autumn, pp. 91–104.

Freud, S. (1905/1960) *Jokes and Their Relation to the Unconscious*. Harmondsworth: Penguin.

Frye, N. (1949) *The Argument of Comedy*. London: English Institute Essays.

Galassi, P. (1996) 'The Complete Untitled Film Stills. Cindy Sherman'. Available at www.MoMA_org/Exhibitions/1997/sherman.htm [accessed 17 February 2005].

Galegroup (n.d.) '*Glossary*'. Available at http://www.galegroup.com/free_resources/glossary/glossary_p.htm#p [accessed 17 February 2005].

Galton, R., and Simpson, A. (1988) *The Best of Steptoe and Son*. London: Pan.

Garfield, S. (2004) *Our Hidden Lives: The Everyday Diaries of a Forgotten Britain, 1945–1948*. London, Sydney and Auckland: Ebury Press.

Genette, G. (1982) *Palimpsestes*. Paris: Editions du Seuil.

Genette, G. (1986) *Théorie des Genres*. Paris: Editions du Seuil.

Gervais, R., and Merchant, S. (2002) *The Office*. London: BBC.

Gervais, R., and Merchant, S. (2003) *The Office, Series Two*. London: BBC.

Gibson, O., and Brook, S. (2005) 'Goodbye Boys!' *The Guardian*, 6 May, p. 5.

Giddens, A. (1992) *The Transformation of Intimacy: Sexuality, Love and Eroticism in Modern Societies*. Cambridge: Polity.

Gilroy, P. (2004) *After Empire*. Abingdon: Routledge.

Giora, R. (1991) 'On the Cognitive Aspect of the Joke', *Journal of Pragmatics*, 16, pp. 463–85.

Goffman, E. (1974) *Frame Analysis*. New York: Harper.

Goldhagen, D. (1997) *Hitler's Willing Executioners*. London: Abacus.

Gray, F. (1994) *Women and Laughter*. Basingstoke and London: Macmillan.

Green, B. (1976) *I've Lost My Little Willie: A Celebration of Comic Postcards*. London: Arrow Books.

Groffman, N. (2001) Letters Page: 'View From China', *The Independent*, 22 September, p. 17.

Guardian, The (2003) 'Welease Bwian', 28 March, 2003. Available at http://film.guardian.co.uk/features/featurepages/0,4120,923997,00.html [accessed 17 February 2005].

Guardian, The (2004) Letters Page: 'No Laughing Matter', 28 February, p 16.

Gundelach, P. (2000) 'Joking Relationships and National Identity in Scandinavia', *Acta Sociologica*, 43, pp. 113–22.

Guthrie, W. N. (1903) 'A Theory of the Comic', *International Quarterly*, 7, pp. 254–64.

Haines, J., and Donnelly, P. (eds) (1986) *Malice in Wonderland: Robert Maxwell v. Private Eye*. London and Sydney: Macdonald.

Hancock, T., and Brent, N. (1986) *Hancock*. London: BBC Ariel Books.

Harding, L. (2003) 'The Joke's On Saddam', *Guardian G2*, 14 March, p. 5.

Hardy, J. (2004) 'Heard the One about the Tory MP, the Whitehall Dinner and the Racist Joke?', *The Guardian*, 27 February, pp. 2–3.

Hay, J. (2000) 'Functions of Humour in the Conversations of Men and Women', *Journal of Pragmatics*, 32, pp. 709–42.

Hay, J. (2001) 'The Pragmatics Of Humor Support', *Humor*, 14(1), pp. 55–82.

Heath, S., and Cleaver, E. (2003) *Young, Free and Single? Twenty-Somethings and Household Change*. Basingstoke: Palgrave Macmillan.

Heider, F. (1958) *The Psychology of Interpersonal Relations*. New York: Wiley.

Heller, Z. (1999) 'Girl Columns'. In Glover, S. (ed.) *Secrets of the Press: Journalists on Journalism*. Harmondsworth: Penguin, pp. 10–17.

Hilbreth, J. (2002) 'The Really Politically Incorrect', *Wall Street Journal*, 10 July, p. 8.

Hillenbrand, F. K. M. (1995) *Underground Humour In Nazi Germany, 1933–1945*. London and New York: Routledge.

Hoggart, S. (2004) 'Simon Hoggart's Diary', The *Guardian*, 28 February, p. 2.

Holden, R. (1993) *Laughter, The Best Medicine*. London: Thorsons.

Hole, A. (2003) 'Performing Identity: Dawn French and the Funny Fat Female Body', *Feminist Media Studies*, 3(3), pp. 316–28.

Howitt, D., and Owusu-Bempah, K. (1990) 'The Pragmatics of Institutional Racism', *Human Relations*, 43, pp. 885–9.

Howitt, D., and Owusu-Bempah, K. (1994) *The Racism of Psychology*. Hemel Hempstead: Harvester Wheatsheaf.

Hudson, B. (ed.) (1996) *Race, Crime and Justice*. Dartmouth: Aldershot.

Husband, C. (1988) 'Racist Humour and Racist Ideology in British Television or I laughed Till You Cried'. In Powell, C., and Paton, G. E. C. (eds) *Humour in Society: Resistance and Control*. Basingstoke: Macmillan, pp. 149–78.

Hutcheon, L. (1985) *A Theory of Parody: The Teachings of Twentieth-Century Art Forms*. London: Methuen.

Hutcheon, L. (1990) 'An Epilogue: Postmodern Parody: History, Subjectivity and Ideology', *Quarterly Review of Film and Video, 22*, pp. 125–33.

Jacobson, H. (1997) *Seriously Funny: From The Ridiculous To The Sublime*. Harmondsworth: Viking.

Jameson, F. (1984) 'Post-Modernism, or the Cultural Logic of Late Capitalism', *New Left Review*, 146, pp. 53–92.

Janik, V. K. (ed.) (1998) *Fools And Jesters In Literature, Art, And History*. Westport, CT: Greenwood Press.

Janus, I. (1972) *Groupthink*. Boston, MA: Houghton Mifflin.

Jaret, C. (1999) 'Attitudes of Whites and Blacks towards Ethnic Humor: A Comparison', *Humor*, 12, pp. 385–409.

Jeffries, S. (1986) *The Spinster and Her Enemies: Feminism and Sexuality, 1880–1930*. New York: Routledge & Kegan Paul.

Jensen, A. R. (1969) 'How Much Can we Boost IQ and Scholastic Achievement?', *Harvard Educational Review*, 39, pp. 1–123.

Kaufmann, J. C. (1994) 'One Person Households in Europe', *Population*, 49(4–5), pp. 935–58.

Kiester, E., Jr. (1986) 'Decked Out in a Sliver Go-go Skirt, Toting a Pistol or Thrashing Motherhood', *TV Guide*, 6 December, pp. 51–6.

Killingsworth, J. M. (1992) 'Discourse Communities, Local And Global', *Rhetoric Review*, 11(1), pp. 110–22.

Klages, M. (1992) 'What To Do With Helen Keller Jokes: A Feminist Act'. In Barreca, R. (ed.) *New Perspectives On Women And Comedy*. Philadelphia: Gordon & Breach, pp. 12–23.

Knorr Cetina, K. (2001) 'Postsocial Relations: Theorising Sociality in a Postsocial Environment'. In Ritzer, G., and Smart, B. (eds) *Handbook of Social Theory*. London: Sage, pp. 520–37.

Koestler, A. (1964) *The Act of Creation*. London and New York: Hutchinson.

Kowallis, J. (1986) Translator's Preface. In *Wit And Humor From Old Cathay*. Beijing: Panda Books.

Kulick, D. (2000) 'Gay and Lesbian Language', *Annual Review of Anthropology*, 29, pp. 243–85.

Lasch, C. (1979) *The Culture of Narcissism*. London: Abacus.

Lauter, P. (ed.) (1964) *Theories Of Comedy*. Garden City, NY: Anchor Books Doubleday.

Lawson, M. (2000) 'When Is A Joke Not A Joke Anymore?', *Guardian G2*, 12 August, p. 7.

Leigh, D. (2000) 'The Real-Life Ali G', The *Guardian*, 1 November, p. 16.

Lewin, K. (1933) 'Environmental Forces'. In Murchinson, C. (ed.) *A Handbook of Child Psychology*. Worcester, MA: Clark University Press, pp. 590–625.

Lezard, N. (2000) 'Is it Because I isn't Funny?' The *Observer*, 5 March, p. 6.

Li, J. (2004) *The Intellectual as Comic Hero*. Unpublished PhD thesis: London Metropolitan University.

Lipman, M. (2000) 'It's the Way You Tell' 'Em', *GM Magazine*, August, p. 216.

Lipman, S. (1991) *Laughter in Hell: The Use of Humour During the Holocaust*. Northvale, NJ: Jason Aronson.

Lloyd, G. (1984) *The Man of Reason: 'Male' and 'Female' in Western Philosophy*. London: Methuen.

Lobo, E. (1978) *Children of Immigrants into Britain: Their Health and Social Problems*. London: Allyn & Unwin.

Lockyer, S., and Pickering, M. (2001) 'Dear Shit-Shovellers: Humour, Censure and the Discourse of Complaint', *Discourse and Society*, 12(5), September, pp. 633–51.

Lodge, D. (1983) *The British Museum is Falling Down*. London: Penguin.

Lorenz, K. (1963) *On Aggression*. New York: Bantam.

Maher, B. (1999) Politically Incorrect. *Channel 4* TV Broadcast, 19 May.

Malik, S. (2002) *Representing Black Britain: Black and Asian Images on Television*. London, Thousand Oaks and New Delhi: Sage.

Maxwell, C. D., Robinson, A. L., and Post, L. A. (2003) 'The Impact of Race on the Adjudication of Sexual Assault and Other Violent Crimes', *Journal of Criminal Justice*, 31(6), pp. 523–38.

McCullough, M. L. (1988) 'Are We Secretly Racist?', *The Psychologist*, November, 1(11), pp. 445–7.

McGhee, P. E. (1980) Development Of The Creative Aspect Of Humour. In McGhee, P. E. (ed.) *Children's Humour*. Chichester: John Wiley and Sons, pp. 127–39.

Milroy, L. (1980) *Language And Social Networks*. Oxford: Basil Blackwell.

Modleski, T. (1999) *Old Wives' Tales: Feminist Re-Visions of Film and Other Fictions*. London: I. B. Tauris.

Montgomery, M. (1999) 'Talk as Entertainment: The Case of *The Mrs Merton Show*'. In Haarman, L. (ed.) *Talk About Shows*. Bologna: Cooperativa Libraria Universitaria Editrive Bolognia, pp. 101–50.

Morreall, J. (1981) 'Humour and Aesthetic Education', *Journal of Aesthetic Education*, 15(1), pp. 55–70.

Morreall, J. (1983a) 'Humor and Emotion', *American Philosophical Quarterly*, 20(3), pp. 297–304.

Morreall, J. (1983b) *Taking Laughter Seriously*. Albany, NY: State University of New York Press.

Morreall, J. (1987a) 'Funny Ha-Ha, Funny Strange, and Other Reactions to Incongruity'. In Morreall, J. (ed.) *The Philosophy of Laughter and Humor*. Albany, NY: State University of New York Press, pp. 188–207.

Morreall, J. (ed.) (1987b) *The Philosophy of Laughter and Humour*. Albany, NY: State University of New York Press.

Morreall, J. (1989) 'Enjoying Incongruity', *Humor*, 2(1), pp. 1–18.

Morreall, J. (1997) *Humor Works*. Amherst MA: Human Resource Development Press.

Morreall, J. (1999a) 'The Resistance of Humor during the Holocaust'. In Hayse, M., Pollefeyt, D., Colijn, G. J., and Sachs Littell, M. (eds) *Hearing the Voices: Teaching the Holocaust to Future Generations*. Merion Station, PA: Merion International, pp. 103–12.

Morreall, J. (1999b) *Comedy, Tragedy, and Religion*. Albany, NY: State University of New York Press.

Mühlhäusler, P., and Harré, R. (1990) *Pronouns and People*. Oxford: Blackwell.

Mulkay, M. (1988) *On Humour: Its Nature and Its Place in Modern Society*. Cambridge: Polity Press.

Mulvey, L. (1975) 'Visual Pleasure and Narrative Cinema', *Screen*, 16(3), Autumn, pp. 6–18.

National Association for the Care and Resettlement of Offenders. (1986) *Black People and the Criminal Justice System*. London: NACRO.

Neale, S., and Krutnik, B. (1990) *Popular Film and Television Comedy*. London and New York: Routledge.

Norrick, N. R. (1993) *Conversational Joking*. Bloomington: Indiana University Press.

Norrick, N. R. (2003) 'Issues in Conversational Joking', *Journal of Pragmatics*, 35, pp. 1333–59.

North, R. (2000) 'It Was No Joke For Me, Ambushed by Ali G', The *Independent*, 4 April, p. 9.

O'Reilly, J. (1989) 'At last! Women Worth Watching', *TV Guide*, 27 May, pp. 18–21.

Office for National Statistics (2003) 'Social Trends 33'. Available at http:www. statistics.gov.uk/socialtrends [accessed 20 February 2005].

Oram, A. (1992) 'Repressed and Thwarted, or Bearer of the New World? The Spinster in Inter-War Feminist Discourses', *Women's History Review*, 1(3), pp. 413–33.

Orwell, G. (1942/1977) 'The Art of Donald McGill', in his *Collected Essays, Journalism and Letters, Vol 2, 1940–1943*. Harmondsworth and New York: Penguin.

Oshima, K. (2000) 'Ethnic Jokes and Social Function in Hawaii', *Humor*, 13, pp. 41–57.

Owusu-Bempah, K. (1994) 'Race, Self-Identity and Social Work', *British Journal of Social Work*, 24, pp. 123–36.

Owusu-Bempah, K. (2001) 'Racism: An Important Factor in Practice with Ethnic Minority Children and Families'. In Foley, P., Roche, J., and Tucker, S. (eds) *Children in Society: Contemporary Theory, Policy and Practice*. Basingstoke: Palgrave Macmillan, pp. 42–51.

Owusu-Bempah, K. (2003) 'Political Correctness: In the Interest of the Child?', *Educational and Child Psychology*, 20, pp. 53–63.

Owusu-Bempah, K., and Howitt, D. (1999) 'Even Their Soul is Defective', *The Psychologist*, 12, pp. 126–30.

Owusu-Bempah, K., and Howitt, D. (2000) *Psychology Beyond Western Perspectives*. Leicester: British Psychological Society Books.

Palmer, D. (1984) *Comedy: Developments in Criticism*. Basingstoke and London: Macmillan.

Palmer, J. (1987) *The Logic of the Absurd*. London: BFI.

Palmer, J. (1994) *Taking Humour Seriously*. London: Routledge.

Palmer, J. (1996) 'Permission to Joke: Some Implications of a Well-Known Principle', *Semiotica*, 110(1/2), pp. 23–36.

Parker, I. (1998) 'They Shoot Arses Don't They?', The *Observer*, 20 September, p. 8.

Pateman, C. (1988) *The Sexual Contract*. Cambridge, Polity Press.

Perelman, C., and Olbrechts-Tyteca, L. (1971) *The New Rhetoric*. Indiana: University of Notre Dame Press.

PhatNav (n.d.) 'God Save the Queen (Sex Pistols Song)'. Available at http://www. phatnav.com/wiki/index.php?title=Sex_Pistols [accessed 17 February 2005].

Pickering, M. (2001) *Stereotyping: The Politics of Representation*. Basingstoke and New York: Palgrave Macmillan.

Pickering, M. (2004) 'Racial Stereotypes'. In Taylor, G., and Spencer, S. (eds) *Social Identities: Multidisciplinary Approaches*, London and New York: Routledge, pp. 91–106.

Pickering, M., and Littlewood, J. (1998) 'Heard the One about the White Middle-Class Heterosexual Father-in-Law? Gender, Ethnicity and Political Correctness in Comedy'. In Wagg, S. (ed.) *Because I Tell a Joke or Two: Comedy, Politics and Social Difference*. London and New York: Routledge, pp. 291–312.

Pilger, J. (1996) 'In a Land Of Fear', *Guardian Weekend*, 4 May, p. 6.

Potter, J., and Wetherell, M. (1987) *Discourse and Social Psychology*. London: Sage.

Powell, C. (1977) 'Humour As A Form Of Social Control: A Deviance Approach'. In Chapman, A., and Foot, H. (eds) *It's A Funny Thing, Humour*. London: Pergamon, pp. 52–67.

Provine, R. (2001) *Laughter: A Scientific Investigation*. Harmondsworth: Penguin.

Purdie, S. (1993) *Comedy: The Mastery of Discourse*. Hemel Hempstead: Harvester Wheatsheaf.

Quillian, L., and Pager, D. (2001) 'Black Neighbours, Higher Crime? The Role of Racial Stereotypes in Evaluations of Neighbourhood Crime', *American Journal of Sociology*, 107, pp. 717–67.

Raju, A. (1991) 'Decoding The Comic'. In Bennett, G. (ed.) *Spoken In Jest*. Sheffield: Academic Press, pp. 71–85.

Raskin, V. (1985) *Semantic Mechanisms of Humour*. Dordrecht: D. Reidel.

Rogin, M. (1996) *Blackface, White Noise: Jewish Immigration and the Hollywood Melting Pot*. Berkeley: California University Press.

Rose, M. (1993) *Parody: Ancient, Modern and Post-Modern*. Cambridge: Cambridge University Press.

Rowe, K. K. (1990) 'Rosanne: Unruly Woman as Domestic Goddess', *Screen*, 31(4), Winter, pp. 408–19.

Rowe, K. K. (1995) *The Unruly Woman: Gender and the Genres of Laughter*. Austin: University of Texas Press.

Roy, S. (2002) 'The Case for and Against the Satanic Verses'. Available at http://www.chowk.com/show_article.cgi?aid=00001720&channel=leafyglade %20inn [accessed 17 February 2005].

Rudolph, I. (1998) 'Sex and the Married Girl', *TV Guide*, 6 June, pp. 12–14.

Rushdie, S. (1988) *The Satanic Verses*. London: Viking.

Russell, C., and Lewis, H. (1900) *The Jew in London*. London: Fisher Unwin.

Russell, I. (1987) 'Parody and Performance'. In Pickering, M., and Green, T. (eds) *Everyday Culture*. Milton Keynes and Philadelphia: Open University Press, pp. 71–104.

Sacks, H. (1992) *Lectures on Conversation*, vol. 2. Oxford: Blackwell.

Samuel, J. (1989) 'Salman Rushdie's *Satanic Verses*'. Available at www.indiastar. com/samuel.html [accessed 17 February 2005].

Sartre, J. P. (1948) *Portrait of the Anti-Semite*. London: Secker & Warburg.

Savage, J. (1991) *England's Dreaming: Sex Pistols and Punk Rock*. London: Faber.

Schutz, C. E. (1995) 'Joking in the Context of Political Correctness', *Humor*, 8(1), pp. 65–76.

Shohat, E., and Stam, R. (1994) *Unthinking Eurocentrism*. London and New York: Routledge.

Spigel, L. (1992) *Make Room for TV: Television and the Family Ideal in Postwar America*. Chicago: University of Chicago Press.

Spigel, L. (1997) 'From Theatre to Space Ship: Metaphors of Suburban Domesticity in Postwar America'. In Silverstone, R. (ed.) *Visions of Suburbia*. London: Routledge, pp. 217–39.

Stallybrass, P., and White, A. (1986) *The Politics and Poetics of Transgression*. London: Methuen.

Stock, Y., and Brotherton, P. (1981) 'Attitudes Towards Single Women', *Sex Roles*, 7(1), pp. 73–8.

Stuart, J. (2000) 'Gettin' Jiggy Wid Da Staines Massive', The *Independent Review*, 4 April, pp. 1 and 7.

Swift, J. (1967) 'A Modest Proposal' in *Satires and Personal Writings*. London, New York and Toronto: Oxford University Press, pp. 19–31.

Thompson, B. (2004) *Sunshine on Putty: The Golden Age of British Comedy from 'Vic Reeves' to 'The Office'*. London: Fourth Estate.

Thompson, E. P. (1967) 'Time, Work-Discipline and Industrial Capitalism', *Past and Present*, 38, pp. 56–97.

Tolson, A. (1991) 'Televised Chat and the Synthetic Personality'. In Scannell, P. (ed.) *Broadcast Talk*. London, Newbury Park and New Delhi: Sage, pp. 178–200.

Veatch, T. C. (1998) 'A Theory of Humour', *Humor*, 11, pp. 161–216.

Waddell, T. (1999) 'Reveling in Dis-Play: The Grotesque in Absolutely Fabulous'. In Mills, A. (ed.) *Seriously Weird: Papers on the Grotesque*. New York: Peter Lang, pp. 207–23.

Ward, G. (1997) *Teach Yourself Postmodernism*. London: Hodder & Stoughton.

Welsford, E. (1935) *The Fool: His Social And Literary History*. London: Faber & Faber.

Whelehan, I. (2000) *Overloaded: Popular Culture and the Future of Feminism*. London: The Women's Press.

Wickberg, D. (1998) *The Senses of Humour: Self and Laughter in Modern America*. Ithaca, NY, and London: Cornell University Press.

Willis, K. (2003) *Making Sense Of Humour: Some Pragmatic And Political Aspects*. PhD Dissertation: London Metropolitan University. Available at www.pragmaticshumour.net

Younge, G. (2000) 'Is It Coz I Is Black?', The *Guardian*, 12 January, pp. 2–3.

Zillman, D. (1983) 'Disparagement Humor'. In McGee, P. E., and Goldstein, J. H. (eds) *Handbook of Humor Research*, vol. 1. New York: Springer, pp. 85–107.

Index